Three Faces of Desire

PHILOSOPHY OF MIND SERIES

Series Editor
David J. Chalmers, University of Arizona

Self Expressions
Minds, Morals, and the Meaning of Life
Owen Flanagan

The Conscious Mind
In Search of a Fundamental Theory
David J. Chalmers

Deconstructing the Mind
Stephen P. Stich

The Human Animal
Personal Identity without Psychology
Eric Olson

Minds and Bodies
Philosophers and Their Ideas
Colin McGinn

What's Within?
Nativism Reconsidered
Fiona Cowie

Purple Haze
The Puzzle of Consciousness
Joseph Levine

Consciousness and Cognition
A Unified Account
Michael Thau

Thinking without Words
José Luis Bermúdez

Identifying the Mind
Selected Papers of U. T. Place
Edited by George Graham and
Elizabeth R. Valentine

A Place for Consciousness
Probing the Deep Structure of the Natural World
Gregg Rosenberg

Gut Reactions
A Perceptual Theory of Emotion
Jesse J. Prinz

Three Faces of Desire
Timothy Schroeder

Three Faces of Desire

Timothy Schroeder

2004

OXFORD
UNIVERSITY PRESS

Oxford   New York
Auckland   Bangkok   Buenos Aires   Cape Town   Chennai
Dar es Salaam   Delhi   Hong Kong   Istanbul   Karachi   Kolkata
Kuala Lumpur   Madrid   Melbourne   Mexico City   Mumbai   Nairobi
São Paulo   Shanghai   Taipei   Tokyo   Toronto

Copyright © 2004 by Oxford University Press, Inc.

Published by Oxford University Press, Inc.
198 Madison Avenue, New York, New York, 10016

www.oup.usa.org

Oxford is a registered trademark of Oxford University Press

All rights reserved. No part of this publication may be reproduced,
stored in a retrieval system, or transmitted, in any form or by any means,
electronic, mechanical, photocopying, recording, or otherwise,
without the prior permission of Oxford University Press.

Library of Congress Cataloging-in-Publication Data
Schroeder, Timothy.
Three faces of desire / Timothy Schroeder.
p. cm.—(Philosophy of mind series)
Includes bibliographical references and index.
ISBN 0-19-517237-X
1. Desire (Philosophy) 2. Desire.   I. Title. II. Series.
B105.D44S37   2004
128'.3—dc22   2004049585

"Fire and Ice" from *The Poetry of Robert Frost*, Copyright 1951
by Robert Frost, copyright 1923, © 1969 by Henry Holt and Company.
Reprinted by permission of Henry Holt and Company, LLC.

2 4 6 8 9 7 5 3 1

Printed in the United States of America
on acid-free paper

*To Hal Schroeder, John Woods,
and Fred Dretske—*

three faces of my philosophical education.

Acknowledgments

As I began to write my dissertation on mental representation, a friend gave me some version of the following wise warning: "Tim, at some point you're going to get sick of your dissertation, and you'll think up a new topic to write on instead. Do not switch to the new topic! Stay with the old topic, and finish it, or you'll never graduate." He was right. Halfway through writing my dissertation, I became convinced I had come up with a much more interesting topic, and I considered switching, but the advice steered me true, and I finished my Ph.D. on time. That more interesting topic stayed with me, however, and eventually became the book you hold in your hands. So the first word of thanks goes to Avrom Faderman, for making sure I didn't write this book until it was time.

Second, I have to acknowledge an enormous intellectual debt owed to Fred Dretske. The first thing I did at the beginning of my graduate education, a full week before classes started, was to read *Explaining Behavior*. Anyone who has read that excellent work will see its influence in these pages—or so I hope. His view that desire has more, at bottom, to do with learning than with directly producing movement is the starting point for all that follows here.

Thanks should also go to a tremendous number of people who have helped me in one way or another with the ideas of *Three Faces*. In addition to Avrom and Dretske, I owe thanks to Nomy Arpaly, Paulette Cassis, David Chalmers, Jon Kaplan, Lisa McCleod, Vance Ricks and Janet Stemwedel for encouragement and discussion (and often patient listening to half-baked ideas) early on. For their more recent intellectual support, I also thank Kent Berridge, Bob Bright, Sarah Buss, Ben Caplan, Karim Dharamsi, Michael Feld, Agnieszka Jaworska, Joyce Jenkins, Stephan Kennepohl, Krista Lawlor, Carl Matheson, David Papineau, Sheila Reynolds, Dan Ryder, Rob Shaver, Ken Taylor, and David Velleman. And Nomy Arpaly needs to be thanked at least once more, if not a dozen times, both for philosophical discussion and for her unflagging confidence in me.

I have also benefited greatly from people who, in one official capacity or another, were induced to give me comments on ideas in development. First on this list belong my research assistants from the last four years: Damien Dowd, Donovan Hulse, Sandra Kumhyr, Jennifer Maw, Cynthia Read, Ramon Rempel, Brendan Ritchie, and Vlad Vlaovic. Commentators on talks I have given on subjects related to this book have also provided very helpful feedback, so thanks to Zsolt Batori, Elizabeth Brake, Andrew Melnyk, Karl Pfeifer, Yonatan Shemmer,

Dennis Stampe, and Christine Tappolet. I have also benefited from having a number of intelligent and sympathetic referees: Ronald de Sousa, Joel Marks, Jesse Prinz, and Shaun Nichols for this book, and three anonymous referees of an earlier essay on pleasure, along with Bill Lycan. Their comments have been invaluable. I must also thank the members of the philosophy departments of the University of Manitoba, Sheffield University, the University of Iceland, and the University of Lethbridge, all of whom heard talks from me on related material.

The University of Manitoba and the Social Sciences and Humanities Research Council of Canada have both provided me with financial support and course release over the last five years, making it possible for me to complete this book, and for that I am very grateful to them.

Parts of chapter 3 are drawn from "Pleasure, Displeasure, and Representation," in the *Canadian Journal of Philosophy*, and are used with the kind permission of that journal. Robert Frost's "Fire and Ice" is reprinted in chapter 1 with the kind permission of Henry Holt and Company.

Finally, I would like to thank Kristín Jóhannsdóttir for putting up with me while I was writing this book. Her patience has been exceeded only by the support she has provided.

Contents

    Preliminaries   3

1   The Standard Theory and Its Rivals   10

2   Reward and Punishment   38

3   Pleasure and Displeasure   71

4   The Production and Prevention of Movement   107

5   Desire and Aversion   131

6   Clean and Messy Theories   162

    Appendix   181

    Notes   183

    References   195

    Index   209

Three Faces of Desire

Preliminaries

Part of the fun of writing a book on desire is announcing one's topic of research to non-philosophers. Friends, relatives, and loquacious strangers open their eyes a little wider when they hear "desire." "Oh," they say, "I'll bet *that's* interesting." And so it should be. Our desires are of unending interest to novelists and playwrights, to the viewers of soap operas and *opera seria*, to advertising executives, to lovers, and to ourselves as people brimming with desires. People want food and shelter, love and self-fulfillment; they crave mangoes and wish for fame, long for the good old days, covet their neighbors' oxen, lust for the unthinkable, desire the impossible, and pine for the fjords. They also need, demand, will, try, intend, seek, and in innumerable manners set their hearts on getting their way.

Though the rest of the world is fascinated, philosophers of mind appear bored by the topic of desire.[1] In what is perhaps the standard view held by these philosophers at present, a desire is just anything that plays the functional role characteristic of desires, which is that of tending to bring about that state of affairs which is the object of the desire.[2] That is, to desire a Monte Cristo sandwich is to have something inside you that tends to make you act so that you get a Monte Cristo sandwich; to desire that your child recover from scarlet fever is to have something inside you that tends to make you act so that your child recovers from scarlet fever; to desire world peace is to have something inside you that tends to make you act so that world peace is obtained; and so on.

The problem, according to the standard account, is not understanding what a desire is, but understanding what it is to have any conception of the world at all: the problem of *original intentionality*, as it is known. In some quarters, this has been understood as the problem of mental representation: what makes it possible for the brain to represent the world?[3] In others, it has been understood as the problem of radical interpretation, the problem of how we can interpret people as thinking about this or wanting that.[4] In still others, the problem is that of understanding the rules of the language game: understanding how social interactions license us to say "he wants this" or "she believes that."[5] But however the problem has been interpreted, one assumption has been widespread: once the universal solvent is discovered that eliminates the problem of original intentionality in general, the application of a few drops will suffice to resolve the nature of desire in particular. This is not to say that the topic of desire has received no recent attention at all from philosophers of mind—Fred Dretske (1988, ch. 5), Denis Stampe (1986), and Galen Strawson (1994, ch. 9) are prominent exceptions—but desires have hardly been the focus of intense research in this field.[6]

Is the neglect of desire deserved or undeserved? If the standard account were correct, then neglect would seem to be desire's just deserts. Other disciplines—action theory, moral psychology, meta-ethics, decision theory, and various branches of psychology—would still have much to say about desire as it bears on other topics, but the philosopher of mind could finish her job with a paragraph or two, plus the all-important theory of original intentionality. On the other hand, if the standard account were mistaken, then there would be some reason to give desire further theoretical attention. Obviously, I think there is something wrong with the standard account—something deeply wrong. Desires are not, by their nature, things that move us to act: their power to move us is merely one of their typical causal effects. Nor, as others think, are desires essentially dispositions to feel pleasure or displeasure: such feelings are, like movements, consequences of having desires, not constitutive of them. The nature of desire is more complex than either the standard account or its best-known rival would suggest, but also—once understood—more explanatory of the complex role desires play within us. Giving a full account of the nature of desire is the goal of this work.

1. Aims

Before I begin, a few more words about aims and methodology are in order, and the first question to answer is this: of what, exactly, is this book meant to provide a theory? In everyday talk, to say that you desire something is to suggest that you are passionate about it, that you are *burning* with desire. In fact, the term 'desire' connotes so much passion and intensity that it is often used to mean 'sexual desire'.[7] This is probably why it would sound ridiculous to walk into a restaurant and say "I desire an egg-salad sandwich." However, this passionate sense of 'desire' is too limited to encapsulate the topic of this book.

A different use of the term 'desire' is popular within philosophical circles. In this sense, any state of mind that can succeed or be fulfilled[8] counts. Wants, plans, intentions, acts of will, cravings, goals, and more are all types of desires, in common philosophical parlance. Donald Davidson (1980) has suggested the term 'pro attitude' for these mental events, since to desire a sandwich, want one, wish for one, and so on, is to have a positive attitude toward getting a sandwich, but even Davidson often resorts to simply lumping the pro attitudes together under the label 'desire'. 'Desire' has simply become a common name for these sorts of mental entities. This sense of 'desire', though having the clarity of a useful stipulative definition, is too broad for present purposes.

I am setting my sights somewhere between the everyday and philosophical extremes. *Three Faces* is a work about a single phenomenon that is more general than passionate yearning, but less general than the whole of the pro attitudes. It is a phenomenon for which everyday usage has at least three labels: 'desiring', 'wanting', and 'wishing'. This phenomenon is a distinct, unified entity, a natural psychological kind. Unfortunately, it has no completely natural label in everyday language or in the specialized jargon of philosophy. I have chosen 'desire' as the best approximation. When I write 'desire', then, the reader is encouraged to see whichever of 'desire', 'want', or 'wish' seems most appropriate in context, if that helps to keep things clear. Paradigm examples are meant to include wanting food, desiring to make a positive contribution to the environment, and wishing that one's father had been more openly affectionate in one's youth.

In fact, my target is really only a proper subset of desires, wants, and wishes: those desires, wants, and wishes that are held *intrinsically*. The standard distinction between intrinsic and instrumental desires (wants, wishes) is between desiring something for its own sake and desiring something only as a means to some distinct, ultimate end. I want my father's welfare just because that is what I want; it is not merely a means to some further end, a tool for achieving some other goal. His welfare is something I desire *intrinsically*. On the other hand, I want his house to remain intact solely because I believe this to be a means to his welfare (comfort, convenience, etc.); were no one to live in the house or be financially dependent upon its condition, I would be indifferent to its fate. I only care about the house *instrumentally*.[9] It should be said that the example will be found controversial by some: there is dispute over what can be desired intrinsically. Some would say that only pleasure can be desired for its own sake, for example, and that everything else that appears to be desired for its own sake is really desired only for the sake of the pleasure it may bring (or the displeasure it may help us avoid). I do not think this particular view is correct: the evidence of both everyday experience and neuroscience suggests that a desire for my father's welfare can be just as intrinsic as a desire for pleasure, as I will argue in chapters 2, 3, and 5. Whatever the truth of the matter is, however, it is only the intrinsic desires that I seek to explain in this work.

So *Three Faces* is a work on intrinsic desires, wants, wishes: on desires, as I will say from now on. It is not, except at occasional points and in passing, a work on instrumental desires, plans, intentions, volitions, values, or the like, insofar as these are distinct from desires. The target, then, is in view.

2. Methods

In order to find out the nature of a thing, there is no more straightforward procedure than to consider its obvious surface features and to attempt to identify the thing itself as the source of these features. In the case of desire, the familiar features surrounding it are complex indeed. People's desires lead them to travel to Cuba, to develop insomnia, to get butterflies in their stomachs; they gain and lose desires by maturing, by painful experience, by massive head injuries; they know what they want, they do not know what they want, they are sure they hate what they actually want very much. But in all this complexity, three phenomena stand out: motivation, pleasure, and reward. Motivation, pleasure, and reward are, as I will say, the three *faces* of desire.

It is uncontroversial and familiar that desiring has something to do with being motivated to act and something to do with feeling pleased or displeased on various occasions. If I want my father to be healthy, for instance, I will tend to do certain things (make sure he sees a doctor when sick, say) and I will be open to certain feelings (unhappiness if he has high blood pressure, relief if a tumor proves to be benign, etc.). It is less familiar, but also true, that desiring has something to do with reward and punishment. If I want to play with my nephew, say, then I can be rewarded for mending my relationship with my sister by being given opportunities to play with my nephew, and I can be punished for quarrelling with her by being denied such opportunities. Most of what we know, or think we know, about desire has something to do with at least one of these three faces, and every leading theory of the nature of desire ties it to one of them. So I will look at desire by looking at its three faces and seeking an account of desire that views desire as the source of its best-known manifestations.

Deciding to focus on desire's three faces will bring little advantage, however, if there are no new facts about them to consider. So I will also be importing a wealth of recent neuroscientific discoveries, along with findings from allied sciences, to the ongoing philosophical discussion. These findings add a tremendous number of additional facts about desire's three faces that any theory of desire must take into account.[10] It is my view that the facts now known about these faces, when combined with the familiar considerations raised by philosophers from Socrates on, support a radical new theory of desire.

My methodology will thus be one familiar—to philosophers, at least—from work in the philosophy of physics, or the philosophy of biology, or recent work in the philosophy of the emotions.[11] I will begin with a combination of familiar philosophy and everyday common sense, describe scientific findings that either support or challenge what is already believed, interpret the findings in the light of previous theory, and conclude with a new view. A philosopher of physics may ask what fields are, or what a physical law is, and a philosopher of biology may ask what natural selection amounts to or what a species is. I approach the nature of desire in the same spirit. Like the authors of such work, I am interested in a question that could be asked by a scientist as well as by a philosopher. In short, I will be treating desire as a *natural kind*, as a meaningful, unified, scientific entity, and investigating it as natural kinds are investigated generally.

Perhaps it is worth pointing out that my methodology is one used in the sciences as well as in philosophy. It is sometimes imagined that science proceeds purely by gathering empirical evidence and drawing the conclusions that the evidence obviously demands, but this is not always even an approximation to the truth. The special theory of relativity and recent theories of consciousness, for example, have been shaped as much by common sense understandings of their subject matters and philosophical presuppositions (a person moving steadily on a train ought to be able to measure the same physical constants as a stationary person; there is a sense in which dreaming is a state of consciousness) as they have been by empirical data.

Not everyone will be happy with this sort of approach. Treating desires as the sort of things that can be studied in the laboratory just as well as they can be studied from the armchair involves a number of controversial philosophical assumptions. These include the following:

1. Desires are part of the natural order.
2. Desires are (probably) useful entities to think about for purposes of causal inference and explanation, at least to the same extent that other scientific kinds such as *electron donor* or *tornado* or *ribosome* are useful.
3. Scientific inquiry may bring to light important facts about the nature of desire not available from the armchair.
4. Many of our presuppositions about desire may prove to be false.
5. In principle, we might discover that 'desire' is an empty natural-kind term, because no existing natural kind fits enough of our pre-theoretic notions to earn the name 'desire'.

At least since the work of Saul Kripke (1972) and Hilary Putnam (1975), such assumptions, particularly assumptions (3) through (5), have enjoyed widespread acceptance in the philosophical investigation of natural kinds, such as (famously) water. No one is ever likely to have doubted that water is a part of the natural order, or that it is useful to think about water for purposes of causal inference and explanation. But many have held that terms such as 'water' have meanings determined entirely by facts about their use that are available to thoughtful native speakers of the language, resting comfortably in armchairs. As a result, it has also been held that it would be impossible for us to have many false beliefs about the nature of water (the nature of the thing referred to by 'water' is up to us to decide, when we determine how we will use this term, after all!), and so, barring gross deception, we could hardly be mistaken about whether or not water exists. But since the 1970s, it has come to be widely agreed that armchair reasoning about water cannot provide all the information there is about the essential nature of water. We may think that water is an infinitely divisible simple substance when in fact it is a finitely divisible compound, for instance. And while it remains unlikely that science will announce the non-existence of water, it has already announced the non-existence of caloric, the ether, and absolute space, in spite of their excellent armchair credentials.

This is the framework within which philosophy of the special sciences (physics, chemistry, biology, etc.) is generally conducted at present. Philosophers interested in fields or natural selection presuppose that these things have one nature, but remain open to scientific evidence that their actual nature is quite different. They presuppose that these things exist, but they remain open, in principle, to scientific evidence that would demonstrate (once interpreted correctly) that they do not. And so on. This is the framework I adopt in my investigation of desire. Desires are natural phenomena, causally interacting with the rest of the natural world, amenable to scientific investigation, vulnerable to surprising scientific results.

I will not offer a defense of this framework here. It places this work within a fruitful philosophical research program that treats the empirical sciences as sources of insight into the nature of mental phenomena,[12] and the fruitfulness of extending this research program to the topic of desire will be tested—and, I hope, demonstrated—in what follows. But in case the reader has serious qualms about treating desires as belonging to a natural kind, let me mention a few controversial philosophical theses to which I do *not* commit myself:

6. Some simple causal theory of reference or meaning is true of 'desire'.
7. Human beings lack first-person, subjective insight into their desires.
8. Scientists know better what we desire than we do ourselves.
9. Desires could turn out to be completely unlike our commonsensical notions of them.

Natural kinds and fairly crude causal theories of meaning have often been associated with one another, but this is an accident, not a matter of necessity, and (6) hardly follows from my modest presuppositions. I have mentioned Kripke and Putnam, but one need not hold to these philosophers' positive theories in order to agree with their insight that we can talk about water or desires without knowing, even implicitly, exactly what water *is* or what desires *are*.

A belief in some reasonable degree of privileged access to our own mental states should also not lead to worries. That (7) and (8) do not follow from assuming that desires form a natural kind is straightforward, for the fact that something is a natural kind says nothing about how facts about the kind are most readily learned. If introspection is good for anything at all, as it obviously is, then it is surely good for gathering information about our desires, and there is no reason to think that methods of epistemic access to desires other than introspection will prove superior merely because one supposes desires to be natural kinds. Assuming that desires are a natural kind strongly suggests that we will not be *incorrigible* in our beliefs about our own desires, but I would think that, at least since Freud, philosophers have been ready to agree that we do not have incorrigible knowledge of our desires.

As for (9), I take it to be an obvious constraint on any theory of a natural kind that it justify the claim that the natural kind has been explained, rather than eliminated. 'The ether' and 'absolute space' were putative natural kind terms, but scientific consensus now holds that there is no ether and no absolute space, not that these natural kinds were quite unlike what we expected them to be. Treating 'desire' as a natural kind is not a license to drag up any old entity from the back pages of some journal of neuroscience and proclaim it a desire, and I will spend part of chapter 6 defending the claim that I have genuinely said what desires are, and not eliminated or ignored them.

One more word on methodology. Throughout this work, I take it for granted that many non-human animals have desires. Cats can desire to drink fresh water, dogs can desire submissive behavior from those below them in pack structure, owls can desire dark sleeping places, and so on. Of course, only humans have certain desires: desires that they had never been born, that lead be transmutable to gold, that U.S. foreign policy be moderated. But this is, I assume, because humans are somewhat better at abstract conceptualizing, not because our minds are so different in kind from those of other animals. As with the other methodological assumptions of this work, I do not propose to defend the existence of desires in other species explicitly: the value of such assumptions will be seen in the work that is to come.

3. Audience

A final, very brief, preliminary remark. *Three Faces* is a book that faces a danger shared by other books importing science into philosophy: that it will be understood only by those who have made a special study of both fields. I have done my best to prevent this from being the case. My hope is that *Three Faces* will be accessible to scientists interested in desire, to philosophers of mind and philosophers of psychology used to thinking about the significance of scientific findings for philosophical theories, and to other philosophers interested in desire but lacking exposure to the relevant sciences. The topic of desire is of such widespread interest, and desires are themselves of such importance, that it seemed a shame to write only for a few.

The perils of writing for a wide audience are just as familiar as those of writing for a narrow one, of course. Some of my remarks about philosophy or science are bound to strike the reader as elementary, in which case I ask the reader to indulge her colleagues across the hall who are grateful for the exposition of what is elsewhere taken for granted. Likewise, some discussions of details are bound to be frustratingly difficult or confusing, in spite of efforts to minimize such episodes. In these cases, I ask the reader for patience: examples and illustrations generally follow, and make clear the point of more technical work.

Enough, then, with the preliminaries. On to desire.

1

The Standard Theory and Its Rivals

> Some say the world will end in fire,
> Some say in ice.
> From what I've tasted of desire
> I side with those who favor fire.
> But if it had to perish twice,
> I think I know enough of hate
> To say that for destruction ice
> Is also great
> And would suffice.
>
> —Robert Frost, "Fire and Ice"

Frost's "Fire and Ice" might be good poetry, but it isn't much as philosophy. So, at least, one might conclude after reading the standard position on desire among many philosophers of mind. Desiring, according to these philosophers, is simply a matter of being disposed to bring the desired end about, and really this has no more to do with fire than with ice. For instance, Michael Smith (1994, 115) suggests that the basic fact about desires is that "a desire that p tends to endure, disposing the subject in that state to bring it about that p," and according to Robert Stalnaker (1984, 15), "to desire that P is to be disposed to act in ways that would tend to bring it about that P in a world in which one's beliefs whatever they are, were true."[1] Passion and hatred are both expressions of desire, since both involve the agent being inclined to bring about specific ends. In the case of passion, one is motivated to attain the end that excites feelings of passion; in the case of hatred, one is motivated to bring about harm to the object of hatred. Hence, at bottom, passion and hatred are really one thing: motivational states. Or, in a word, desires.

That desiring is purely a matter of being motivated to attain an end is such a commonplace in many quarters of the philosophy of mind that it is not even defended; its truth is imagined to be self-evident upon a moment's reflection. Observations like Frost's, that there is an important distinction between burning desire and chilly aversion, are neither explained nor dismissed—they simply do not appear within the theoretical horizons of these philosophers. I shall call the motivational theory "the standard theory" of desire. The standard theory is lean, simple, and elegant. It is also false. Showing that the theory is, at the least, far from ideal is the main work of this chapter. Once this has been done, I will deal briefly with the standard theory's main rival, the hedonic theory of desire, and then sketch out some of the recent neuroscience that hints at an alternative theory of desire, the theory that will take up the rest of this book.

1. The Standard Theory of Desire

Before attacking the standard theory, however, it is only right to first present the theory in detail, and to show that the theory is not without its merits. Though the standard theory of desire is open to attack on a number of fronts, and ultimately inadequate to the task of explaining the wealth of commonsensical and scientific facts surrounding desire, it is far from obvious that the theory is doomed. On the contrary, the leanness, simplicity, and elegance of the standard theory are virtues that make it quite appealing. To the standard theory, then, I turn first.

According to the simplest version of the standard theory of desire, to have a desire that P is to have something inside you that plays the causal role characteristic of desires that P, that of moving you to bring it about that P (in some fairly straightforward way). Other versions of the standard theory (interpretationist, behaviorist, representationalist) modify this basic formulation, but the differences will be ignored for the moment, as the commonalities are substantial.

Standard Theory 1 (ST1): To desire that P is to be disposed to bring it about that P.

The standard theory has two central features. First, it holds that all desires are desires that P, for some proposition P. One cannot desire sex, an apple, Darren, or peace *simpliciter*, but must desire that one have sexual intercourse with one's partner that very minute, or that one eat an apple sometime that day, or that Darren fall in love with one and commit himself to a lasting relationship, or that all wars cease on Earth. This is a consequence that standard theorists find congenial. They, like many other philosophers, hold that what is desired can always be expressed with a complete proposition in a 'that-clause'. It may be that Eve desires an apple, but this is always shorthand for Eve's desiring that some state of affairs obtain[2]—some state that would count as satisfying Eve's desire—and to express this state of affairs (that Eve eat the apple at once, or that Eve eventually obtain an apple) requires a complete proposition.

The other central feature of desires on the standard theory is that they are action-guiding. Desires can play all sorts of causal roles within our heads, but there is just one role definitive of desiring, and that is of engaging the mental machinery in such a way as to tend to bring it about that P, for the P that is the content of the desire. Desires are distinguished by what they do, and what they do is move us to act. If I drive to San Francisco, that surely means that I wanted to go to San Francisco; if I had not wanted to go (for fun, to do my duty, or whatnot), I just would not have gone. Of course, in addition to motivating action, desires also cause us to worry, or to feel guilt, or to think about how far it is to San Francisco, but these are secondary effects of desires. According to the standard theory, these are side effects that do not appropriately distinguish desires from other things, such as beliefs. And indeed, beliefs may also cause feelings of worry or guilt, and thoughts about San Francisco, but beliefs alone do not seem to move us to action. The motivational power of desires is thus a natural point to seize upon in distinguishing desires from beliefs, and this is what the standard theory does.

Desiring is a rich and varied phenomenon, and these two features—propositional content and motivational force—making up as they do the whole of the standard theory, are a lean, economical duo. It would be a mistake, however, to criticize the theory for excessive parsimony on just these grounds. After all, the standard theory is a philosophical theory of desire, not a psychological theory. It says what it is for any creature whatsoever to have a desire, not what human desires are like in all their complexities. And this is quite right and proper. In human beings, desires come and go, they are sometimes stronger, sometimes weaker, they are desires that Ann have dinner with me, that you see a rare bird, that the neighbors turn down their stereo, it's one in the morning, goddamn it! And on one could go, for pages and pages, in loving natural-historical detail. But if it is possible for others—those afflicted with brain injuries, dolphins, robots, aliens, superintelligent shades of the color blue, or whatever might be out there—to have desires without having desires that change, or that have variable strength, or to have desires without caring at all about bodily needs, or in other ways to have desires without having the characteristic features of human desires, then these rich and varied phenomena have nothing to do with what desires *are*, and only tell us some of the incidental facts about desires. These incidental facts are quite interesting and may be needed for theoretical work in other areas (in moral theory or clinical psychology, for instance), but they need be of no particular importance to a philosophical theory of desire per se.

Still, it must be admitted that desire *is* a rich and varied part of the human mind, and while the standard theory of desire is not committed to giving an account of this richness and variety, it is not forbidden from doing so either. Indeed, there is a fairly standard supplementary account of human desire that tags along with the doctrinally central theory of desires in general. This supplementary story helps add a measure of plausibility to the standard theory of desire by showing that, lean as the standard theory is, it is readily supplemented in a manner that is consistent and that makes for a well-rounded account of desires in actual human beings. The supplementary story usually has a number of details.

According to the standard theory, there is no bar in principle to organisms desiring only pleasure, or desiring only their own reproductive success, or desiring only that bell-bottomed pants be retired from fashion forever. In actual human beings, however, the standard theory holds that desires are for many things, both sensuous (desires to smell a certain way or empty one's bladder) and abstract (desires to make something of oneself or to refute Gödel's incompleteness result). In particular, they are not restricted to sexual longings, or to the satisfaction of basic bodily needs. Desires for sex, desires to make something of oneself, desires to confront reality and desires to walk to work all share the common, two-part core of desiring: they all involve some state of affairs, and being motivated to bring that state of affairs about. Because they share this common core, the standard theory calls them all 'desires'.

All desires play the role of tending to get the agent to bring about their contents. But some desires are better poised for bringing about their ends than others, all else being equal. Such desires are *stronger* than others, and other desires are *weaker*. If Brad desires both to own a new car and to avoid debt, and his desires ultimately move him to purchase a new car even though that involves acquiring debt, then that shows he wanted the car more than he wanted to avoid debt, at least in the normal case. Cases in which a weaker desire moves an agent to action in the face of a stronger and directly competing desire are, by their nature, cases of some sort of failure of the action-producing system (according to the standard theory). If Brad were to read too many stories of personal bankruptcies on the day he was intending to purchase his car, he could lose his nerve and be moved to avoid debt instead, but this sort of outcome would have to be the product of some sort of processing failure within Brad, given that his desire to purchase a new car is stronger.

Being rather more careful, a standard-theory description of Brad would talk about coalitions of desires and perceived likelihoods of outcomes. Brad does not have just two desires: to own a new car and to avoid debt. He has, surely, scores of desires: desires to someday visit India, to enjoy a comfortable retirement, to be perceived as manly, to keep the love of those who love him, to be fit, and so on. Additionally, Brad has various rough estimates of how likely he would be to attain, or make progress toward attaining, these various ends given particular actions. Signing an appropriate piece of paper, then, is taken to be a surefire way of satisfying the desire to own a new car, and a moderately effective way of making others perceive him as manly, while also being seen as rather detrimental to getting to India and slightly detrimental to enjoying a comfortable retirement, and so on. These coalitions of desires and guesses about the impact a particular action would have upon their satisfaction or frustration are what really weigh in against one another in determining motivation, according to the standard theory. But given the types of choices people actually make, a model of choice as competition between desires with the strongest winning is not such a poor first approximation.

The fact that desires can be stronger or weaker invites obvious questions, to which the standard theory has conventional answers. The limit of desire weakness is, of course, zero—not having a desire at all. Desire strength, on the other hand, has no limit, since it is a relational matter: there is no limit to how much stronger the tendency to act on one desire might be as compared to the tendency to act on another. These basic facts about desires, while not entailed by the standard account, are a natural supplement to it, needed for anything like a full explanation of human desires. Another challenging question—how to compare desire strength between individuals (possibly of different species)—is the topic of ongoing research by decision theorists and utilitarians,[3] but one on which the standard theory is silent.

Then there is the fact that desires are involved in the causation of pleasure and displeasure. If I desire to own a plot of land, coming to own it will cause me pleasure, and missing a chance to buy it will cause me displeasure.[4] Conceptually speaking this is an accident, according to the standard theory of desire, but an "accident" natural selection has chosen for non-arbitrary reasons. Exactly why desire has a hedonic face is not generally explained by standard theorists of desire, but this face is not ignored by the standard theory.

Critics of the standard theory sometimes appear to misunderstand the standard theory's commitments when it comes to pleasure and displeasure. For instance, in moral theory there is an ongoing debate about whether moral beliefs can, without the assistance of desires, motivate action.[5] One sometimes hears support for the thesis that they can do so given along the following lines: when I eat chocolate, say, I do what I desire, but when I refrain from speaking sharply to an annoying student, I do *not* do what I desire; I act solely out of my sense of duty. Thus, it is possible to be moved by duty in the absence of desire. This distinction between acting out of duty and out of desire is sometimes imagined to be supported on the grounds of phenomenology, including hedonic phenomenology: the agent gets pleasure out of eating chocolate, but does not get pleasure from refraining from sharp words, and so, it is thought, one can reasonably infer that a desire is acted upon in the first case but not the second.[6] This style of argument need have no force against the standard theorist, however. The standard theorist will simply interpret the story of the person who refrains from speaking sharply to the student as a story about two conflicting desires, one of which (the desire to do the right thing) wins out but does not lead to pleasure. The standard theorist may claim that satisfying a desire typically causes pleasure, but it is no part of the standard theory that satisfying a desire always causes pleasure, much less that it essentially causes pleasure (or is even disposed to do so all else being equal). Because she connects pleasure to desire only by the causal structure of individual minds, it is open to the standard theorist to imagine individuals who are full of desires but who never take pleasure in their satisfaction. The fact that a particular person takes no pleasure from acting morally on some occasion is a fact needing to be explained, but on the standard theory the fact cannot entail anything about the presence or absence of a desire.

For the same reasons, the standard theory holds that strength of feeling and strength of desire cannot be expected to map infallibly onto one another. The fact that Todd suffers greatly from being forced to pay for the ottoman that he had expected to come free with the reclining chair he is purchasing—even the fact that he suffers far more from this experience than he does from many others—does not demonstrate that Todd's desire for a free ottoman is stronger than many of his other desires. The strength of Todd's feeling may present some evidence that his desire is strong, but it could just be the case that Todd is prone to strong feelings on the subject of discount furniture, and that this desire is much weaker than many other desires that stir up weaker feelings.

Pleasure and displeasure are just a portion of the total contribution desires make to consciousness, on the standard theory. One can be aware of a desire by feeling the disappointment that its frustration causes or the elation produced by its satisfaction, one can experience the effects of a desire by experiencing the movements one is impelled to make by desires, and one's desires can cause one to think to oneself "I want . . ."; these are all fairly direct ways in which desires can affect one's conscious life. One can also feel things such as the tension and readiness to act that come before actual actions in some cases, and sometimes one can feel the control desire can take over the focus of attention, bringing one's eyes or thoughts back to a particular person or scene again and again. That said, it is an equally familiar claim made by the standard theory that desires need not appear in consciousness at all, as is the case with most of our standing desires (for the well-being of our loved ones, for example). Desires can even have baroque, disguised effects upon consciousness (as in the case of desires that show themselves only in nineteenth-century hysterias, or in dreams). These phenomena are a treasure trove for the novelist to draw upon and might seem to present a problem for the lean standard theory. As with the relation of pleasure and displeasure to desire, however, it is again open to the standard theorist to hold that these phenomena are all linked to desire through non-necessary, though eminently reasonable, evolutionary happenstance.

It must be noted that there is a view of desire according to which the only real, full-blooded desires are those which are a part of consciousness, unconscious desires being mere dispositions to token true desires in consciousness,[7] but this view is rejected by the standard theory. The standard theory of desire holds that desires do not depend upon consciousness for their existence but upon motivational structures, and the involvement of a desire in consciousness is not necessary for it to carry out its functional role. Accordingly, a desire is a desire whether it is part of consciousness or not.

The third face of desire, stressed by Fred Dretske in his *Explaining Behavior* (1988) but largely neglected by both popular thinking and philosophical research, is that there is a link between desire and reward: desires determine what counts as a reward and what counts as a punishment for an organism. A rat, according to this view, can only be rewarded with food when it wants food; when it does not want food, food is no reward, and indeed force-feeding a satiated rat would constitute a punishment. In the standard theory, this can be accommodated as another accidental, but evolutionarily sensible, feature of desires. Just as it makes sense for pleasure and displeasure to be linked to desire, so it makes sense for desires to determine what will serve to operantly condition an organism.

2. Objections to the Standard Theory

The standard theory of desire is spare, while the lived experience of desire is rich and complex. The standard theory works hard to incorporate this richness by holding that while the nature of desire is simple, desire happens to play a very complex role within actual human beings, but a number of problems remain for the theory. Seven will be canvassed here, ranging from the purely philosophical through to the neuroscientific. Not all of these objections will apply equally to all versions of the standard theory of desire, and they are not intended as a decisive refutation of the standard theory. Even so, I hope that they will shake the reader's confidence in the standard theory. There may be a correct lean and economical theory of desire, but it is not obvious that the standard theory is it.

Motivation Is Not Essential to Desire

The first series of objections I want to make against the standard theory of desire stems from the thought that it ties desire too closely to motivation. Desires typically involve motivation in some manner, true enough. But to hold that a motivational component is necessary to all desires seems to take things too far.

First, think of some simple desires that would appear to lack connection to an agent's motivation. Think, for example, of an ancient Greek mathematician who is uncertain about the value of π but who desires that it not be expressible as a fraction of two natural numbers. What motivational complex could possibly correspond to this desire? There is nothing our mathematician can do, and nothing he believes he can do, to affect the value of π. He can affect what is believed about the value of π, of course, but wanting π to be irrational is not the same as wanting π to be believed to be irrational, and our mathematician desires the former, not the latter. Desires regarding the necessary facts of the world, such as the facts of mathematics, are admittedly scarce, but not as scarce as might be imagined. In addition to contemporary mathematicians and logicians wanting that the logical facts be this way or that, there are people who desire, say, that there be superconductors that are ductile and that conduct at over 40° Celsius, or that superstring theory be a close approximation to a correct theory of the fundamental constitution of the universe. These desires, like desires about logical facts, are desires about necessities, though they are desires about physical necessities rather than logical ones. Still, there is nothing an agent can do to change whether or not a certain material can, in principle, be constructed, or whether an existing physical theory is, in fact, correct, and few are deluded otherwise. Nonetheless, people have these desires.

Even more prosaic examples can be found if we turn to desires relating to our own personal timelines. I might desire that I had never been born, or that my parents had never met, or that, right now, life exist elsewhere in the universe (or, to be more prosaic still, I might desire that my girlfriend, away at a conference, not be having an affair at this very moment). Because of the necessary facts about causation, these are also desires for ends I can do nothing to bring about, and so are problematic for the standard theory to accommodate. As with our imagined ancient Greek mathematician, it should be pointed out that these desires should not be mistaken for related desires. If I desire that my girlfriend not be having an affair at this very moment, this is not a desire that can be satisfied by it being the case that my girlfriend is not having an affair ten seconds later, after I have called her on her cell phone: my desire can only be satisfied if no affair is taking place just then, before I have dialed her number. No doubt I would also desire that my girlfriend not be having an affair at other times, but these would be other desires, not identical to the desire that might suddenly seize control of my consciousness in a moment of panicky doubt: I hope she isn't making love to some suave Hegelian *right now* while I'm stuck here in traffic! In the same way, the desire that there exist a material with certain special properties is not the desire that one discover it, or that someone discover it, or that one have experiences as if the material existed. These are all desires fulfilled under readily distinguished conditions from the desired condition, that there be arrangements of atoms having certain electrical conduction and ductility properties.

The standard theory of desire cannot accommodate these sorts of desires with any ease. The standard theory says that to desire that I had never been born is to be disposed to bring it about that I had never been born, but obviously no such disposition is possible. The standard theory might appeal to contrary-to-possibility counterfactuals, holding that a desire for some causally inaccessible state of affairs would act to cause me to bring that state of affairs about, if only it were possible to affect things in this way. But such a cure appears worse than the disease it is supposed to remedy. How does one determine how an agent would behave in a universe in which basic logical or metaphysical facts did not hold?

A more conservative and more credible response to objections like those just raised might look something like the following:

> **ST2**: To desire that *P* is to be so disposed that, if one were to believe that taking action *A* would be an effective method for bringing it about that *P*, then one would take *A*.

This constitutes quite an improvement over the more standard formulation, in that it deals with objections derived from the impossibility of bringing it about that *P*. Although no one has a disposition to change mathematical truths, some people might have dispositions to take actions they *believe* would change mathematical truths. However, the theory has trouble with ends that the agent hopes obtain, but that the agent would not be willing, under any circumstances, to cause to obtain. Suppose I desire that a committee make up its mind in my favor without my intervention. This is a state of affairs I might want very much, yet because of the very nature of the desire it makes no sense to try to act so as to satisfy it. What I want is that the committee make a certain decision *without* my needing to do anything.

The defender of the standard view could answer that, even though it would be tremendously irrational of me to believe that I could intervene to make the committee reach a decision without my own intervention, this level of irrationality is possible. Yet almost anything is possible at this level of irrationality. At this level of irrationality, it is certainly possible that I have the requisite belief and desire and not intervene, for instance. Weakness of will and sheer incompetence are known to exist, after all. What can the defender of the standard view say in response? He cannot just add another clause requiring that the agent be rational. If I were rational, then I would not take any action regarding the committee at all, certainly not an action designed to influence the committee's decision-making process. Similarly, the defender of the standard view cannot simply add a clause saying that the desire is effective, or has its characteristic effects. Just what the characteristic effects are of desires—just what it is for a desire to be effective—is what is under debate at present, and it would beg the question for a defender of the standard theory to presuppose that an effective desire is one which moves an agent to action.

For a similar moral, imagine I desire that I had never been born. If I had this desire, would I push a button I believed would make it true that I had never been born, even if I also believed that nothing else mattering to me would be affected? Specifically, would I prefer to push this button rather than push another button simply ending my existence? If my reason for wishing never to have been born is self-regarding (I wish I had never had the experiences I did) as opposed to other-regarding (I wish I had never hurt my beloved the way I did), then why would I be disposed to push the first button rather than the second, however rational I might be?

No version of the standard theory which requires that an agent desiring that P aim at bringing it about that P under any non-question-begging circumstances easily answers these objections. But if the standard theory were to hold that desiring that P need not always involve being disposed to (try to) bring it about that P, the question would arise what one *did* have to be disposed to bring about, in order to desire that P. One could hold that, for P's regarding necessities, one desires that P so long as one is disposed to sigh with relief upon hearing that P, or to assent that one desires that P when questioned by someone one believes deserves to hear the truth, or something of the sort. But this would both involve introducing an artificial distinction between desires regarding things one believes one could, in principle, change and desires regarding things one believes one could not, and would also require behaviors—sighing, assenting, or the like—with no clear intrinsic connection to the actual content of the desire. It does not take much imagination to conjure up scenarios in which a person would desire that P but not be the least inclined to assent to desiring that P under any conditions (people lacking the capacity to make assertions leap to mind here, though other, more convoluted scenarios will also do), or to engage in any behavior other than bringing P about. But since not all desires will move the agent (under any conditions) to bring it about that P or even try to do so, there seems to be no sort of action at all necessarily associated with desiring.

One final theoretical twist: this first objection could be answered by a teleofunctional version of the standard theory. This sort of theory, championed by Millikan (1984, 1993) and Papineau (1987), holds that desires need not *tend* to realize their ends, they need only have the biological *function* of realizing their ends. ST3 presents the simplest version of such a theory.[8]

ST3: To desire that P is to have a structure inside one whose biological function is to bring it about that P.

If an ancient Greek mathematician desires that the value of π be irrational, that desire might have no tendency to move the mathematician to action, but it might still be a neural structure whose *function* is to move the mathematician to action, and so be counted as a desire by ST3. The structure might not be able to perform its function, true, but this no more entails that it lacks the function than the inability of a particular sperm cell to fertilize an egg (due to malformation or the like) entails that the cell lacks the function of fertilizing eggs. Admittedly, one does not normally think of the brain as containing structures whose biological function is to bring about mathematical necessities. But there are possible answers here. The advocate of ST3 can hold that particular neural systems have the function of moving one to bring it about that *P* for whatever states of affairs *P* one comes to associate with the so-called primary reinforcers: things such as food, water, and sex, for instance. Through a suitably complex chain of associations, food, water, or sex might come to be associated in a particular person's mind with π being irrational, and so give a person a structure with the function of moving her to bring it about that π be irrational. This structure would not, of course, be capable of carrying out its function, but that would not deprive it of the function. And so the structure would count as a desire that π be irrational.[9]

Though ST3 solves one problem for the standard theory of desire, it seems to saddle the theory with an even worse problem. As has been much discussed in the philosophical literature, there is a high price to pay if one makes having biological functions a strictly necessary requirement for having desires or other states of mind. If one assumes, as Millikan and Papineau do, that biological functions are derived from histories of natural selection, then it turns out that no creature can have a mind unless it is the product of a long biological lineage, and that has seemed implausible to many. Surely a mad scientist making a very lifelike human brain out of protoplasm would be able to make a mind with desires if she simply got the arrangement of protoplasm right. Surely a being that coalesced by pure accident out of randomly moving molecules would have a mind if it were an atom-for-atom duplicate of Donald Davidson. Surely a creature recovering from massive injuries to the brain, whose brain is doing things it was never adapted to do, nonetheless still has the mind it seems to have.[10] There is room to debate these points, but the challenge facing the teleofunctional theorist of desire is daunting, and not evidently easier to meet than the challenge facing the more dispositional defender of the standard theory.

After all these technical details have been considered, there is also the commonsensical observation that desires regarding mathematical truths, one's never having been born, and the like just obviously do *not* play the same role in one's motivational economy as other desires (which is, perhaps, why they are commonly called "wishes" rather than "desires"), and in fact seem to play perfectly appropriate non-motivational roles instead. Some desires can, perhaps, be thought of as driving forces behind behavior, but wishes regarding the known necessary facts of the world simply do not seem to act in this way. Wishes one has about mathematical facts, or one's own birth, play important roles in guiding thought and feeling, in sensitizing one to certain related issues, in drawing one's attention to particular items of information and so on, but they simply do not feel like they are impotently driving one toward doing what it is impossible to do. I see no reason not to take this observation at face value other than the fact that the standard theory is the best theory of desire available, and it requires a non-obvious interpretation of the phenomenology. Since it is the project of this book to show that there is a superior competitor theory to the standard theory, this reason hardly carries much weight in the present context.

The claim that desires are, necessarily, things that dispose us to action gives rise to other problems as well. Why could there not exist beings quite incapable of action who nonetheless had desires? This question forms the basis for a second objection to the standard theory. In *Mental Reality* (1994), Galen Strawson asks us to imagine a race of "Weather Watchers," beings whose internal states have no dispositions to cause their owners to act, and have never (neither phylogenetically nor ontogenetically) had such dispositions. He imagines that such creatures might have beliefs about what the weather is and desires that it be one way or another; such a life, though evolutionarily unlikely, does not seem a metaphysical impossibility. Surely, we might have naively thought, a creature who had an experience as of having soaring hopes upon seeing a break in the clouds, only to feel something just like bitter despair when the sky again became overcast, would be a creature who wanted something, who had certain desires. Yet it also seems possible that these feelings should exist in the absence of any biological structure directed at bringing about ends. Intuitively, it seems plausible that a being could be of a sort to lack limbs or other behavioral capacities, while still having the ability to feel just what we feel when our hopes soar, or when despair comes crashing down on us. And since appropriate dispositions to these experiences would seem to entail that a being has desires, it would seem to follow that desires can exist in the absence of any motivational capacities whatsoever.

In response, it is open to the standard theorist to hold that the imagined scenario is not a real metaphysical possibility—either because the person imagining it does not realize that to be conscious metaphysically requires the capacity to act (as some functionalists might have it) or because the person imagining the Weather Watchers does not realize that he is not imagining a being with desires, but only a being with certain feelings. There is nothing internally inconsistent in such a response, but it does seem prima facie implausible. It is, once again, a response that we could accept if the standard theory of desire were by far the best available theory, but it once again demonstrates that there is room for an intuitively more attractive theory of desire.[11]

Motivation Is Not Sufficient for Desiring

A third problem for the standard theory of desire might be put as follows: Intending that *P* and trying to bring it about that *P*, just as much as desiring that *P*, involve structures playing functional roles such that, when the actor's beliefs are true, his actions will tend to bring it about that *P*. What is it, then, that separates desires from other pro attitudes? The answer generally offered by the standard theory is that there is exactly one basic pro attitude, namely desire, and any other pro attitude is a complex of desires and other things. So, for instance, it is sometimes held that to will that *P* is simply for one's strongest (first-order) desire to be a desire that *P*,[12] that intending that *P* is desiring that *P* and believing that one will bring it about that *P*,[13] that hoping that *P* is desiring that *P* while believing *P* not very likely,[14] and so on. Thus, providing motivational *oomph* is uniquely distinctive of desiring, and so can characterize what it is to desire. Unfortunately for the standard theory of desire, these proposals are not uniformly satisfactory. At the very least, intending and trying are not so easily reduced to complexes containing desires.

In defense of trying as an autonomous mental event, Alfred Mele (1990) has argued that a person may try to do something without actually wanting to do it. For instance, imagine a person offered money if she will try to bench-press sixty kilograms. While she is indifferent to the accomplishment, she would like the money. She thus tries to lift the weight without particularly desiring to lift the weight, and so trying must be distinct from desiring. There is room for the standard theorist to object that the weight lifter is *really* trying to get some money, but if it is accepted that she is trying to do so by means of trying to lift the weight, then Mele's point stands: the weight lifter tries to do something she does not, in any sense, desire to do: she has a pro attitude toward a state of affairs that is not a desired state of affairs. If so, then trying cannot readily be understood as a composite entity made up, in part or in whole, of an individual's desires.

Turning to intentions, Michael Bratman (1987, 15–20) has argued that considerations of when an intention is rational show that intentions cannot be reduced to complexes of beliefs and desires. Bratman holds that, while there need be nothing irrational in failing to act on a desire to drink a milkshake for lunch when lunchtime comes (after all, one's desire might be outweighed by other desires), there would be something irrational in an agent who intended to drink a milkshake for lunch, assuming certain conditions obtained, but who, when lunchtime came, did nothing about drinking a milkshake in spite of the fact that circumstances were evidently just as expected. Hence, if intentions are to be thought of as involving desires, they must be thought of as involving desires of sufficient strength relative to other desires that they decisively control action in rational actors. That is, if intentions involve desires at all, they must involve an agent's predominant desire, the one that it would be irrational to act against (in the expected circumstances). Yet intentions can conflict (in less than ideally rational agents), while predominant desires cannot conflict by definition, and so intention cannot be analyzed in terms of predominant desire after all, making it seem that intention cannot be analyzed in terms of any sort of desires.[15]

If we are convinced to accept the existence of trying and intending as pro attitudes distinct from desiring, and we accept that trying and intending have the motivational force they appear to, it follows straightforwardly that motivation cannot be all there is to the nature of desiring. Now, this in itself is not a criticism of everyone who has held something like the standard theory, since not everyone advocating something like the standard theory has had the goal of explaining the nature of *desire*, in the sense at stake here. Often, advocates of something like the standard theory have really intended it only as a theory of the nature of having a pro attitude. But some standard theorists—those inclined to reduce all pro attitudes to complexes of desires and other things, for instance—are vulnerable to the points raised by Mele and Bratman, and in any case, this third objection at least shows that if one wants a theory of desires specifically, one must think twice before simply accepting the standard theory as adequate.

There are sources of motivational impulses other than trying and intending that also look unlike desires, and that provide a fourth objection to the standard theory. Take, for instance, habits. A person may ingrain a habit, such as turning left at a particular intersection, through many years of repetitive action. Once ingrained, the habit may retain a certain motivational power even in the absence of any relevant desire. For example, imagine a man who ingrained the habit of turning left at a particular intersection because that was the direction he took to work for years. Taking a job elsewhere in the city, the man may be left with no desire whatsoever that would be satisfied by turning left at that very intersection (the former place of work need hold no fond memories, the scenery of the route need evoke no nostalgia, etc.). Yet on returning to the familiar intersection on some errand, say, to fetch some tea from the local Chinese grocery found if one turns *right* at the intersection, the man may find himself turning left purely out of habit, without any desire required to provide the impetus to make the left turn. Examples such as this would seem to show that too much stress has been placed upon the motivational face of desire. The ability to get the body moving in a coordinated way is not exclusive to desiring, or even to pro attitudes more generally, for a habit is no sort of attitude at all, much less a pro attitude.[16] Of course, behavior produced out of habit is not a clear counterexample to the standard theory of desire, because it is quite unclear how such behavior is produced, or even whether it should be called 'acting'. Yet the phenomenon should be worrying to friends of the standard theory, if only because it suggests that there are yet further sources of motivational force to which they have not given sufficient attention.

A fifth and related problem comes from the phenomenon of stuttering.[17] In stuttering, it is often the case that anxiety about stuttering itself is a principal cause of stuttering. If we take this anxiety to involve, at a minimum, a belief with the content that one is going to stutter, then it seems to turn out, on the standard theory of desire, that this belief is a desire to stutter. After all, the belief has the content that one will stutter, and the belief does play a functional role such that it tends to produce stuttering, and this is the entire nature of desiring according to the standard theory. This example, like those before, seems to be an example of being moved without really desiring that the end-state be brought about, and so another counterexample to the sufficiency of the standard theory.

The response could be made that this fifth objection is really just a variant on a standard problem for action theory, namely that of so-called deviant causal chains. In the theory of action, there is a puzzle about how to draw a principled distinction between two sorts of cases, in both of which a belief and a desire combine to produce a rationalized behavior, but in one of which the behavior is the product of a deviant causal chain and, intuitively, is not a genuine action. For example, imagine that Kristín is skiing downhill at high speed. Frightened about a possible high-speed crash, she has conflicting desires: both to fall down in a safe manner and to continue skiing and test her limits. It suddenly occurs to her that if she were to turn *thus* and fall now, she would fall safely and avoid all danger of a crash. The thought causes her to lose her nerve, and she takes the turn badly, *thus*, resulting in a safe fall. The poor turn and safe fall (Q) are caused, it seems, by her desire that she avoid a crash (P) and her belief that $Q \rightarrow P$, but nonetheless do not seem to be a genuine action. What is wrong with the fall is that it is produced through a deviant causal chain—through a chain that involves her belief causing her to lose her nerve, and her loss of nerve causing her to take a turn badly—rather than through a normal decision that falling now would be better than continuing on. This sort of problem is a familiar one to action theorists, and though there is no widespread agreement about how to address it, there is widespread agreement that there must be some way to address it.

Because a belief that one is going to stutter can cause one to stutter without any accompanying desire, it might be said that the "stuttering" objection is just a version of the deviant causal chains problem. There is a deviant causal chain that leads from a belief about future stuttering to stuttering itself, just as there is a deviant causal chain that leads from Kristín's thought that she could be safe by falling down to her falling down. And since it is universally agreed that there has to be some solution to the deviant causal chains problem, it should also be agreed that there will be some solution to the stuttering problem for the standard theory of desire. The problem with this response is that the action-theory literature only presupposes that there is some way to distinguish appropriate causal chains producing actions from inappropriate ones producing mere behavior: there is no presupposition that the distinction can be made while maintaining any particular theory of action or of desire. In the same way, I would agree that there must be some solution to the problem raised, since a belief that one is going to stutter certainly is not a desire to stutter, but this presupposition does not entail that the solution will be compatible with any particular theory of desire. And in fact, the problem suggests that the best way to distinguish a motivating belief from a motivating desire is to have a theory of what it is to desire other than merely to be motivated.

Mental Representation

Perhaps the most popular version of the standard theory among philosophers of mind at present is the representationalist version, presented in ST4:

ST4: To desire that P is to have a mental representation that P which plays a certain causal role, namely, that of disposing one to bring it about that P.

According to the philosophers of mind who have theorized about them, mental representations are structures found in organisms' heads that have the capacity to represent particular states of affairs, allowing them to believe, desire, intend, think, and so on, that P, for various states of affairs P.[18] On the representationalist version of the standard theory, beliefs, desires, and so on are created by individual mental representations playing appropriate functional roles. Believing that P involves a mental representation that P playing one functional role, while desiring that P involves a distinct representing object (token) with the same content playing a different functional role, desiring that Q involves a distinct token with a different content, and so on.

Of course, ST4 faces the problems confronted by other versions of the standard theory, but in spite of its popularity, it also faces some special problems of its own. Looking at the brain, for instance, there arises a sixth problem: where are the mental representations found in desires *tokened*? That is, where are desires found within the brain? Kandel, Schwartz, and Jessell (2000), a leading text in neuroscience, describes the major functional areas of the cerebral cortex as containing primary sensory cortex, sensory association areas, primary motor cortex, motor association areas, and three "multimodal sensory association areas" (351). The sensory areas are held to be the home of sensory/perceptual representations, while the motor areas are held to be the home of representations demanding immediate, simple actions of the body: simple bodily movements and short sequences of movements.[19] Neither sort of representational structure is suited to be the seat of mental states such as desires for a prosperous future or desires to consume baked brie: these are not sensory representations, but they are also not commands to the body for simple behaviors, even according to the standard theorist. This leaves only the remaining three multimodal (i.e., receiving input from multiple sensory modalities) sensory association areas as likely homes of desire. The first of these association areas, in the parietotemporal region, is believed to function in "visuospatial localization, language, attention"—in domains distant from desire, in other words. The second of these, the pre-frontal portion of the frontal lobe, is dominated by working memory and short-term action planning systems (Goldman-Rakic 1987, 1998). The third association area, the limbic association area, contains straightforward memory systems (in the hippocampus and related cortex), the amygdala, which is the center for the classical conditioning of fear responses and related responses (LeDoux 1996, 2000), and the cingulate cortex, only the anterior half of which is linked to any emotional or motivational functions, and which proves to be the home primarily of pleasure and displeasure (see chapter 3) and a short-term motor preparation area (see chapter 4). If we take most desires to be achievable in any number of manners, and so not identifiable with any particular representation commanding a limb movement or short sequence of such movements, and we take most desires to be more than classically conditioned responses or desires for pleasure, then we are left with a puzzle. In the whole of the cerebral cortex, there is no plausible home for the scores of mental representations required by our scores of desires. This is not to say that desires have no home in the brain, of course. This is rather to say that the most straightforward version of the representationalist standard theory, with its simple picture of a distinct set of mental representations making up our desires, is a biologically implausible picture.

The same point can be made by pointing out that, although brain regions have been found whose stimulation causes sensory hallucinations or brief motor responses, no region of the brain has been found whose stimulation causes a person to become motivated to tend to her child's well-being, or to see to it that humans colonize Mars, or do other things that people take as ultimate ends.[20] If the simple representationalist version of the standard theory were correct, one would expect such "desire centers" to be discoverable at least in principle, and by now to have been discovered in fact. Yet scientific studies on humans have not yet turned up such centers.

A standard theorist of desire not committed to representationalism could readily meet the biological challenge just presented by pointing out that, clearly enough, people *are* moved to meet their goals on at least some occasions, and so how the brain accomplishes this, and why it cannot be electrically stimulated into replicating these effects, is irrelevant. But a representationalist standard theorist commits to a very particular set of claims about the realization of desires in the brain (with differences depending upon the particular representationalist in question), and she finds herself in hot water when it becomes hard to make good on these claims by identifying where, exactly, the desire-forming representations are to be found. Of course, representationalists can claim that the representations underlying desires are unlike the representations underlying perception, memory, and short-term movement production in that they are *very* non-localized structures. But why believe that the brain uses one type of representational system for desires and a different type of representational system for everything else? The failure of the brain to reveal a distinct collection of representations connected to its desires poses a challenge to the would-be representationalist that cannot be ignored.

A Phenomenon That Fits Poorly

For a seventh and, for the present, final objection to the standard theory of desire, one could certainly do worse than return to Robert Frost and the poem that began this chapter. This objection leaves behind the debate between representational and non-representational formulations of the standard theory, and comes back to phenomenological issues challenging to any version of the theory. One way of reading Frost's distinction between fire and ice, between what he calls "desire" and "hate," is to distinguish between appetites and aversions, and then to align fire and desire with an appetitive, positive stance toward a state of affairs, while aligning ice and hatred with an aversive, negative attitude toward a state of affairs. This way of reading Frost is not the only one—certainly, there are forms of hatred that amount to an appetite for destruction, rather than icy aversion—but it strikes me as a plausible reading, one that makes sense of the metaphors of fire and ice. In any case, the interpretation is one that points to a legitimate phenomenological distinction: the distinction of desire-like attitudes into positive and negative is readily recognized.

How, then, would the standard theory go about explaining this distinction? One option would be to distinguish between appetite and aversion by distinguishing between desires that P and desires that not-P. To have an appetite for pie is to have a desire that I eat pie, on this view, while to have an aversion to eating pie is to have a desire that I not eat pie. This might seem the natural way for the standard theory to accommodate Frost's distinction, but a moment's reflection will show that it is not. After all, why not think of the person with an appetite for pie as the person who desires not to go without pie, and the person with an aversion to pie as the person who desires to go without pie? One can play with where the negation symbol appears in the content of a person's desire without changing whether the desire is more appetitive or more aversive in nature. Likewise, imagine a bodyguard who desires that his charge remain safe from harm. This is a desire that P. But does the bodyguard really have an appetite for his charge's safety? This certainly need not be the case. The bodyguard might be indifferent to his charge as a person, yet be highly averse to his charge being harmed. Although there is no negation symbol in the content of his desire, his demeanor suggests ice more than fire. If ice and fire are good metaphors, they are not metaphors for mental contents with or without negation symbols in front of them, but for something to do with the role the desires play within our own minds.

At this point, a defender of the standard theory is likely to point out that the distinction between positive appetite and negative aversion need not be found in the essential nature of desire. It could instead be found, say, in the syndrome of associated experiences that cluster around a desire. If the primary phenomenology of desire satisfaction is itself positive—joy, or contentment, for example—then the desire may be counted a positive appetite. If, on the other hand, the primary phenomenology of desire satisfaction is emotionally flat, or a sensation of relief, and fear or dislike of non-satisfaction is a central phenomenon, then the desire may be counted as a negative aversion. This way of characterizing the dichotomy may be a little crude (one needs to account for desires never satisfied, and so on), but it is plausible that it could be refined. Thus, the standard theory could accept the distinction: there are two kinds of desires, one kind having a more passionate, fiery phenomenology, the other a more aversive, glacial phenomenology.

Reinterpreting the thesis that there is a deep distinction between positive appetite and negative aversion as the thesis that there is a superficial distinction between desires that cause certain syndromes of pleasure and desires that cause certain syndromes of displeasure may not strike the reader as a reinterpretation that stays close to the original intuitions. The very fact that some desires provoke one syndrome of experiences, while others provoke quite different experiences, seems a fact needing explanation, of a sort that might naturally be thought to stem from a theory of desire. That is, the most natural way to read the phenomenology is as suggesting the existence of a distinction in kind between positive and negative desire-like attitudes. The standard theory can draw a corresponding distinction, but identifies it with the distinction in phenomenology. Thus, the standard theory treats the phenomenology as constitutive of a superficial distinction, rather than indicative of a deeper distinction. This is not self-evidently a fault of the standard theory, but it does not sit especially well with every aspect of everyday experience, and so is yet another reason to be discontented with the standard theory.

3. The Hedonic Theory of Desire

The arguments of the previous section suggest that the motivational face of desire is not its essence. A possible conclusion to draw would be that the arguments thereby show that the hedonic face of desire is its essential aspect: desiring is to be explained in terms of feelings of pleasure and displeasure, rather than motivation.[21] After all, though the hedonic theory of desire has never been the dominant theory, it has a certain appeal. John Stuart Mill appears to lean toward something like a hedonic theory of desire in writing, "desiring a thing and finding it pleasant, aversion to it and thinking of it as painful, are phenomena entirely inseparable or, rather, two parts of the same phenomenon" (Mill 1861/1957, 49), and Mill is not the only distinguished historical figure to have considered such a view.[22] More recently, Galen Strawson (1994) has also defended a hedonic theory of desire.

A straightforward hedonic theory of desire might look something like the following:

Hedonic Theory 1 (HT1): To desire that P is to be so disposed that one will tend to feel pleasure if it seems that P, and/or displeasure if it seems that not-P.

Or, for those philosophers who prefer to reify desires rather than identify them with dispositions:

HT2: To desire that P is to contain some structure (this being the desire) which so disposes one that one will tend to feel pleasure if it seems that P, and/or displeasure if it seems that not-P.

A theory of desire such as HT1 or HT2 draws upon a number of lines of evidence for its support. First, there is the simple observation that desires are *felt*. To be hungry or thirsty, to pick two paradigmatic desires, is at least to have certain feelings. And these feelings are distinguished from the feeling of a mere rumble in the stomach, or the feeling of a throat that is dry, by the fact that one feels displeasure when one is hungry or thirsty, and pleasure when the desire is satisfied.

Perhaps hunger and thirst involve more, in their essence, than the salient collection of feelings that accompany them, but perhaps not: it is not obviously unreasonable to hold that hunger and thirst can be identified with dispositions to the appropriate feelings, and this is just what is proposed by the hedonic theorist.

Looking beyond hunger and thirst, there is the fact that all sorts of desired states are sources of pleasure when they obtain, and all sorts of states of affairs one desires to avoid are sources of displeasure when they obtain. Defeat and illness are unpleasant, a needed hug and the return of a loved one from a long journey are pleasant, and so on. Admittedly, there are many occasions on which illness is not unpleasant, the return of a loved one is not pleasant, and so on, but a virtue of the hedonic theory is that it can accommodate such cases by holding that people have many desires, capable of coming into conflict in a variety of circumstances. If one desires the company of one's spouse, that will incline one to pleasure at the return of one's spouse from a trip. But if one also desires not to argue with one's spouse, and believes that the spouse's return will likely be the occasion for a ferocious argument, then that will incline one to displeasure at the spouse's return. These competing inclinations to pleasure and displeasure will result in the complex phenomenology that frequently surrounds desire: fleeting pleasure interspersed with fleeting pain, rising hope and sinking dread, and so on. But this welter of complexity, says the hedonic theorist, is simply a consequence of the fact that each desire inclines one to pleasure at its apparent fulfilment, and displeasure at its apparent frustration, once it is also understood that an individual may have many different and potentially conflicting desires. It therefore does nothing to undermine the basic idea of the hedonic theory.

The standard theory of desire, it should be said, is capable of saying much of what was just said about pleasure and displeasure, since the standard theory accepts that desires are causally related to pleasure and displeasure, thanks to our history of natural selection. But this might seem to underrate the significance of the connection between pleasure and desire. A hedonic theory of desire avoids underrating hedonic tone by elevating it to the essential face of desire. Desires are felt, according to hedonic theories of desire, because to desire *is* to feel (to be disposed to, or possess something disposing one to feel). This is hardly a necessary consequence of accepting that desires are felt, but the suggestion has intuitive force.

As a second point in its favor, it can be pointed out that the epistemology of desire in everyday contexts relies heavily upon dispositions to feel pleasure and displeasure. If Phil enjoys thinking about the misfortunes of a colleague, the enjoyment suggests that he desires the ill fortune of his colleague, however much he might deny it or be unmoved to actually bring about misfortunes. Likewise, if Kim feels displeasure as a result of her cat's affectionate display toward a stranger, that will suggest to most people that Kim is jealous, that she wants all of her cat's affectionate displays for herself, and this diagnosis will be maintained even in the face of Kim's own denials or in the face of the evident absurdity of being jealous of such a thing. Tendencies to pleasure and displeasure are taken to be very powerful evidence of desire, often overriding other sources of evidence such as statements of what one desires (even honest statements), behavioral evidence, and so on. This does not entail that desires are to be identified with tendencies to pleasure or displeasure (or the grounds of such tendencies), any more than the fact that desires are felt does, but it is further support for the thesis. If hedonic dispositions are a very reliable form of epistemic access to our desires and the desires of others, perhaps this is because desires consist of something like hedonic dispositions.

Third, a number of the arguments just made against the standard, motivational theory of desire pointed to facts a hedonic theory of desire incorporates with ease.

Our imaginary Greek mathematician was not motivated to make it the case that π be irrational, but he would certainly have been happy to learn that it is. His desire thus seems manifested in his hedonic dispositions in a way that it is not manifested in his behavior, and this is a point in favor of a hedonic theory of desire. Similarly, the argument that Strawson's (1994) Weather Watchers are possible beings, possessed of desires, got its intuitive force from the fact that they could be imagined to feel joy or sorrow upon seeing the weather turn this way or that. That also seems some reason to draw the conclusion that desiring is just a matter of dispositions to joy, sorrow, and other hedonic states.

The arguments against the motivational theory on the grounds that there are other sources of motivation than desire are of no concern if the hedonic theory of desire is adopted. After all, doing what one was trying to do, or intending to do, or already doing out of habit, is not normally a source of pleasure unless one also *wanted* to do what one was trying to do, intending to do, or doing out of habit. Desire, it seems, is connected to pleasure and displeasure in a fashion in which volition, intention, and habit are not. It can also be noted that acting from desire can be readily distinguished from acting out of a sense of moral duty on hedonic grounds, if the hedonic theory of desire is correct.

As for the neurological argument, sophisticated hedonic theories such as HT1 and HT2 can answer it without strain. If to desire that P is to be disposed to pleasure if it seems to one that P, then desiring presupposes the prior existence of the capacity to bear the content P in a perceptual or cognitive form—in the form of it *seeming* to be the case that P. By making perceptual and cognitive representations a part of what constitutes a desire, a hedonic theory can answer the question of where desires can be found in the brain. If the representational capacities involved in desiring are found just where the representational capacities for perception and belief are found, then all that needs to be added to the brain in order to have desires is a hedonic center and neurons connecting the representational capacities to the hedonic center, and this is a much more modest demand on brain space than that apparently called for by the representationalist version of the standard theory.

Finally, it could also be pointed out that dispositions to pleasure differ from dispositions to displeasure in just the way that fire differs from ice, and so the hedonic theorist of desire can make a fundamental distinction between desire and aversion along these lines, thus responding to the objection from Robert Frost.

In sketching the virtues of a hedonic theory of desire, it is, of course, important to distinguish better forms of the theory from worse. I have selected HT1 and HT2 as representative formulations of the theory because they avoid a number of obstacles faced by other formulations. For instance, neither theory holds that desires are to be identified with episodes of pleasure or displeasure themselves. Instead, both identify desires with dispositions to such episodes or the grounds of such dispositions. This saves the theories from the embarrassment of being forced to hold that one does not desire when one has no occurrent pleasure or displeasure. Common sense says that one continues to desire the welfare of one's child while one is asleep or distracted by other, hedonically neutral topics, and both theories can endorse this thesis.

It is also a virtue of HT1 and HT2 that they do not hold that to desire that P is simply to be disposed to pleasure if it is the case that P. Instead, they hold that to desire that P entails being disposed to pleasure if it *seems to be the case* that P. To see the significance of this difference, consider the obvious fact that many desires are for states of affairs that can be realized without one noticing that they have been realized. If I desire that Jon be safe, then my desire is satisfied by Jon's being so, but this will hardly cause me any pleasure unless I learn that it is the case. If to desire P were simply to be disposed to pleasure at P, then it would be better to interpret my desire for Jon's safety as actually being a desire to hear that Jon is safe, since the latter correlates far better with actual pleasure than the former. Yet it is a thesis of common sense that I more typically desire things such as Jon's safety than the news of it: if Jon were to have died in a car crash, then things would not have turned out as I wished, whether or not I ever learned about the crash. Of course, I can also desire to hear that Jon is safe, but generally I want Jon's safety itself *more* than I want to hear of it: these are quite distinct desires. HT1 and HT2 allow one to maintain what seems common sense. Building desires out of seemings is also what allows the hedonic theory to explain desires for impossibilities. Though it makes little sense to talk of someone's being disposed to pleasure if π is a rational number, it makes much more to talk of it *seeming* to someone that π is rational.

The standard theory of desire holds that the only essential feature of desires is that they motivate, but it allows that desire has various accidental features, such as coming in different strengths, conducing to pleasure or displeasure, and so on. Similarly, a hedonic theory of desire is free to hold that while the nature of desire is a tendency to influence hedonic tone, desires as they are found in human beings and other animals have a wide variety of other, non-necessary but familiar, features. Perhaps the hedonic theorist would suggest something along the following lines: desires generally come in different strengths, with strength of desire corresponding to the strength of feeling one tends to have, all else being equal, when it seems to one that P. Desires can be limitlessly strong, since there is no ceiling to how intense a feeling of pleasure or displeasure can be, but the limit to weakness is set by neutral hedonic tone: if its seeming that *P* does not tend to move one in the slightest, one has no desire regarding it. Desires have typical motivational effects, such that we are moved to seek out and promote desired states of affairs and avoid or prevent those to which we are averse, and these motivational effects exist for obvious evolutionary reasons. Desires also have typical but not essential effects upon our conscious lives beyond pleasure and displeasure: they cause us to think about how to obtain our ends, they cause us to think "I want . . ." to ourselves, they cause us to attend to some things and not to others, and so on. Finally, it is also an inessential but interesting fact about pleasure and displeasure that the former defines what is a reward for purposes of operant conditioning, while the latter defines what is a punishment.

In spite of the advantages of a hedonic theory of desire, I think it is just as mistaken as the standard theory. The main argument for this conclusion is to be found in chapter 3, which deals with the nature of pleasure and displeasure at length. There I argue that pleasure and displeasure are best interpreted as sensory representations of the difference between actual and expected desire satisfaction, and are thus a type of sense experience whose object is the subject's own desires. Just as vision gives us the ability to perceive the shape, location, and light-reflectance properties of distant objects, so hedonic tone gives us the ability to perceive changes in how well satisfied our desires are. If this is right, and desires are the representational object of pleasure and displeasure, then desiring itself cannot be identified with tendencies to feel pleasure or displeasure, and hence hedonic theories of desire must be mistaken. But until chapter 3 has been reached, this will hardly suffice as an argument against the hedonic theory of desire. So consider, in the interim, a few objections to the hedonic theory derived from the gap between something that *is* one's desire and something that is merely *responsive to* one's desire.

Consider a man who has just had a number of powerfully negative life experiences, say, the death of both parents and the loss of a meaningful occupation, and who as a result has become depressed. This man once took great pleasure in many things, including his wife's successes, but now is only slightly pleased by these things. Need we hold that he cares less about his wife now than before? That he has fewer, or weaker, desires for her success? Normally, this is not held to be the case. Normally, one views a person who has become moderately depressed as not capable of appropriate feelings until the depression has lifted, rather than as having the appropriate feelings for one who now hardly cares what happens to his loved ones. Feelings are often taken to be the true measure of one's desires, but in the case of depression, folk wisdom holds that a moderately depressed person is just temporarily unable to appreciate the things he does care about. "Of course I still want you to succeed, I'm just having a bad patch" is the sort of thing the moderately depressed husband might say to his wife, after being criticized for failing to show happiness upon learning that she has been promoted, and he is likely to be believed. Perhaps extremely severe depression, of the sort that leaves the sufferer unable to rise from bed to perform even vital tasks, can be said to take away all desire along with all positive feeling. But more commonplace depressions, in which the sufferer feels leaden but still functions, and still holds certain things to be meaningful to him and other things not, seems unlike this. Yet the depressed person does not tend to feel happiness upon learning of his wife's success and does not tend to feel distress upon learning of her setbacks—or, at least, feels these things far, far less when depressed than when not. As a result, a hedonic theory must say that the depressed person has lost some of his desires, or suffered a diminution of desire, when this does not seem correct. The discrepancy between everyday thinking about such cases and the hedonic theory's commitments should give the hedonic theorist pause.[23]

A defender of a hedonic theory of desire might try to argue that desiring only requires dispositions to pleasure or displeasure under normal conditions, and when an individual is depressed, conditions are not normal. But making such a claim stick is very difficult when one's theory of desire makes tendencies to pleasure and displeasure the essence of desire, rather than a causal consequence of desiring. If desires are, in principle, independent of dispositions to pleasure and displeasure, then what makes depression an abnormal condition is straightforward: desires still exist when one is depressed, but their apparent fulfillment and frustration no longer have appropriate hedonic effects. If, however, dispositions to pleasure and displeasure are constitutive of the existence of desires, then it becomes very problematic to say what the difference could be between having a substantial loss of desire and having a constant desire that, because of the abnormal conditions created by depression, does not have its normal hedonic effects. After all, desires can change in strength, and be restored to their former strengths. What makes this an incorrect interpretation of a case of everyday depression? Not the fact, if it is one, that the depression is induced by an abnormality of brain chemistry or neurotransmission, since such abnormalities seem capable, in principle, of modifying what desires an individual possesses just as much as surgical intervention is capable, in principle, of modifying one's desires. Let me take a moment to justify this assertion. Sacks (1970, 102–4) relates the story of an eighty-nine-year-old woman who, at the age of eighty-eight, felt a strong renewal of sexual desire. It turned out that she was experiencing the effects of a latent syphilitic infection. The woman's request to Sacks was not that she be "cured" but that the infection be treated (to prevent dementia) without altering her new personality. Reading the case, one is given the impression of a person whose sexual desires were significantly strengthened by a biological disorder, but whose new desires were as real as anything else. "Mere" biological change can, it seems, produce real changes in desire and desire strength. The same moral is presented by Damasio's (1994) detailed case history of Phineas Gage, a man who survived having a railway spike driven through the front of his brain, but who turned from a hard-working, responsible, decorous man into an irresponsible, wanton man as a direct result of the damage to his brain. His change also cries out to be treated as a genuine change in desires, following radical interference with the brain. What resources, then, does the hedonic theorist have to repel an interpretation of the moderately depressed person as genuinely ceasing to care about his wife's fortunes?

The case of individuals who have been rendered incapable of pleasure or displeasure by surgical procedures is also worth considering. The most extreme forms of frontal lobotomy surgery result in individuals who seem largely or entirely incapable of happiness or sadness in any form, and who are likewise listless, incapable of caring for themselves, and unmotivated to do much. Such individuals present no difficulties for a hedonic theory of desire, for according to such theories, the loss of the capacity for pleasure and displeasure is tantamount to a loss of desire, and a failure of motivation is a normal consequence of the loss of desire. Other individuals, recipients of less radical surgeries, present more puzzling cases. Foltz and White (1962) describe the results of a much more restricted procedure, cingulumotomy, upon patients suffering from chronic and intractable pain. In a number of patients, this procedure had the effect of severely reducing or eliminating the patient's capacity for displeasure without having any other apparent harmful effects upon the psyche. Thus, one patient who had been bedridden in hospital for nine months as a result of chronic pain and who received the surgery was able to leave hospital two weeks later and return to her role as homemaker. She continued to feel the formerly unpleasant sensations she had felt before surgery, but reported that they "did not concern her now." This was a typical result if the surgery was successful. Foltz and White write (1962, 97):

> It must be accepted that these patients are changed persons after the cingulumotomy, but the change is indeed subtle. It is most difficult to classify and describe the change that occurs, but it is obvious that effective lesions produced a definite stabilization of emotional lability that was present before operation. Much of the anxiety, which is so manifest in these ill, unhappy people, is no longer apparent. The patient with a good result simply is not as precipitously reactive to his own environment and his own situation as he was prior to operation. The anguished faces and evidence of suffering are modified markedly. The perception of pain as such does not appear to be modified, but the patient's total reaction to pain and the threat to existence that it represents is modified markedly. Most of the patients stated they continued to have pain but it was "not distressing," "not particularly bothersome," "doesn't worry me anymore," etc.

In the same vein, there is the case report by Sprengelmeyer et al. (1999) of a man who became nearly incapable of experiencing fear or anger after damage to a region of his brain. The man, N. M., would engage in activities such as "hunting deer in Siberia while hanging on a rope under a helicopter" without fear, and in fact could only recall feeling fear once in the twenty years prior to his clinical examination, and this under genuinely terrifying circumstances. His capacity for anger was similarly blunted. "He stated that he adopted an 'Eastern philosophy' approach to life, and was able to cope with difficult and frustrating situations without becoming angry." While N. M. still had the ability to feel pleasure and displeasure, this ability was limited in situations normally arousing anger or fear.

Of course, it is hard to know what to say about cases such as N. M. or recipients of cingulumotomies, but at first glance they do not appear to be cases in which the individuals have been deprived of the capacity to desire, or to have suffered a diminution of that capacity. They are still motivated to feed and otherwise care for themselves, they can initiate and carry out apparently meaningful projects, they affirm having desires, and so on. The changes are "subtle." Yet the changes in capacity to feel pleasure and displeasure are gross. N. M. appears to care about whether he lives or dies, to care about whether or not he is cheated in business dealings, and so on, but his emotions do not respond as though he does care. Recipients of cingulumotomies would rather not have their bodies cut or bruised, but they lose the ability to feel any distress as a result of such injury. In these cases, changes in dispositions to pleasure appear disproportionate to changes in desire. Surely gross damage to one's capacity to desire would, in a normal human being, have more profound effects than these.

As a final objection to the hedonic theory of desire, consider a somewhat different point. Desires, like beliefs, are generally agreed to have a "direction of fit." As the point is usually put, beliefs are things that are supposed to accord with the world: if the belief does not fit the world, it is the belief that is in the wrong, not the world, and a rational person changes beliefs when confronted with the mismatch. Desires, on the other hand, are things the world is supposed to accord with: if the world is not as desired, something is wrong with the world (from the point of view of the agent with the desire; needless to say, this is not a moral claim). A rational person who finds that the world is not as she desires sets off to change the world, if possible, not to find some way to revise her desires.[24] Explaining where direction of fit comes from, either in belief or desire, is a nontrivial problem, but in the case of desires, the standard theorist can give an answer with a certain measure of plausibility. Michael Smith (1994, 115) suggests that desires set a standard for how the world is to be because "a desire that p tends to endure, disposing the subject in that state to bring it about that p." By disposing the agent to bring it about that P, a desire that P makes it true that the world accommodates the desire, rather than the desire accommodating the world (as beliefs do). It is not clear how a hedonic theorist is to explain direction of fit, however. Why is it that a rational person who suffers as a result of it not being the case that P should make it the case that P? Why is it not equally rational to change oneself so as not to suffer from the realization that P? It might well be that suffering and pleasure both influence what a rational person would do, but it does not seem given by the nature of suffering or pleasure themselves that a rational person strives to change the world, rather than herself, in order to avoid suffering and attain pleasure. In fact, common sense suggests that a rational person sometimes takes the one tack, and sometimes the other. And as for creating dispositions to modify the world, suffering and pleasure certainly do this, but they are considerably less reliable at doing so than are motivational states aimed at making it the case that P. If I want to eat the cake, and get pleasure from eating it, that is just as likely to cause me to stop eating the cake (so that I can have some tomorrow, thus maximizing pleasure) as it is to cause me to continue eating the cake. Given that I want people not to starve, and that I am suffering because I am seeing starving people on television, I am much more likely to end the suffering by changing channels than by sending money to help. These objections hardly show it to be impossible for the hedonic theorist to explain direction of fit, but the task is not trivial. The standard theory of desire is not perfect, but there remain a number of reasons not to leap to its historical rival.

4. A New Theory of Desire

The previous sections have presented objections to the standard, motivational theory of desire and its leading rival, the hedonic theory. None of these objections are decisive. Though some of them are quite strong, and all should concern the relevant theorists to some degree, even their collective weight does not constitute a good enough reason to reject the basic spirit of either theory. After all, many theories suffer from well-known defects. Faced with imperfect theories, a theorist may surely decide to stick with one that has other virtues and hope that someday someone will come along and answer the objections. Still, when enough anomalies pile up, there is also reason to be open to revolution: to a new theory that can save what was good in the old theories and incorporate the anomalous facts as well.[25] In this section, I present a candidate for such a theory. The remainder of this book will explore the justification for and consequences of accepting it.

The standard theory and the hedonic theory each place exclusive emphasis on one face of desire. There is the motivational face of desire: desires are involved in moving us to act, or to refrain from acting. There is also the hedonic face of desire: desires are involved in our feelings of pleasure and displeasure. Both faces of desire are salient. But there remains the third, less salient, neglected face of desire: the role of desire in reward and punishment. In spite of its humble status at present, this third face of desire is also the best candidate for the core of desire, for the very nature of desire.

The suggestion is likely to be met with howls of protest. Reward and punishment are suitable notions for rats, perhaps, but people? Are not 'reward' and 'punishment' simply crude names for pleasure and displeasure? Is a return to *behaviorism* proposed? Such skepticism is the just reward for a philosopher who would put these notions to work again in the philosophy of mind. The advocates of reward and punishment had their moment in the mid-twentieth century, and squandered it on implausible philosophical theories and ultimately sterile science. If a deep mistrust of theorists invoking reward and punishment lingers on in philosophy, it is because trust has not yet been earned back.[26] In this section, I want to attempt to win back the first, smallest measure of that trust. A return to behaviorism is not proposed. Nevertheless, reward and punishment *are* linked to desire, and are linked in a way that distinguishes them from motivation and hedonic tone. They thus present a third face from which a theory of desire may be generated.

Let me begin with a brief description of recent scientific findings on reward, pleasure, and motivation. Work over the last decade or so has decisively identified a pair of dopamine-releasing structures deep inside the brain, known as the *ventral tegmental area*, or *VTA*, and *substantia nigra pars compacta*, or *SNpc*, as the neural basis of reward in animals like ourselves (see appendix, fig.1). The effect of VTA/SNpc activity that makes it the basis of reward is, most centrally, that it causes a certain form of *learning*, but this is learning in a very specific and perhaps unfamiliar sense. The learning mediated by the activity of the VTA/SNpc is not rote memorization of facts for conscious retrieval. Rather, this is learning triggered by specific types of events in the environment, causing changes in perceptual and motor capacities, changes in associations of ideas, and changes in behavioral dispositions.

Because this form of learning includes behavioral learning of the sort B. F. Skinner made the center of his research program, one might think that this sort of reward system could exist only in those creatures capable of movement, but this would be hasty. Reward-driven learning modifies behavioral tendencies, but this function is not essential to it. A creature lacking the capacity to move, such as Strawson's Weather Watchers, can still engage in reward-driven learning by learning to see the difference between dark clouds that presage rain and dark clouds that do not, and by learning to associate the season with the location at which the sun rises above the horizon, for example. By having a structure analogous to the VTA/SNpc that, by acting just as the VTA/SNpc acts, causes changes in perceptual sensitivities and the association of ideas, Weather Watchers can engage in this sort of learning as much as motile organisms can. What makes the VTA/SNpc the neural basis for reward is that it produces a characteristic learning effect within the organism. The fact that this characteristic learning effect results in behavioral modification in many cases is not essential to the effect itself.

As for pleasure, work done in localizing the neural basis of hedonic tone has strongly implicated a structure on the inner surface of each hemisphere in the frontal lobe, in a region known as the *perigenual anterior cingulate cortex*, or *PGAC* (see appendix, fig. 2). This structure is the one that is responsible for the capacity of animals like us to feel pleasure and displeasure. There are at least two tremendously important facts about the PGAC. The first is that it is wholly distinct from the VTA/SNpc: that the neural basis of pleasure, therefore, is not identical to the neural basis of reward, and so pleasure is not identical to a reward signal. The second is that the PGAC is far from the only source of excitatory input to the VTA/SNpc: that pleasure, therefore, is not the only thing that is rewarding. In fact, what appears much more likely, given the way connections are found in the brain, is that the activity of the reward system is a normal *cause* of pleasure. These findings are supported in large part by scientific findings available only since the later 1990s, and so overturn earlier philosophical interpretations of these systems based on incomplete evidence (Morillo 1990), as well as common scientific preconceptions.

Work done in localizing the neural basis of motivation has centered around the *motor cortex*, the main region of the brain sending signals directly to the spinal neurons controlling the voluntary muscles (see appendix, fig. 2). However, the selection of an actual action from the range of plausible actions is not performed by the motor cortex, but by another structure deep in the brain, known as the motor center of the *basal ganglia*. The basal ganglia guide both conscious, preplanned action and spontaneous action. It may come as a surprise to learn that the connections between the neural basis of pleasure, in the PGAC, and control of the voluntary muscles appears to be fairly modest. Instead of pleasure dominating motivation, motivation appears much more influenced by the neural basis of reward, in the VTA/SNpc. Reward signals from the VTA/SNpc appear to have a very important influence upon the basal ganglia, both in the short term (influencing immediate motivation) and in the long term (guiding the formation of behavioral tendencies).

It thus turns out that of the three faces of desire, it is desire's neglected face, reward, which causally guides the other two faces. The neural basis of reward is the normal cause of pleasure and an important cause of motivation, while pleasure and motivation have much less influence upon one another and neither exerts a dominating influence upon the reward structure. This striking finding is a fairly recent revelation of scientific work, and it has not yet been given an interpretation by the scientific community in terms of desire. Yet some such interpretation seems called for. Here we have the three faces of desire: what then shall we make of desire itself, knowing how the causal relationships stand between its faces? Common sense holds that desires are at least one normal cause of actual and attempted behaviors, and that they contribute to causal explanations of why we feel joy or sorrow on a given occasion. Perhaps, then, desires are realized within our brains by the structure that plays just these causal roles: that is, by the biological reward system.

The facts about the causal interaction of the three faces of desire are suggestive, but far from conclusive. Yet I am convinced that there is something deep to them. The coming chapters will say why. Chapters 2, 3, and 4 will look at the three faces of desire in depth: their phenomenology, their neural underpinnings, and other scientific findings about them. Chapter 5 will use their conclusions to present a detailed version of the theory of desire just sketched and will answer the long list of questions appropriate to every theory of desire: what it says about objects of desire, desire strength, change in desire, instrumental desire, direction of fit, and so on. Finally, chapter 6 will answer the lingering questions about the divide between theoretical reduction and elimination, and about the justifications for insisting on placing a single face of desire at the center of a theory of desire. It will, I hope, add up to a clear and attractive third theory of desire.

2

Reward and Punishment

In a restaurant, Victoria rewards her waiter for his honesty about the failings of today's special with a large tip. In a laboratory, a scientist rewards a rat for reaching a certain point in a maze by feeding it rat chow. Are these two actions genuinely of the same type, namely, that of bestowing a reward? Or is it a misleading fact about the English language that the term 'reward' is used for both? The latter seems a natural answer. After all, the waiter knows he is being rewarded, the rat does not; the waiter deserves his reward, the rat does not; the waiter belongs to a social system in which certain rewards are the norm, the rat does not; and so on.

Upon reflection, though, one might conclude that the issue is less clear-cut. The waiter might not know, or even guess, he is being rewarded: he might believe that the tip is merely money that was left behind by accident, and yet Victoria would still be rewarding him for his honesty, rewarding him without his realizing it. The waiter might not deserve his reward: he might have been lying about the special, trying to convince Victoria to order something more expensive, in which case she would inadvertently be rewarding him for his dishonesty. The waiter might not even belong to a social network with tipping conventions: perhaps Victoria is dining in a country without such norms, but this would also not change the fact that she rewards the waiter's honesty. These considerations invite us to reverse our initial judgement, and hold that the tip and the rat chow might really be rewards in an unequivocal sense of 'reward'.

Questions about the nature of reward are difficult to answer: not because there is too little known about reward but because what is known is scattered between different systems of knowledge that have rarely been brought into fruitful dialogue. Common sense has a host of insights about reward and punishment, including the psychology of reward and punishment, but is ignorant of science and not trusted by scientists. Behaviorists[1] make their careers studying the abstract structure of reward and punishment and applying this knowledge in therapeutic contexts, but on methodological grounds they disdain both common sense and more biological approaches. Neuroscientists have made tremendous strides in understanding the operation of the brain in rewarding and punishing contexts, but have rarely linked their findings to what is known to common sense or to behaviorists. In short, the study of reward is a mess.

This chapter begins with three sections dedicated to the three main fields of knowledge about the psychology of reward and punishment. The findings of common sense, behaviorism, and neuroscience will be surveyed in turn, and found to have much in common. These commonalities will then be used to produce a more unified theory of the nature of reward. For there really is a unified theory waiting to be produced. A wide variety of organisms, including both rats and people, appear capable of constituting some things as rewards and others as punishments, in a sense that is perfectly unified, and perfectly compatible with common sense. Uncovering this common core of reward will be this chapter's task.

1. The Folk Psychology of Reward and Punishment

Living in a world that includes Skinner's *Beyond Freedom and Dignity*, Burgess's *A Clockwork Orange*, behavior modification therapy, popular works on child psychology, and popular scientific magazines publishing occasional stories about the rat sciences, it can be hard to come to the topic of reward and punishment without thinking about it in these popularized parascientific terms. Nonetheless, it takes only a moment's reflection to remind ourselves that there is a vast reservoir of commonsensical thought on the topic, encompassing moral claims, parenting lore, personal experience, and more.

Rewards and punishments, as they are commonly understood, can be deserved or undeserved, miserly, public, gratuitous, private, reprehensible, salutary, and much, much, more, but all that is relevant for present purposes is their psychological aspect. What sorts of things count as rewards and punishments for particular organisms, what psychological and behavioral effects do rewards and punishments have, and why do they have these effects? Folk psychology—the body of claims common sense makes about the mind—has some simple, standard ideas. Perhaps the most obvious of these is that rewards and punishments are diverse. Rewards typically include being given sweets (though not if one is unwilling or unable to eat them), praise, money, and recognition of valued achievement, while punishments may be corporal (spanking, whipping, and the like) or not, with public and private condemnation being favored forms of non-corporal punishment, though one can punish one's enemies for their misdeeds in grosser or more subtle ways as well. The obvious incompleteness of this catalog reminds us indirectly of what is known to everyone: that while there are common rewards and punishments, rewards and punishments may in principle be almost endlessly varied.

The main limitations on what can be a reward or punishment appear, if one follows common sense, to be set largely by the nature of the person being rewarded or punished. Being given an opportunity to eat a certain species of termite might be a reward for some hardworking boys in Nigeria, while not being any such thing for the boys living downstairs from me. Being sent to summer camp might be a reward for some children and a punishment for others. And so on. Provisionally, one might speculate that what links rewards together is that the recipients of rewards have a certain psychological response to, or take some special attitude toward, the things they receive that makes those things rewards, and similarly for punishments. What to make of this idea is something to which I will return before the end of this chapter. But since common sense rarely deals in the essence of things, no further attempt will be made to say what common sense thinks *makes* something a reward.

The effects of rewards and punishments are known to be, like rewards and punishments themselves, diverse, but they can be roughly grouped into emotional, behavioral and non-emotional psychological effects. The emotional effects are obvious: receiving a reward is generally pleasant—sometimes an occasion for euphoria, sometimes something less—while being punished is generally unpleasant. The greater the reward, the more powerful the feeling of pleasure, typically, and the more severe the punishment, the greater the displeasure. To this it can be added that rewards and punishments that take one by surprise tend to be more powerful in their emotional effects, whereas familiarity has a tendency to breed contempt: the fifth medal won by a child who skis competitively tends to have less effect than the first, and a child's terror of being spanked tends to be much greater the less often the punishment is actually administered. This mention of terror reminds us that the generic terms 'pleasure' and 'displeasure' are rather limiting when one describes the emotional effects of rewards and punishments. Less generically, passive sadness and anger are both common effects of punishment, though if one feels the punishment was merited one may also feel unburdened or cleansed by it, and so pleased to some degree. Pride commonly follows reward, or a sense of satisfaction, though these emotions may also be undercut in particular circumstances—think of a person receiving a coveted award who believes she has cheated her best friend out of it, and feeling nothing but unhappiness and shame. In short, while rewards and punishments have familiar characteristic emotional effects, their full range of effects spans the whole range of emotions.

Obvious behavioral effects of rewards and punishments include those which tend to be associated with the emotional effects: a rewarded person smiles, a punished person looks downcast, or perhaps cringes, and so on. There are also pure motivational effects: people make an effort to get rewarded and to avoid being punished, all else being equal. As with emotional responses to reward and punishment, these immediate behavioral responses are highly variable in a way that depends upon the individual and the circumstances: stoics will not flinch when punished, depressives will not smile when rewarded, some people seek out punishment, others reject the opportunity to be rewarded, and so on.

The effects of reward and punishment on *dispositions* to behave are also familiar: "spare the rod and spoil the child" is a saying that predates scientific theories of behavior modification. A young boy rewarded with praise and attention for helping his little sister will be more likely to help his sister on future occasions, to choose a piece of folk-psychological wisdom at random, though of course there are many, many layers of complexity here (to which I will turn in a moment). Interesting in this regard is the fact that folk wisdom recognizes two sorts of changes in behavioral dispositions brought about by rewards and punishments: those mediated by memory, conscious choice, planning, and the like, and those not so mediated. The former sorts of changes are straightforward: a person rewarded by her boss with praise for writing terse memoranda is likely to recall this praise and, wanting further praise, or a raise or the like, is likely to decide to continue writing terse memoranda. Or, in a contrary spirit, she may decide to cease writing terse memoranda, perhaps because she dislikes her boss and wishes to do what will displease him. Rewards and punishments are, in this respect, not much different from any other sort of event: they are remembered, and factored into decision-making whenever it seems appropriate. The other sort of change in behavioral dispositions that rewards and punishments are held to inculcate is more subtle. Paradigms of it can be found in changes in the behavioral dispositions of children as they are taught how to act. These changes are called learning—"he has to learn she has feelings too," and so on—but it is not learning in the sense of memorization or in the sense of acquiring general knowledge about the world, and it is not learning which is effective through the consideration of reasons in conscious decision-making. Rather, it is a form of learning demonstrated first and foremost in behavior that is not premeditated. Think of a child who would dearly love to be allowed to join the adults at a dinner party, but whose akratic[2] tendencies to wriggling, getting up, bouncing up and down, and so on have resulted in banishment. "When you've learned to sit still, you can join the adults at the table" means something more like "when you have mastered the art of sitting still" than "when you know that sitting still is valued," and reward and punishment have long been thought excellent teachers of such arts.

Inculcating behavioral tendencies in the second of the two above manners via reward and punishment is known to have a number of complications. As many parents notice, if the rewards are too crude, or too crudely connected to the act that brings them about, then the child learns the wrong thing—to act helpful only when he wants attention or a cookie, for instance—though if the rewards are sufficiently subtle, the child will come to be inclined to help his little sister or otherwise do what is expected of him, whether an adult can be counted upon to reward him or not. It could be speculated that crude rewards and punishments, being so blatant, only affect behavior via memory and deliberation, while subtlety is necessary for rewards to take effect via the unconscious route, but this particular speculation is perhaps a little too complex to be true "folklore": it was not part of the folklore of my family, at least. More familiar is a different complication: the idea that, for a child feeling deprived of attention, punishments may also be rewards, as they involve attending to a child. "Don't react," goes a common admonishment. "You'll only encourage her." Similarly, it is said that for a teenager wishing to rebel, a verbal reprimand intended as a punishment may be taken as a sign of successful rebellion, and hence actually be a reward, even though the teenager complains about the reprimand when it is issued.

Reward and punishment also have non-emotional but still psychological effects of which folk psychology is aware, though here common wisdom gets rather thinner. One very interesting, if implicit, thesis of folk psychology is that reward and punishment can inculcate or eliminate intrinsic desires, as well as behavioral tendencies. Returning for a moment to the boy who is rewarded for being kind to his little sister, it is commonly assumed that, while the boy may be very selfish as a two- or three-year-old, if his parents encourage him to be kind to his sister in sufficiently subtle ways (e.g., reward him indirectly for kind acts, reward him for displaying empathy by talking about him positively in front of others, punish him for acts of unkindness and thoughtlessness by sharp words, allow themselves to engage him via Strawson's [1962] "reactive attitudes," etc.), he will come to intrinsically desire his sister's welfare. More generally, one of the goals of parenting is to inculcate socially and morally preferable intrinsic desires in children who initially lack them, and to strengthen such desires in children who display them to some degree without prompting, and it is assumed that rewards and punishments are effective in this process (along with other things). Parents have often been discomfited to find their young children without intrinsic aversions to public masturbation, to the ingestion of insects, to shouting, and so on, and similarly to find their offspring lacking intrinsic concern for animal welfare, for cleanliness, or for the physical integrity of their clothing. Throughout the ages, parents have sought to inculcate the relevant intrinsic desires and aversions, and have used rewards and punishments to do so—admittedly, with mixed success.

Parents are not the only members of the folk-psychological community who implicitly believe they can inculcate intrinsic desires through suitably sophisticated rewards and punishments. This is also the attitude of many athletic coaches who wish to instill, say, team spirit—an intrinsic desire for the team's success, independent of desires for personal athletic success and stronger than them—and the attitude of those teachers who praise and encourage reluctant students in the hopes of "igniting" an interest in the subject being taught. Of course, folk psychology holds that there are also other means of inculcating intrinsic desires— role modeling, rational discourse, and so on—and I do not mean to diminish their importance in the folk-psychological scheme of things. But it is significant that everyday thinking assumes, explicitly or implicitly, that reward and punishment also have the power to change what people intrinsically desire.

It is a more familiar idea that intellectual tendencies, like tendencies to overt behavior, are also susceptible to reward and punishment: this is another form of psychological modification rewards and punishments are believed to bring about. If a girl has a tendency to daydream, goes an all-too familiar line of thinking, it can be beaten out of her—her psychological tendency can be brought into line, as her overt behavior can, with the aid of the strap (though once again, the process is not thought infallible: perhaps the girl will retreat further into her daydreams). Less grimly, teachers also hope to encourage habits of attention to novelty and inquiry into mystery through praise and attention. Familiar psychological tendencies include the practice some people have of counting to ten before acting when angry, and the tendency others have of mentally rehearsing unsatisfactory conversations until just the right phrasing—the one I *should* have used to put that so-and-so in his place—is found.

At the limits of folk wisdom, there are even hints that sensory capacities can be influenced by reward and punishment. Imagine two oenological novices, with identical taste sensitivities, asked to sample a variety of similar wines and learn to discriminate between them. To the students, many of the wines taste just the same at the beginning. They cannot detect differences between different glasses that exceed the differences they seem to taste when trying the same wine twice in a row. Imagine that both students receive feedback about whether their discriminative guesses have been better or worse, but that one also receives praise and encouragement with each improvement, while the other student receives feedback in a bored-sounding monotone. In such a scenario, two things seem likely: that the encouraged student will do better than the one lacking encouragement, all else being equal, and that, at the end of the exercise, the encouraged student will actually be able to taste some of the differences he was not formerly able to taste. That is, it is easy to imagine that praise and encouragement—that rewards for successful discriminations—will be at least partly responsible for a change in sensory sensitivities. This notion may not be a centerpiece of folk psychological wisdom about rewards and punishments, but the example just given, and related ideas about appreciating complex music or being able to feel Braille characters, have a certain plausibility about them, and the plausibility is certainly not owed to popular awareness of the relevant scientific studies (more on which later). The extent to which this story is plausible is thus the extent to which common sense implicitly holds that rewards are effective ways to modify our minds, even to the extent of modifying sensory capacities.

The behavioral, emotional, and other psychological features associated with reward and punishment are thus familiar and rich. They do not tell us exactly what reward and punishment might be, and they offer a very mixed verdict about the usefulness of reward and punishment, but they give us enough information to make progress. Perhaps most important, they remind us that the notions *reward* and *punishment* are not the property of rat-obsessed scientists. They are part of our common knowledge of the psychological world, and any theory of the mind that explains everything we know about the mind will have to spend a fair amount of time discussing the psychology of reward and punishment.

2. Behaviorism, Reward, and Punishment

Unlike the previous section, this section *will* be dealing with rats and mazes, but before beginning, a word should be said about labels. Philosophers have generally had a neat view of behaviorists as divided into philosophical behaviorists (e.g., Ryle 1949), who were often interesting but errant philosophers; methodological behaviorists, who were often uninteresting but useful scientists; and B. F. Skinner (see, e.g., his 1938, 1971), who combined the best and worst of both worlds in an infuriating mix. Non-behaviorist psychologists have held similar views.[3] The fact is that few scientists now fit these philosophically familiar categories, and fewer than one might believe ever did. In spite of this, philosophers still think of behaviorists in their own terms, and I will not resist this trend. In what follows, I will generally use the term 'behaviorist' to refer to what might be called *ideologically pure* behaviorists: those few who believe that the entirety of the mind is to be found in overt behavior and dispositions to behave, and that therefore the study of the mind is simply the study of behavior and behavioral dispositions. I will use the broader term 'behavioral scientist' to include all those who fall within intellectual spitting distance of ideologically pure behaviorists: those who run rats through mazes, talk in terms of operant conditioning, forbear from asking human subjects about their feelings, and so on, whether they are ideologically pure or not.

If one accepts that food is a reward for hungry rats, water a reward for thirsty rats, tail-pinch and foot-shock a punishment for any rat, and so on, and that rats (pigeons, mice, and so on) are suitable model animals, then behavioral scientists have added substantially to our knowledge of what rewards and punishments are and what they can do. Unfortunately, there is also a tremendous amount of confusion within behavioral science that makes it unclear exactly what that science has learned about reward and punishment per se. To see this, begin by considering the contrast between Pavlovian (classical) conditioning and Skinnerian (operant) conditioning. The paradigm of Pavlovian conditioning is found in Pavlov's (1927) experiment with dogs, who naturally salivated upon tasting meat, learned to associate the ringing of a bell with tasting meat, and eventually came to salivate upon hearing the bell regardless of the presence or absence of meat. Compare this with a paradigm of Skinnerian conditioning, found in Skinner's (1948) work with pigeons. Skinner placed hungry pigeons in a cage that released food every fifteen seconds regardless of the pigeon's behavior. After a number of trials each pigeon had developed distinctive and consistent behavior patterns. One pigeon made repeated turns about the cage, another continually thrust its head into a corner, and so on. Each behavior had been produced spontaneously by the pigeon and had been (purely by coincidence) immediately followed by food; the coincidence between spontaneous behavior and food had caused the pigeon to produce the spontaneous behavior more frequently, which led to another coincidence of behavior and food, and so on. Each pigeon's behavior was thus shaped by the pattern of reinforcements it received following its spontaneous behavior.

There are two key differences between these paradigmatic experiments, only one of which is always noted by behavioral scientists. Pavlov's experiment (1) involves an effect, salivation, over which the organism has no voluntary control, and (2) involves a cause, a ringing bell, which is (intuitively) neither a reward nor a punishment, but merely a neutral stimulus. Skinner's experiment (1) involves effects, such as walking in circles, over which the organism has voluntary control, and (2) involves a cause, food for hungry pigeons, which is (intuitively) the sort of thing that can be a reward. Behavioral scientists generally discriminate between the two experiments solely in terms of their effects: innate, nonvoluntary, reflex-like responses can be controlled by classical conditioning, while voluntary, spontaneous behaviors (not necessarily responses to anything) can be controlled by operant conditioning.

This reduction of two differences to one creates a problem interpreting certain experiments. Take Watson and Rayner's (1920) famous demonstration of "conditioned emotional responses." They conditioned an 11-month-old boy named Albert to fear laboratory rats by pairing the sight of the rats (an apparently neutral stimulus) with a loud crashing sound (intuitively, a punishing stimulus). Of course, the sound frightened Albert (an effect over which Albert had no voluntary control), and eventually the sight of the rat was enough to frighten him without the crashing sound. Watson and Rayner's work has been taken to be a paradigm of Pavlovian conditioning, since it involves the learning of an involuntary response. Clearly no voluntary response is learned, and so the experiment is not properly Skinnerian. Yet the basis for ignoring the experiment's second dimension, as an experiment involving a punishment, is unclear.

A deep and principled investigation into paradigms of behaviorism is not what is needed at present; a rough and ready guide will be more helpful. If we take our lead from the common sense notion of reward, then Pavlovian conditioning, in its purest form, seems to have nothing to do with rewards or punishments, as it investigates the effects of causes that have no connection to everyday notions of reward. Skinnerian conditioning, in its purest form, is the study of the impact of rewards and punishments upon behavior, and so *is* relevant to the study of reward. Since conditioned emotional responses are responses to what (intuitively) are rewards and punishments, they too, presumably, should be treated as a part of the scientific endeavor of interest at present: the study of the effects of rewards and punishments upon organisms like ourselves. So all Skinnerian and some Pavlovian work is relevant for present purposes. The doctrinaire objection to such a proposal would be that rewards are identical to states of affairs that increase operant responding, and since emotional responses are not operant responses, reward and emotional conditioning can have no connection to one another. But in section 3 I will argue that this theory of reward is hopeless, and so the objection will not detain us.

Now that we know where to look, what can behavioral science tell us about rewards and punishments? The lore here is as rich as it is amongst people of common sense, and runs surprisingly parallel to it.

The stock rewards of the behavioral scientist's trade are straightforwardly biological in character: food for food-deprived organisms, water for water-deprived organisms, and so on. Likewise for punishments: foot-shock, tail-pinch, loud noises, and bright lights are all part of the repertoire. But like the person of common sense, the behavioral scientist holds that there are all sorts of rewards and punishments. Mason, Cooper, and Clarebrough (2001) found that, for minks, being allowed to swim was a reward by behavioral measures, and Homme et al. (1963) found that being allowed to run around and make noise was a reward for children. The diversity of possible rewards and possible punishments is, it seems, enormous—even according to behavioral scientists—and depends upon facts particular to each organism.

Turning to the emotional impact of rewards and punishments, Watson and Rayner's (1920) experiment on little Albert has been repeated and elaborated upon (though generally with non-human subjects), producing a rich store of knowledge as to how, exactly, rewarding and punishing stimuli become, by association, linked to previously neutral stimuli, until the emotional effects produced by the rewards or punishments are now also produced by the formerly neutral stimuli. The range of emotional impacts rewards and punishments are capable of causing has been less studied by behavioral scientists, naturally enough, since there is considerable difficulty in observing these effects.

Scientists have also learned a little about how emotional expressions follow from reward and punishment. It turns out, for instance, that rats have facial expressions, and food rewards cause rats to display characteristically pleased faces, while food punishments cause rats to display displeased faces (Grill and Berridge 1985). These facial expressions are quite unlike their counterpart human expressions in many respects, but their correlation with paradigmatic rewards and punishments, plus their deep evolutionary relationship to human facial expressions, allows the connection to be made.

Beyond facial expressions, non-human animals generally try to attain rewards and avoid punishments, just as much as people do. Whether it be peck at vertical lines in order to get food (Honig et al. 1963), jump the barrier separating two halves of a room in order to escape foot shock (Seligman and Maier 1967), or glance to the right in order to indicate the apparent majority direction of dot movement on a television display (Celebrini and Newsome 1995), animals will do quite a lot for a reward or to avoid a punishment. But just as in human beings, this behavior has some complications. Seligman and Maier (1967) famously discovered "learned helplessness," for example. Although dogs will normally do whatever it takes to escape from electrical foot shock, dogs exposed to unavoidable shocks quit trying to escape, and will not try to escape shocks delivered at a later time, even though these *could* be avoided: they learn to behave as though helpless. In a less depressing vein, Breland and Breland (1961) found that pigs who had learned to put wooden "coins" in a slot in return for food had a strong tendency to begin rooting the coins, tossing them into the air and dropping them (i.e., treating them like natural pig foods), to the extent that the pigs got too little food and began losing weight. Thus open-minded behaviorists, like the rest of us, arrived at the conclusion that animals do not *always* seek to maximize rewards and minimize punishments.

It must be admitted that the mere fact that animals work to attain rewards and avoid punishments indicates little that is special about reward and punishment. Although one cannot ask the rat, pig, or monkey why it does what it does, the most obvious answer is that it is aware that getting off of the electrified floor would be a lot more comfortable, that depositing coins will bring food, and so on, and it is thereby motivated to get off the floor, deposit the coin, and the like. But behavioral scientists have also turned up some fairly striking results, indicative of effects of reward and punishment upon voluntary behavior that are not readily explained in terms of their subjects desiring Q and being aware that P would bring Q. The common lore of parenting suggests that rewards and punishments can modify unthinking behavioral dispositions, inculcate intrinsic desires, and modify patterns of thought, and scientists working on behavior have supplied model experiments—often on humans—in support.

In a model study of unthinking behavioral dispositions, Hefferline et al. (1959) performed an operant conditioning study on human subjects specifically designed to eliminate the possibility that conscious decision-making, rather than operant conditioning, was producing the observed behavior. In the study, subjects listened to music over headphones, and the music was occasionally interrupted by an irritating noise. However, the irritating noise could be stopped or postponed so long as subjects made small twitches of the thumb at the right times. These twitches were very small, and occurred spontaneously in all subjects without effort: they were the sort of thing that one normally does not notice one is doing. One group of test subjects was told that the study was merely measuring muscular tension produced by noise superimposed on music, and another group was told that there was something they could do to stop the noise, but got no hint as to what it might be (and subsequent questioning demonstrated that they never guessed). Yet in both groups, the rate at which minor thumb twitches were produced soared dramatically. One other group, given clear instructions and assistance monitoring the production of exactly the right sort of thumb twitches (to supplement proprioception), did even better at producing the thumb twitches, demonstrating that they could be produced voluntarily (though not reliably: the sort of twitch required was very precise, in addition to being very small). Thus, on the reasonable assumption that having the music to which one is listening interrupted by loud noise is a punishment, the study demonstrated that the unthinking behavioral dispositions of human subjects were manipulated by the punishments they were administered.

In a study of intrinsic desires, Johnsrude et al. (1999) performed an experiment in which they presented human subjects with numerous abstract images. Subjects were told they were participating in a counting task, with corresponding rewards and punishments. What subjects were not told was that they were being frequently but not always rewarded after seeing one picture, rewarded and punished equally often after seeing a second, and frequently but not always punished after seeing a third. After the "counting task" was over, subjects were asked which of the three images they found most appealing, and they found the image most often followed by reward most appealing. Asked why, however, subjects responded with explanations in terms of the intrinsic qualities of the abstract image, "indicating that subjects were not completely aware of the effects of the conditioning procedure on their subsequent behavior" (251). That is, subjects came to prefer some images over others simply intrinsically, as a result of being rewarded or punished in a way they did not consciously relate to the objects themselves.

As for patterns of thought, in an experiment conducted by Greenspoon (1955), human subjects were asked to produce as many words as they could over an extended period of time (a total of fifty minutes). The experimenter responded to some subjects by saying an encouraging "mmm-hmm" whenever the subjects mentioned a plural noun, while nothing was said to other subjects.[4] After the experiment was over, subjects were explicitly asked about what they thought the purpose of the experiment was, whether they had noticed any changes in frequency of word production, the purpose of the experimenter saying "mmm-hmm," and so on. The results from the sole subject who discerned the pattern in the experimenter's responses were discarded. Among the remaining subjects, it was found that those hearing "mmm-hmm" after mentioning a plural noun had a small but statistically significant tendency to produce more plural nouns in total. Thus, in response to a small encouraging noise, subjects who were casting about in their minds for all the words they could think of tended to think of slightly more plural nouns than they would otherwise have done. This minor reward manipulated, to a small but real degree, subjects' spontaneous thoughts.

As a whole, these findings suggest that, although behaviorism has always been hostile to common sense, its findings about human behavior are in accord with common sense to a surprising degree.

3. The Neuroscience of Reward and Punishment

To a neuroscientist, reward and punishment look very different from the way they do to a behaviorist. Insofar as she is doctrinaire, the behaviorist can think of rewards and punishments only in terms of their impact upon behavior. The neuroscientist, however, looks into the brains of rewarded and punished organisms and attempts to locate and describe the common mechanism, if there is one, by means of which diverse rewards and punishments have their similar effects.[5] For most of the twentieth century, knowledge of the neuroscience of reward and punishment was radically incomplete. There were a few hints: centers in the brain that rats would work to activate, even to the exclusion of food; clusters of cells releasing distinctive active compounds; drugs known to create dependence; surgical procedures known to eliminate motivation in human beings; and the like.[6] But toward the end of the century, a tremendous burst of investigative work led to the creation of a very detailed picture of the neuroscience of reward. Unfortunately, as of the beginning of the twenty-first century, knowledge of the neuroscience of punishment lags behind, but I will say as much about punishment as is possible at this time.

Neuroscientists have added nothing of note to the stock list of rewards and punishments compiled by behaviorists and common sense.[7] They have not found new emotional expressions induced by rewards or new behavioral patterns induced by punishments. What they *have* done is traced the mechanisms by which rewards and punishments have their effects. The story is complex, but worth understanding.

Begin with reward. When an organism like us is rewarded by, say, being given a bicycle, the first thing that happens in its brain is that it represents being given a bicycle.[8] This representation causes activity elsewhere in the brain, that categorizes the represented event as a reward. Meanwhile, other brain structures have been attempting to predict the rewards and punishments the organism was going to receive at this moment. The combination of current reward information and predicted reward information is used by the brain to calculate the difference between the rewards that had previously been predicted and the rewards that have actually materialized. The result is released to the rest of the brain in the form of a very specific signal, one causing a very specific form of learning. This signal has effects upon the short-term operation of the brain and upon its long-term dispositions, effects that, in organisms like us, affect our feelings and modify dispositions to act, think, and experience, all in ways that tend to increase the acquisition of rewards and the avoidance of punishments.

Each stage of reward has been described by neuroscientists. The capacity to represent the world is the starting point, and at least one feature of it is worth mentioning: the capacity is found in two quite distinct locations, according to the scientists. One collection of representational capacities, those corresponding to familiar sense perception and everyday cognition, is found throughout sensory and much of association cortex (KSJ[9] 2000, chs. 17–32). These capacities allow us to be aware that we are hearing a tone at a given frequency, or seeing a dog, or being awarded the Nobel Prize for chemistry. The other collection of representational capacities is found in a structure deep in the brain known as the *hypothalamus*. The hypothalamus has a number of functions, but among these is the monitoring of blood sugar, body temperature, salt levels, and other, similar conditions (KSJ 2000, ch. 49). We do not perceive these qualities of our bodies directly (though we may become indirectly aware of them, through being more directly aware of a lack of energy, or a dry mouth, etc.), but nonetheless they are represented[10] by the hypothalamus. The brain's perceptual/cognitive and hypothalamic representational capacities are all connected to diverse other structures: to one another (allowing for complex perceptual processing and chains of ideas), to motor structures (allowing for perception and cognition to guide action), to endocrine structures (this is especially the role of representational structures in the hypothalamus), and so on (KSJ 2000, ch. 49). Most important for present purposes, they are also connected to the biological underpinnings of the reward system.

There are two output structures of the biological reward system in organisms like us, twin structures found immediately adjacent to one another deep in the brain: the *ventral tegmental area*, or *VTA*, and the *pars compacta* of the *substantia nigra*, or *SNpc* (see appendix, fig.1).[11] The VTA and SNpc have several properties that define them as the output structures for the brain's reward system. First, their principal neurons reach out to almost every structure in the brain, including almost the entire cortex, and many sub-cortical structures,[12] and these structures have receptors for dopamine, the chemical released by these neurons (Haber and Fudge 1997; KSJ 2000, ch. 45). Thus, the VTA and SNpc have the reach necessary to distribute a reward signal, and the signal can be received.

Second, the pattern in which dopamine is released by the VTA/SNpc is exactly the pattern required to transmit information about reward that is useful as a learning signal, as a signal that can cause useful change at the neural level. The pattern has been studied extensively by a number of researchers, especially Wolfram Schultz and colleagues.[13] Their finding is that the dopamine-releasing neurons of the VTA/SNpc have a baseline level of activity (fairly low), and that these neurons sometimes fire more rapidly than this baseline, and sometimes more slowly. When an organism receives an unexpected stimulus that would, intuitively, be called rewarding (such as some fruit juice received by a hungry organism), VTA/SNpc neurons briefly fire at above-baseline rates. When an intuitively rewarding stimulus is regularly preceded by a signal that fully predicts the stimulus (say, a light that comes on always and only when the juice is about to be given to the test subject), then these same neurons come to fire at above-baseline rates when the predicting stimulus is perceived (the light), but not when the reward (the juice) is received. Thus, the elevated firing rate of VTA/SNpc neurons corresponds to the time at which information is received that an *unpredicted* reward has been received *or* is coming. A fully predicted reward, however, causes no deviation in VTA/SNpc activity. Punishment as such has no effect upon the VTA/SNpc,[14] but absence of reward can. Absence of reward when no reward is predicted by the organism has no effect, but when a predicted reward fails to materialize, VTA/SNpc activity immediately drops. Hence, VTA/SNpc neurons fire in a pattern that carries information about the difference, at time t, between the rewards received and expected at t versus those rewards the organism was predicting (at t-1) it would receive or expect at t. Or, to put things in a more intuitive if less precise manner, VTA/SNpc neurons signal the difference between how good the world was predicted to look at t and how good it in fact looks at t. Such a signal has been shown to be exactly the sort of signal required for reward-based reinforcement learning (Houk, Adams, and Barto 1995; Montague, Dayan, and Sejnowski 1996; Schultz, Dayan, and Montague 1997). That is, such a signal is exactly what is most computationally useful if a system is going to modify itself adaptively on the basis of rewards received.

Third, dopamine from the VTA/SNpc has actually been observed changing neural connection strengths, in exactly the sort of fashion required by the computational theory of reward-based learning. Bao, Chan, and Merzenich (2001) conducted a study upon rats, in which they controlled activity in the auditory cortex (by making a sound at a given frequency, known to activate specific neurons in auditory cortex) and dopamine release from the VTA/SNpc (by electrically stimulating dopamine-releasing neurons found there). The experimental conditions included rats hearing the tone and then receiving VTA/SNpc stimulation, rats hearing the tone after prior VTA/SNpc stimulation, rats hearing the tone without any VTA/SNpc stimulation, rats receiving VTA/SNpc stimulation without hearing a tone, and rats exposed to no experimental condition. The finding was that only one condition differed from the control condition, and that was when rats were first exposed to a sound, then received VTA/SNpc stimulation.[15] Under this condition, the area of the rat cortex that responds first to sounds, namely, primary auditory cortex, was found to have modified its connections, such that more of the cortex was dedicated to processing sounds of the same frequency as the experimental tone. Furthermore, a region of rat cortex responsible for higher auditory processing was also reorganized when the tone was followed by VTA/SNpc stimulation, and this was found to be a region that received input from the affected region of primary auditory cortex. In order to confirm that these changes were the result of dopamine released by the VTA/SNpc, the experiments were repeated while chemicals were administered to the rats blocking their dopamine receptors (structures found on neurons, required for dopamine from the VTA/SNpc to have its effects). Under this condition, no change in rat cortex was observed. Finally, it should be noted that the neurons of the rat auditory cortex are very similar, in kind, to neurons found elsewhere in the rat and in the human cortex, and in many sub-cortical structures as well. Hence, there is no reason to expect this effect to be restricted to rats, or to auditory regions in the brain.[16] As a whole, this study demonstrated that the release of dopamine by the VTA/SNpc can be expected to reorganize neural structures (and hence the psychological structures implemented by them); given the fact that the pattern of elevated dopamine release from the VTA/SNpc corresponds to the theoretical requirements of a reward-based learning signal, the conclusion that the VTA/SNpc is responsible for releasing a reward signal is powerfully supported. It also strikingly vindicates the commonsensical hunch that rewards can help to change discriminative capacities.

The study by Bao, Chan, and Merzenich is a decisive demonstration of the power of the reward signal observed by Schultz and colleagues. Once the demonstration has been made, however, it is possible to go back to other work and read it as showing other powers of the reward system. For instance, Merzenich and Jenkins (1993) demonstrated a reorganization in somatosensory (touch) cortex that was reward-dependent, though they did not trace the source of the reward signal back to the VTA/SNpc.

More striking examples come from a series of studies conducted by Norman White, Mark Packard, and colleagues (Packard and Teather 1997, 1999; Packard and McGaugh 1992; Packard and White 1991; White 1996, 1997). In these experiments, researchers distinguished two discrete "memory" systems, one responsible for episodic/spatial memory (in the hippocampus), the other responsible for behavioral/habit learning (in the dorsal *striatum* [appendix, fig.1], a motor region of the basal ganglia, to which we will return in chapter 4). They found that some forms of learning relied upon explicit memory stored through the action of the hippocampus: learning the absolute spatial location of a safe place, for example. Other forms of learning relied upon implicit memory stored through connections in the dorsal striatum: learning to swim toward a marker with one distinctive appearance rather than another, regardless of absolute location, in order to reach safety, for example. These latter forms of learning, that they interpreted as behavioral habit learning, depended upon dopamine reaching the dorsal striatum. Knowing what we do from the studies just mentioned, we can reasonably speculate that it was dopamine from the VTA/SNpc, carrying reward information, that inculcated the behavioral learning Packard, White, and their colleagues observed. If this interpretation of their findings is correct, then they have observed the reward signal shaping unthinking behavioral response tendencies—tendencies that persist even without conscious declarative memory of the benefits of one action over another—of exactly the sort common sense holds can be modified by reward and punishment.

Another study, by Knowlton, Mangles, and Squire (1996), also strongly suggests that dopamine release is involved in what its authors call "the gradual, incremental learning characteristic of habit learning," but in this case, the learning of *mental* dispositions. In their experiment, human subjects were confronted with one of a number of arbitrary stimuli and asked to learn, by trial and error, whether the stimuli presaged "rain" or "shine" (all this being displayed on a computer); after guessing, subjects received feedback telling them whether they had been right or wrong. None of the stimuli were infallible signs of the weather—they were either 75% or 57% reliable. Anterograde amnesiacs—people without the ability to form new declarative memories—were found to learn to perform this guessing task quite well, comparably to control subjects, though they retained no declarative knowledge of previous guesses beyond a moment. But subjects with Parkinson's disease—a disorder selectively destroying the dopamine-releasing neurons of the SNpc—who had excellent episodic memories turned out to be nearly random in their attempts to predict the "weather." They were unable to learn in a very specific sense of "learn," one more closely linked to learning to offer another person help than to learning the capitals of European countries. Once again, common sense receives vindication from neuroscience, and the mechanism for the sort of learning described by common sense is found to be the VTA/SNpc.

It can also be added that there is evidence that dopamine release directly modifies receptive neurons in a way that mediates pure operant conditioning in the sea slug *Aplysia* (Brembs et al. 2002), that dopamine is involved in creating synapse-specific strengthening of neural connections (Otmakhova and Lisman 1996), and that dopamine is required for certain forms of long-term changes in connection strengths between neurons (Frey, Schroeder, and Matthies 1990). Extra details such as these, confirming the role of dopamine release and the VTA/SNpc in changing connections between cells, and so changing organisms' psychologies, is now fairly widespread in the neuroscientific literature; this has been only a review of selected highlights.

So the brain's reward system starts with representation and ends with a reinforcement signal emitted by the VTA/SNpc. But between representation and reinforcement there are a number of complications. For instance, somehow the brain must keep track of expected rewards, so that it may calculate the difference between rewards known or expected at t, and those previously predicted to be known or expected at t. A number of lines of evidence suggest that this role may be performed by another deep-brain structure known as the *nucleus accumbens*, perhaps in conjunction with the *caudate nucleus* (appendix, fig.1).[17] But however this calculation is performed, it is clear that some version of it must be performed, since the dopamine neurons of the VTA/SNpc express the results. Exactly how the calculation is performed will not detain us, however, as it will not bear on the philosophical conclusions drawn in this work.

Another layer of complication is found in the *orbitofrontal cortex*, or OFC (appendix, fig. 2). The OFC is a portion of the frontal cortex that receives signals from almost all perceptual and cognitive representational structures in the brain (Rolls 2000; Cavada et al. 2000). It takes this input and appears to categorize it as indicating a reward or coming reward, or as indicating a punishment or coming punishment, or else does not respond, if the brain's cognitive and perceptual representations deliver it no information about states of affairs it recognizes as rewarding or punishing. That is, the OFC responds selectively to stimuli that we, as observers, would intuitively call "rewards" and "punishments," doing so after the rewards or punishments (or signs of coming rewards or punishments) have been represented as more particular things elsewhere in the brain.[18] It can respond to simple stimuli such as rewarding or punishing tastes and smells, to more complex stimuli such as fractal computer images known to precede the delivery of a reward, and even to monetary rewards and punishments (Rolls 2000; Schultz et al. 2000). The OFC sends its signals about these rewards and punishments on to motor regions of the brain (the motor regions of the basal ganglia and the pre-frontal cortex, discussed in chapter 4), to a structure (the amygdala) whose outputs control visceral responses to rewards and punishments, and, most important, to the nucleus accumbens and the ventral tegmental area (Haber et al. 1995).[19] By sending output to the structures responsible for generating the reward signal, it allows representations of tastes, fractal images, and money to cause the release of reward signals.

The focus so far has been on the structures neuroscientists have identified as the core of the brain's reward system. This system is conceived of as one that contributes to a certain form of learning: incremental, non-conscious learning from rewards, also known as 'reinforcement learning' or (when punishment is included) 'contingency-based learning'. It is in these terms that I have focused upon the reward system. But the reward system has many more impacts upon the organism than merely causing a special sort of learning. The neuroscientist's reward system is also held to be a biological cause of emotional effects and behavioral effects that everyday thinking attributes to rewards.

Take contributions to pleasure. The pleasurable effects of cocaine appear to be mediated by its effect on dopamine (Gawin 1991), and the same is true of MDMA, or "ecstasy" (Liechti and Vollenweider 2000), and a number of other pleasure-causing drugs (KSJ 2000, ch. 51), suggesting that dopamine release is a contributing cause to pleasure under normal circumstances as well. This conclusion is also supported by the fact that there are sites in the brain that animals (including humans) will voluntarily stimulate electrically, and most of these sites have some connection to dopamine transmission (Stellar and Stellar 1985). This is a topic to which we will return in chapter 3, when pleasure is the focus.

As for behavioral effects of the more immediate, obvious sort, there is work arguing on theoretical and experimental grounds that dopamine release guides decision-making in humans (Egelman, Person, and Montague 1999) and action-selection in non-human animals (Berridge and Robinson 1998), and there is the striking fact that individuals whose dopamine-releasing cells are mostly destroyed are thereby rendered Parkinsonian, impaired and slow in voluntary movement, or unable to move voluntarily at all (KSJ 2000, ch. 43). There is no doubt that the release of dopamine in the brain from the VTA/SNpc is central to making voluntary movement possible, a matter that will be discussed further in chapter 4.

To summarize: the commonsensical view of reward is that rewards (generally) make people happy, motivate them directly in a manner mediated by conscious deliberation, inculcate behavioral tendencies unconsciously, create intrinsic desires, inculcate intellectual tendencies, and perhaps modify sensory capacities. And, strikingly, the neuroscientific view of reward confirms common sense at many points, while also explaining the mechanism by which these effects are brought about.

Turning now from reward to punishment, the story becomes less clear. No investigation of the neural basis of punishment has put forward evidence for a punishment center with the persuasive force of the evidence for the reward center. But given the apparent fact that the OFC and nucleus accumbens generate both reward and punishment information (Rolls 2000), there surely must be a structure somewhere in the brain that makes use of this information to produce a punishment signal, a counterpart to the VTA/SNpc reward signal. The leading candidate for a punishment center is found in the *dorsal raphe nucleus*, or *DRN* (appendix, fig. 1), located high in the brainstem, near the reward center (see, e.g., Wise, Berger, and Stein, 1973; Deakin 1983; Deakin 1998). A distinctive feature of the DRN is that almost all of the cells in the brain that release serotonin are found in it or in related neighboring cell clusters (KSJ 2000, ch. 45). Hence, serotonin has been thought to be the messenger carrying the neural punishment signal, just as dopamine is the messenger carrying the reward signal.

Anatomically, the DRN appears to receive information from the orbitofrontal cortex (Coffield et al. 1992; Peyron et al. 1998; but see Cavada et al. 2000); the hypothalamus (Abramson and Moore 2001); and striatum, which contains the nucleus accumbens and caudate nucleus (O'Hearn and Molliver 1984). Thus, all the key sources of information used by the VTA/SNpc are also used by the DRN.

The DRN, in turn, projects to targets throughout cortical and sub-cortical regions (KSJ 2000, ch. 45), where receptors for serotonin are widespread, just as in the case of the VTA/SNpc. Thus, the DRN is appropriately poised to receive and send information about punishment.

Unfortunately, there are no studies parallel to those by Schultz and colleagues demonstrating that the serotonin-releasing neurons of the DRN change their activity in a manner that corresponds to deviations from expected punishment, and no studies parallel to that by Bao, Chan, and Merzenich demonstrating that serotonin released by the DRN directly controls the organization of neural connections in the cortex. There is, thus, no "smoking gun" demonstrating that the DRN carries a punishment signal. Even so, there are important findings.

Microdialysis studies performed on non-human subjects come closest to repeating Schultz-style microelectrode recordings of activity patterns in the VTA. In microdialysis studies, minute probes measure the concentrations of chemicals, such as serotonin, floating freely in particular regions of the brain. Since the release of such compounds into the brain is normally caused only by neural activity, microdialysis is believed to indirectly measure the activity of neurons containing the chemicals under study. In the case of serotonin, only a small group of cells in the brain release serotonin, and so elevated serotonin levels in the brain indicate elevated activity in those cells. Unfortunately, these studies have not looked at the sorts of conditions Schultz and colleagues studied, with unpredicted versus predicted punishments, and absence of expected punishment, but correlations between punishments and serotonin have nonetheless been observed. Stressors such as immobilization and restraint (Shimizu et al 1992; Shintani et al. 1995; Vahabzadeh and Fillenz 1994), tail pinch (Reuter and Jacobs 1996; Vahabzadeh and Fillenz 1994), forced swim (Reuter and Jacobs 1996; Jordan et al. 1994), and exposure to a known predictor of aversive stimuli (Wilkinson et al. 1996; Yoshioka et al. 1995; West et al. 1991) all cause release of serotonin in the brain at above-normal levels, suggesting that punishing events are a normal cause of activity for serotonin-releasing cells.[20]

It should be noted, however, that a review of the evidence from microdialysis studies (Rueter et al. 1997) found that being awake and being fed were both conditions capable of producing quite significant increases in serotonin release, and the authors concluded that serotonin was more likely to play a role in behavioral arousal than in punishment per se. Though appropriately cautionary, this interpretation has difficulties of its own. For instance, it does not explain the fact that increased serotonin levels have been found to increase behavioral inhibition (Engleman et al. 1995), and decreased serotonin levels have been found to decrease inhibition (Higgins et al. 1988, Thiébot et al. 1982)—just the opposite of what one would expect if serotonin release correlated purely with behavioral arousal. Just to take one instance, it was found that rats receiving a chemical that selectively blocks the activity of serotonin at certain cells are less sensitive to punishment than untreated rats (Cervo and Samanin 1995). This behavioral evidence is reviewed at length in Soubrié (1986).

As for studies on the impact of serotonin on learning, once again the literature is deficient, although there are again interesting hints. Rogers et al. (1999) found that serotonin depletion impaired human subjects who had to learn that a previously rewarded response was no longer rewarded, and that a new response was needed, suggesting that serotonin is needed for some forms of learning. In a similar vein, Hensman et al. (1991) found that ritanserin, a drug blocking the effects of serotonin at certain cells,[21] largely prevented human subjects from forming a Pavlovian association between a neutral stimulus and an aversive one. There have also been a few findings regarding the effects of serotonin upon neural connections in very simple organisms (Liu et al. 1997; Zhang and Endo 1997) and in the *cerebellum* (Mitoma and Konishi 1999), a structure involved in movement production (appendix fig. 1; mentioned again in chapter 4).

The effects of antidepressant drugs such as fluoxetine (Prozac) have raised a number of questions for the view that serotonin release by the DRN is a punishment signal.[22] Fluoxetine and many other antidepressants have the effect of raising serotonin levels in the brain while decreasing displeasure, something one would not expect were serotonin the mediator of a punishment signal. In fact, experiments have shown that individuals using antidepressants or otherwise vulnerable to depression who are suddenly deprived of the ability to make serotonin, and whose overall levels of serotonin in the brain fall as a result, rapidly become depressed, an effect reversed by the return of the ability to make serotonin (see, e.g., Delgado and Moreno 1999). Surely, one might think, if serotonin were the carrier of a punishment signal, then being deprived of serotonin would deprive one of information about punishment, which ought to cause optimism, not depression. Bill Deakin, the scientist most prominently defending the role of the DRN in anxiety at present, has no simple answer to this objection. Still, there are a few things that can be said. For instance, it can be pointed out that individuals who are completely well do not fall into depression when deprived of the ability to make serotonin (Delgado and Moreno 1999). This suggests that the depressant effect of serotonin deprivation in vulnerable individuals may not indicate anything general about the role of serotonin in the normal human being. It can also be pointed out that antidepressants acting on serotonin generally increase serotonin levels rapidly, but can take weeks in order to have psychological effects (KSJ 2000, ch. 61), again rendering their mode of action mysterious, and potentially compatible with a role for briefly elevated serotonin release in a punishment signal.[23] Finally, and perhaps most powerfully, it can be pointed out that many anti-anxiety drugs suppress the release of serotonin in the brain (Deakin 1983). Thus, anti-anxiety drugs decrease serotonin availability, while antidepression drugs increase serotonin availability. How to square these results remains mysterious. Deakin (1998) has speculated that there are two roles for serotonin, one (for serotonin released from the DRN) in anxiety (a candidate punishment signal), the other (for serotonin released from the *medial raphe nucleus*, a neighboring structure) in resistance to depression (a candidate to explain the action of SSRIs), but at present this remains fairly speculative. Even so, the conflicting findings seem to leave open the possibility that serotonin does mediate a punishment signal as much as they suggest it does not.

4. From Phenomena to Theory

We now have an impressive collection of data, acquired through naturalistic observation and scientific study, about the character and causal powers of rewards and punishments. All that we lack is a theory that says what it is for something to *be* a reward or punishment. That is the topic of this section. Because their theories are the best known, and because they were the first to produce systematic theories of reward and punishment, the first word will go to the behaviorists.

Reward and Behaviorism

According to familiar behaviorist doctrine, a reward is a stimulus which, when it follows behavior, increases an organism's tendency to produce the same behavior again in similar circumstances. Likewise, a punishment is a stimulus which, when it follows behavior, decreases an organism's tendency to produce the same behavior again in similar circumstances.[24] Characterized in this way, *reward* and *punishment* are explanatorily worthless concepts for explaining behavior, for reasons so familiar that they need be only briefly rehearsed.[25] On the definition just given, the fact that an organism was rewarded cannot explain why its behavioral dispositions changed, since rewards change dispositions by definition. Had the stimulus not had the power to change the organism's dispositions, it would not have been a reward for that organism. The same problem holds for punishments. The fact that pinching a rat's tail changes its behavioral dispositions is what makes a tail-pinch a punishment, and so the fact that a tail-pinch is a punishment cannot serve to causally explain why the pinch changes dispositions.

To make matters worse, it is also clear that this theory of reward and punishment misses the mark extensionally: it misjudges particular cases. Smith and Duffy (1957) observed that hungry rats would lick quite a lot of saccharine solution from a drinking spout, and were forced by their behaviorist scruples to conclude that, for hungry rats, saccharine is highly rewarding. If all there were to something being a reward was that it promoted repetitions of acquisition behavior, this would be right, but of course other explanations leap to mind. Perhaps the rats could taste the sweetness of the saccharine but remained calorie-deprived even after drinking the solution, and so continued to drink in the hope of ceasing to be hungry. In this (perhaps more plausible) case, there would be nothing particularly rewarding about saccharine for the rats in this condition, in spite of their repeated behavior. Or consider the cases described by Heath (1963), in which human subjects were allowed to stimulate regions of their own brains. One subject's self-stimulation behavior was sometimes "frantic," entailing (on this theory of reward) that at that point self-stimulation must have been maximally rewarding. Yet the subject's self-report was that his self-stimulation caused a feeling of building to orgasm; his highest self-stimulation rates were an attempt to actually achieve orgasm, an attempt that was "futile," "frustrating," and the cause of a "nervous feeling." Such circumstances hardly suggest maximal reward. Another subject described by Heath self-stimulated maximally in an attempt to recall something: apparently, self-stimulation gave the subject the feeling of almost, but not quite, recalling something, and the subject tried, but failed, to achieve a clear memory. The effort "induced irritability," as one can well imagine. Once again, the cause of maximal responding is something one can hardly dignify with the name 'reward.' Of course, one can *stipulate* that 'reward' will mean nothing more than the usual behaviorist's definition, but such a stipulation tells us nothing about the real phenomenon also known as 'reward', and in fact is obfuscating if the means to understand the real phenomenon are at hand.

The final nail in the coffin of the motivational theory of reward comes from the neuroscience of reward: the biological system identified as the reward system is one that could exist whether or not an organism had the capacity to behave. One branch of the reward system, based in the SNpc, has a powerful influence upon behavior. But the other branch, based in the VTA, reaches out through the cortex to have effects such as the one measured by Bao, Chan, and Merzenich, in which reward signals change sensory capacities. Even in the absence of the SNpc, even in the absence of the ability to move, the activity of the VTA would continue to conform to learning rules. Even in the absence of any capacity for behavior whatsoever, neural change induced by the VTA would continue to exemplify what is called 'reward-based learning'. Why would the normal sorts of events triggering bursts of VTA firing not count as rewards, then? Behavioral change is not the only thing the reward system does in the brain. Given the conceptual difficulties, why should we treat it as the sole *essential* function of the reward system?

Reward and Pleasure

Perhaps this failure of behaviorism seems obvious. One might say that rewards and punishments were not understood by behaviorists precisely because they are causes of characteristic sensations, namely, pleasure and displeasure. For something to be a reward is simply for that thing to be a source of pleasure, and for something to be a punishment is simply for it to be a source of displeasure. Since the behaviorists forbade themselves to talk openly about feelings of pleasure and displeasure, they had no way of expressing these simple truths, but simple truths they remain—according to this view, which can be called the *hedonic* theory of reward and punishment.

Unfortunately for the hedonic theory of reward, it faces just the same sorts of problems the behaviorist theory faced: reward and punishment are explanatorily significant *causes* of pleasure and displeasure, and so cannot be identified with things causing pleasure. If a child is crying, or a dog's tail lies listlessly between its legs, or a criminal shouts obscenities, one common explanation goes like this: the behavior is an expression of displeasure, and the displeasure can be causally explained by a recent punishment—being told to leave the table and sit in the corner, being struck on the nose with a newspaper, or being sent to solitary confinement, as the case may be. Likewise, the fact of reward is thought to causally explain pleasure, which in turn may cause the sorts of behaviors we normally associate with being rewarded—exuberance, boasting, or whatnot. These explanations cannot be literally correct and informative, if rewards *just are* causes of pleasure, and punishments causes of displeasure.

The hedonic reward theorist could object that the true causal explanation in these cases is not that reward or punishment per se causes pleasure or displeasure, but only that certain events, which can be described as rewards or punishments but which can also be described in other ways, are the causes of pleasure or displeasure. To continue with one of these examples, it was said that a dog may feel displeasure as a causal consequence of being punished, which would not make sense if feeling displeasure as a result of some event was what constituted that event as a punishment. However, the hedonic theorist might reply that it is the fact that the dog is struck on the nose which is the truly explanatory cause of its displeasure. Nose striking is what explains the dog's displeasure, not the fact of being punished. Hence, the explanation of the dog's displeasure in terms of punishment is misleading. It identifies the event that causes the displeasure, but does not identify it in terms that make clear the causal relation between the event and the onset of the dog's displeasure. When understood correctly, all that common sense requires is that hitting the dog on the nose causes displeasure, and hitting the dog on the nose can, as a result, be correctly described as "punishing the dog." Thus, in an indirect fashion, it can be said that punishing the dog caused displeasure, but this does nothing to show that the hedonic theory of reward and punishment is unable to explain the causal relations between events that happen to be delivery of rewards or punishments and pleasure or displeasure.

The problem with this answer is that it is mistaken in holding that it allows for all the explanations common sense requires. Imagine visiting a neighbor and seeing his young son busily raking leaves. After a while, the child comes in and announces he has finished his chore. "Wonderful," says the father. "Now you can cook dinner!" The boy beams in delight. Curious, you asked why the boy was so happy, and the father explains the situation by saying "Oh, for Andrew, being allowed to cook is a reward." In this vignette, the fact that being allowed to cook is a reward for Andrew is held to explain why it is that it pleases Andrew. That is, it is the fact that being allowed to cook possesses a property, that of being a reward for Andrew, which is held to explain the fact that being allowed to cook caused pleasure. If the hedonic theory of reward were correct, this explanation would be as empty as an explanation of morphine's soporific qualities in terms of its dormitive virtue. This strikes me as mistaken. The fact that one has been rewarded is enough, under normal conditions, to causally explain one's happiness, and the fact that one has been punished explains unhappiness. Although one *can* mention what the reward or punishment consisted in, it is not necessary to do so in order to produce a genuine explanation. As before, this theory of reward and punishment falls short by *identifying* them with phenomena that ought rather to be *explained* by them.

Also against the hedonic theory of reward and punishment, it can be pointed out that there are many exceptions to the generalization that rewards cause pleasure and punishments cause displeasure, though here the discussion must proceed carefully. On one way of using the words 'reward' and 'punishment', it is trivial that a reward can be suffered by, and a punishment enjoyed by, the person rewarded or punished, but this is not the relevant sense for present purposes. Consider a criminal living in Winnipeg, seeking to murder a person in the Stony Mountain prison. He may commit a crime and allow himself to be caught, so that he will be punished by being placed in that same prison. This punishment, however, is just what the criminal seeks, for it brings him within reach of his intended victim. In the same way, a shy person may attempt to avoid receiving a public reward for his good works, because he would find the process (the speeches, the plaque) intolerable. These cases suggest that there is a sense in which what is a reward and what a punishment is determined by something like the public function of an act, or the intention of the rewarding or punishing agent. But this is obviously not the sense of 'reward' or 'punishment' of interest to a philosopher of mind. In that sense, the would-be murderer will not be punished for his misdeed, but in fact rewarded, if he is sent to the prison he desires to reach, though of course the authorities will be rewarding him unwittingly. Likewise, a well-meaning group might inadvertently punish a shy man for his good deeds by insisting on a large, public ceremony to recognize his contributions to society.[26]

Even with potential confusions eliminated, however, there are still examples of non-conventional punishments that please and rewards that do not. In this regard, it is instructive to learn of experiments conducted by Fischman and Foltin (1992) and by Lamb et al. (1991). In these experiments, users of euphorigenic drugs (cocaine, heroin, and morphine) were found to preferentially engage in activities in return for euphorigenic drug injections that contained so little of the drug that the experimental subjects subjectively experienced the injections as causing no pleasure. The best interpretation of the experiments appears to be that low doses of certain drugs remain sufficiently potent rewards to motivate behavior even when they do not cause pleasure, showing that rewards are not constituted by their relation to pleasure. In the study by Lamb and colleagues, hospitalized heroin addicts could receive injections of an unknown (to them) quantity of morphine. The quantity might be zero or some higher dose, and that quantity would be available for a week, from Monday through to Friday. The next Monday, a new dose would be available. Subjects on Monday thus did not know what dose of morphine they might receive, but by Wednesday it should have been fairly clear to them, through their subjective experience of it. Subjects who wanted doses on Thursday and Friday were required to press a lever three thousand times within forty-five minutes in order to obtain the dose. Lamb and colleagues found that subjects would press the lever for any dose of morphine offered, but would not press it for saline. This result extended to a dose of 3.75 milligrams of morphine, the smallest offered, which the addicts worked to obtain *but which they also subjectively rated as worthless, containing no drug*. Hence, while they derived no pleasure from getting the smallest dose, and could not discriminate it from saline, getting it was somehow a reward.

The final argument against the hedonic theory of reward returns to the structure of the brain. Though nothing has yet been said about pleasure, chapter 3 will show that the biological basis for pleasure is independent of the reward system described here. From the brain's general representational capacities, through the OFC and nucleus accumbens, to the VTA/SNpc, there is nothing that can be called a pleasure center: the biological seat of pleasure is elsewhere. The reward system might cause pleasure, and it might be activated by pleasure, but it is not identical to, or constituted by, a hedonic system of any sort. Even in an organism with no capacity for pleasure or displeasure (such as the aforementioned sea slug *Aplysia*), a reward system of the sort described by neuroscientists can exist, modifying short-term and long-term behavior patterns, modifying sensory capacities and associations of ideas, all via the implementation of reward- and punishment-based learning algorithms.

Reward and Learning

At this point, the neuroscience of the reward system seems the obvious place to turn. But how much help can neuroscience be to a philosopher in characterizing a phenomenon like reward? Like most contemporary philosophers of mind, I stand by the idea that mental categories are multiply realizable: that there is nothing in principle barring an organism made of polymers, silicon chips, or pure energy (if such can exist) from having desires, being conscious, or constituting events as rewards.[27] So long as such beings have the right features in common,[28] they can all have minds: neurons are not *essential*, but rather an implementation detail. Given this commitment, I can hardly hold that for X to be a reward is for X to cause firings of the VTA/SNpc. The VTA/SNpc can only be the implementation, in beings like us, of (part of) a reward system that could be implemented differently.

The neuroscience of reward nevertheless has something special to offer philosophy. By identifying the reward system *as a system computing information for the purposes of producing a particular teaching signal*, it offers a way of understanding the essential nature of reward independently of reward's connections to behavior and to pleasure. Specifically, it offers the idea that perhaps what makes something a reward is that it triggers a specific sort of learning. The fact that the outputs of the reward system are used to influence action, on the one hand, and feelings, on the other, is not essential to it: even if the rest of an organism consisted of nothing but perceptual capacities and VTA/SNpc,[29] it could nonetheless have a reward system, because it could have a system emitting a characteristic teaching signal.

Schultz and colleagues have, it seems to me, been looking at the reward system in exactly this way: as a system defined by its production of a special learning signal, a signal that in turn is used by, for example, the behavior-production system, without being defined by this use. Not being philosophers, they have not explicitly characterized the reward system in these terms: necessary and sufficient conditions for being a reward system are not their business. Yet in practice, this is how they have treated their object of study. The evidence that powerfully demonstrates that the VTA/SNpc is the output end of the reward system, according to Dayan, Montague, Schultz, and others is not the fact that it drives behavior, or the fact that it is involved in pleasure, but simply the fact that it fires in the pattern required by the best existing mathematical models of reinforcement learning.[30]

Encouraged by the neuroscientific opinion, I want to argue that reward and punishment *should* be looked at in this way: as tied, at bottom, to contingency-based learning. The argument will have two stages. In the first, I will argue that there are straightforward theoretical benefits to thinking of contingency-based learning as the nature of reward and punishment. In the second, I will give a detailed theory of reward and punishment in these terms, and develop it with the help of possible objections.

To start: there are at least four major benefits of treating contingency-based learning as the core nature of reward and punishment. The first two are tied to the criticisms just made of behaviorist and hedonic theories of reward. If the essence of the reward system is that it is a system driving contingency-based learning, then the claims that behavioral change can be causally explained by the fact of reward and that pleasure can be causally explained by the fact of reward can turn out to be true, not distorted expressions of trivialities. Since they appear to be basic but important contingent empirical discoveries, rather than poorly stated necessary truths, this is a happy consequence, and one that must be given up if one of the foregoing theories of reward is preferred over the learning-theoretic one offered here. The power of the learning-theoretic account to make these claims warranted and interesting should not be discounted.

One could object that if the learning-theoretic account of reward is accepted, there will be other apparently good causal explanations that will turn out to be ultimately non-causal and trivial. The objection is correct. If the learning-theoretic account of reward is accepted, then contingency-based learning per se cannot be given a non-trivial causal explanation in terms of the fact of reward. But how significant is this? One can still causally explain learning in terms of events, such as the receipt of a pellet of rat chow, that trigger the learning system. Only explanations of learning in terms of rewards *as such* turn out to be vacuous. Furthermore, one can still give non-trivial causal explanations of the *effects* of learning in terms of rewards. For instance, the fact that James now wants to have clean hands, and the fact that Jennifer has a tendency to smile at people coming to her desk, may still receive non-trivial causal explanation in terms of rewards. The fact that James was rewarded for having clean hands does not guarantee that he now has an intrinsic desire for them, and the fact that Jennifer has been rewarded for smiling at strangers does not guarantee that she now does so out of habit. All that is guaranteed is that reward signals have been released in the past. The effects of reward signals upon a psyche depend as much on the psyche as upon the reward signals, and so the fact of past reward is always a partial, and so meaningful, contribution to the explanation of any particular effect. Hence, if the learning theory of reward is correct, the sorts of causal explanations that are rendered trivial are the sort that common sense has never made much of. The explanations common sense *has* focused on in terms of reward all turn out to be perfectly good, non-trivial explanations, if the reward theory is correct.

This brings us to the third benefit of a learning-theoretic account of reward: such a theory is quite compatible with the existing, commonsensical theory of reward held by most people. According to everyday thought, rewards cause emotional changes, they directly motivate via deliberation and inculcate unconsciously effective behavioral dispositions, they inculcate intrinsic desires, they modify intellectual dispositions, and they can, perhaps, modify sensory capacities. The neuroscientists working on the reinforcement learning system have demonstrated that most of these effects can be caused, directly or indirectly, through the action of the system. And, if all forms of unconscious learning observed by behaviorists prove to be mediated by the same biological reward system (as seems likely), then the few remaining phenomena of reward that neuroscientists have not yet directly observed to be manipulated by VTA/SNpc teaching signals (the inculcation of intrinsic desires and the unconscious modification of intellectual dispositions) will eventually be observed, as appropriate experiments are performed. That is, neuroscientists have shown that the reinforcement learning system mediates most effects that common sense attributes to rewards, and seem likely to show that all such effects are mediated by the reinforcement learning system. Since it is always theoretically preferable to produce a theory of X that preserves as many apparent truths about X as is possible, all else being equal, this is a strong mark in favor of the reinforcement-based learning theory of reward.

It can also be pointed out that the same cannot be said of other theories of reward. The faults, in the eyes of common sense, of the familiar behavioristic theory of reward need hardly be rehearsed. This theory has whatever appeal it does in spite of its hostility to common sense, not because of it. But the hedonic theory of reward also fares badly when compared to the claims of common sense. Hedonic structures in the brain cannot explain the power of reward to shape unconsciously effective behavioral dispositions and have nothing to do with sensory modification. They also appear unlikely to have much to say about the shaping of unconscious intellectual dispositions or the formation of new intrinsic desires. This is because hedonic structures in the brain are all distinct from the VTA/SNpc (again, see chapter 3 for the argument for this), and it is the VTA/SNpc that is the proximal cause of these effects. Hence, unconscious dispositions to overt behavior and deliberation, changes in intrinsic desires, and sensory modifications are all caused by something other than reward, according to the hedonic theory of reward. This is quite a lot for the theory to give up, and substantially detracts from its appeal as a commonsensical theory.

The fourth benefit of treating contingency-based learning as essential to reward is that none of what behaviorism learned about reward need be abandoned, though some of it must be redescribed, if we follow this theoretical path. The paradigmatic rewards and punishments used by behaviorists all turn out to be paradigmatic rewards and punishments, if the contingency-based learning theory of reward is correct. The findings that rewards modify immediate behavior and behavioral dispositions, that organisms will learn to do all sorts of things for rewards, that intellectual dispositions can be modified by rewards—all of these things turn out to be true, according to the theory being defended. It seems that there is every reason in the world to want a learning theory of reward. On, then, to the details.

Suppose that we were to hold that for an event or state of affairs X to be a reward (or punishment) for an organism O is for X to cause the release of a characteristic learning signal, of the sort currently labeled 'reinforcement learning' by scientists.[31] What would follow? The immediate answer is "problems." At least two arguments prevent any such simple identification. First, because the first step of reinforcement learning is the representation of the world, it is possible to activate the system by means of misrepresentation. Such an erroneous triggering of the system would not seem to constitute the cause as a reward. Think of a woman who locates a notorious criminal and assists the police in arresting him. In return, the police send her what is supposed to be a reward, but which is actually (because of a clerical error) a check for zero dollars. Yet the woman does not notice the low amount, and in an unfortunate mishap loses the check, and so never learns the truth. In this context, though the woman believes she was financially rewarded for her services, in truth she was not.[32] The fact that the arrival of the check caused her brain to release a reinforcement signal does not suffice to show that she really was rewarded; rather, it shows that simple dispositions to cause the release of reinforcement signals do not suffice for a thing to be a reward.

The second immediate argument against identifying rewards and punishments with triggers of the neural reinforcement and extinction signals is that rewards and punishments can go quite undetected by the individual. A doctor can punish a patient for being obnoxious by prescribing him a pleasant drug with a nasty tendency to cause blood clots, and the patient may never discover he was punished. Likewise, one can reward a soldier for her kindness by arranging that she be assigned to a unit likely to avoid combat, and the soldier may never realize she was rewarded. It is important to note that these punishments and rewards are not merely conventional. Like many other punishments, the doctor succeeds in punishing the patient only if the patient takes a negative stance to being harmed; if the patient's only wish is to be harmed by a malicious doctor, so that his family will be able to sue and so restore its fortunes, then the doctor's attempted punishment is a failure—the doctor has instead granted the patient a precious and sought-after opportunity. And like many other rewards, the soldier is rewarded only if she takes a positive stance toward avoiding combat: she has been inadvertently punished for her kindness if it was her greatest wish to enter combat with the enemy. It is true that these rewards and punishments do not have the psychological effects characteristic of other rewards and punishments, but they are rewards and punishments in the same sense as rewards and punishments *having* typical psychological effects, and so should not be eliminated from any theory of reward and punishment, if at all possible.

How can an account of reward and punishment derived from contingency-based learning accommodate the fact that rewards and punishments need not be represented, or be represented accurately, in order to be given to (or visited upon) us? An answer can be found in the representational capacities involved in reward learning. The first step in the operation of the mechanism of reward learning is a representation of the world as being this way or that. But representational capacities are not always exercised without error or omission. On the contrary, one of the characteristic features of representational systems is precisely that they have the capacity to misrepresent the world, or to fail to represent it (Dretske 1986). These two characteristic failings of representational systems correspond to our two prima facie problems for a theory of reward in terms of reward-based learning, suggesting a simple modification of the theory. Instead of holding that rewards and punishments are things that contribute to triggering the release of reinforcement or extinction signals, it should rather be held that rewards are those states of affairs whose representation by the organism directly contributes to causing the release of a reinforcement signal, and punishments are those states of affairs whose representation by the organism directly contributes to causing the release of an extinction signal.

By incorporating the representational step in contingency-based learning into the theory of reward and punishment, the prima facie problems for such a theory are made to disappear. The woman who receives a check for no money at all is not thereby rewarded, because representing *that*—the receipt of a worthless check—would not have directly contributed to the release of a reinforcement signal within the woman. What *would* have rewarded the woman is the receipt of a financial gift, as representation of that state of affairs would have directly contributed to the release of a reinforcement signal within the woman, but that state of affairs was not the one that obtained. What actually happened was that the woman accurately represented various states of affairs (a check has been given to her, it comes from the police, etc.), none of which would directly contribute to the release of a reinforcement signal in her, and these accurate representations caused the tokening of a misrepresentation, that she has been given a financial gift. The inaccurately tokened representation then caused the release of a reinforcement signal directly. Being tricked into thinking she has been given a financial gift does not turn out to be a reward for the woman, on this account, because an accurate representation of *that* state of affairs has no tendency to cause the release of a reinforcement signal. In a similar spirit, the story of the soldier rewarded for her kindness in a way she never realizes can also be explained. Representing that she has been given an assignment specially chosen to keep her out of combat would have directly contributed to the release of a reinforcement signal in the soldier, and that is what makes it true that being so assigned is a reward for that soldier, even though she never actually tokens that representation.

There remain a few wrinkles to iron out. Reinforcement learning is driven directly, not by information about contingencies, but by information about the difference between actual and expected contingencies, by information about previously predicted versus currently predicted future contingencies, and by the net calculation of such differences. But these details are just that: details. In particular, they are the details of mathematical models of reinforcement learning, and there is no reason to think that one very specific mathematical model should be identified with such learning, while other models differing only slightly should not. So I propose to gloss over the particular mathematical details, leaving them to those interested in computational theories of learning and neural modeling. For philosophical purposes, all that is important is that such theories exist, and provide good theories of the functions of particular structures in the brain. The following theory will be ample:

Contingency-based Learning Theory of Reward (CLT): For an event[33] to be a reward for an organism is for representations of that event to tend to contribute to the production of a reinforcement signal in the organism, in the sense made clear by computational theories of what is called 'reinforcement learning'.

A few points about ordinary language should now be faced. Ordinarily, we talk about a reward or punishment only when the rewarded or punished person has done something to bring about the reward or punishment, and only when the connection between the act and the reward or punishment makes some sort of sense. By the standards of common sense, a person who goes looking for fish in a distant stream may be rewarded for her efforts by finding several fat trout; a person who is fleeing in terror from imagined ghosts and falls into a stream, there discovering several fat trout, is not rewarded for imagining the ghosts. Similarly, a person who goes looking for fish in a distant stream and who finds nothing may be punished by having missed a chance to gather berries; a person who goes looking for fish and inhales a stray carcinogen that ultimately causes her to develop liver cancer, though, has not been punished. In the same spirit, a mathematician can be punished by being shown that his putative theorem is false, but he is not punished just by the fact that the putative theorem is false. Yet the current theoretical account of reward and punishment diverges with common sense over these cases. The discovery of trout will count as a reward for a person on the present theory if and only if that representation contributes to a reinforcement signal; how the trout are discovered is theoretically irrelevant.

If it were my central project to give necessary and sufficient conditions for a state of affairs to be a reward or a punishment for an organism, something would have to be done about this; presumably, I would need to clarify what sorts of connections between actions and candidate rewards or punishments make enough sense for the candidate rewards and punishments to be actual rewards and punishments. But I have a rather different target in mind. My goal has been to give a theory of the psychological aspect of reward: what must be the case inside an organism in order for it to make things into rewards. What must be the case outside the organism may, as these everyday examples seem to show, also be relevant to what counts as a true reward or punishment, but that is not the concern of the present work, and so I will ignore these details. A theory of the psychological aspect of reward will be theory enough.

Reward and Desire

We have now examined three theories of reward and punishment. Two, I have argued, are flawed both conceptually and empirically, while the third has virtues in both domains. But there is a fourth plausible theory of reward and punishment that has not yet received discussion: a reward is a state of affairs desired by the organism, and a punishment is a state of affairs to which the organism is averse (roughly, has a desire to avoid). If a manatee desires to eat biscuits intended for captive monkeys,[34] then being allowed to eat such biscuits is a reward for the manatee; if a person hates the music of Mozart, then being forced to hear Mozart is a punishment for that person, and so on. Forget, for the moment, that I have been arguing that rewards and punishments are connected to the mechanism for contingency-based learning, and consider this proposal on its own merits. What is there to be said in its favor or against it?

In favor of the theory that rewards and punishments are constituted by an organism's desires are the commonsensical thoughts that if you want to reward someone, the best way is to give that person something she really wants, and if you want to punish someone, the best way is to find out what that person would hate done and then do it. Likewise, it is widely believed that a common failure in rewarding a person is to give him what the giver would like to be given, rather than what the recipient actually *wants*. Just think of a well-meaning person, Donald, whose boyfriend has spent hours baking things to contribute to Donald's favorite charity's bake sale. As a reward for all the hard work, Donald gives his boyfriend a gift certificate for a weekend of lessons in in-line roller skating, something Donald himself would love to try. The intended reward will prove to be no reward at all if the boyfriend desires nothing more than to enjoy fine cuisine and the company of sophisticated thinkers, and has an aversion to all things sporting. Such scenarios are familiar, and are often couched in terms that equate successful attempts to reward with gifts of things desired by the recipient of the reward, and successful punishments with things to which the recipient is averse. Common sense, then, gives at least some support to the idea that rewards and punishments just are things desired by the organism, or to which it is averse.

Furthermore, according to common sense, the causal consequences of getting what one wants are by and large the same as the causal consequences of being rewarded. Rewards cause people to feel pleased and dance for joy; getting what one desires does the same. The opportunity to get a reward is motivating; the opportunity to get what one wants is the same. People decide what to do by thinking about how they were rewarded in the past; they likewise think about how they were given what they want in the past. Rewarding a child can influence her future thinking and actions through unconscious processes; giving a child things she wants does the same.

It could also be noted that a desire-based theory of rewards and punishments, like the contingency-based learning theory, has the resources to explain how one can be rewarded without one's knowledge, or not rewarded even though one believes one has been. If I desire that P, and, knowing that, someone decides to thank me for something by making it the case that P, I have been given something I desire, and so rewarded, though I may not be aware of the fact. If I am averse to it being the case that P, and, knowing that, someone decides to punish me for some misdeed by making it the case that P, then I have been punished if he tells me Q but actually makes it true that P, though I may even be tricked into thinking that I have been rewarded.

It could be objected that, if rewards are essentially things that satisfy desires, then certain standard explanatory practices are rendered trivial—that the proposed identification falls victim to just the same sort of problem as other unsuccessful identifications. However, this is not the case. Consider, this time for the case of desire, how the objection might go. Holding rewards to be things that satisfy desires renders trivial explanations such as "getting a reward caused a desire of his to be satisfied," the objection might run. But put thus, the putative explanation sounds odd. Getting a reward might satisfy a desire, but it isn't a *cause* of desire satisfaction. Surely getting a reward just *is* an event that satisfies a desire. The style of objection that worked for other attempts to get at the nature of reward is not plausible here.

Still, it might seem problematic that one can desire a reward (or be averse to a punishment, or even desire a punishment or be averse to a reward), given that rewards are being understood as things satisfying desires. Would there not be some sort of vicious circularity in desiring something that would satisfy a desire? Actually, this is not circularity but hierarchy. A desire for a reward is, according to the current proposal, a desire for something that would satisfy one's desires. This would be incoherent as one's *only* desire, but if one already has other intrinsic desires, which constitute various ends as rewards, then to have a further desire to be rewarded is just to have a desire that one of the other desires (any of them) be satisfied. A desire for reward per se is thus an implicit second-order desire, a desire which, of necessity, is satisfied only if there is satisfaction of at least one of one's other desires.[35] The same story can be told, mutatis mutandis, for desiring punishment, aversion to punishment, and aversion to reward. In each case, one has a desire regarding the satisfaction or frustration of one's other desires (or aversions). Hence, there is only a problem for the desire-based theory of reward and punishment if our only (intrinsic) desire is for reward, and our only (intrinsic) aversion is to punishment, and this strikes me as quite implausible. It seems to me, as it seems to most others, that people also have intrinsic desires to be well-fed and sheltered and loved, desires that their loved ones be safe, and so on. In the absence of any reason to override common sense, it seems plausible to agree with it that a desire to be rewarded is only one of many desires a person might have.

Perhaps an attack can be made on the grounds that the theory is extensionally incorrect. There is certainly room to do so, but the evidence is quite interesting, for the obvious failures of the desire-based theory of reward are the same as the obvious failures of the contingency-based learning theory of reward. Common sense requires that rewards and punishments have some sort of intelligible connection to the rewarded or punished individual, but desire satisfaction is more general. A person who would like to meet the prime minister of Iceland and who is sitting in her own living room minding her own business when, lo and behold, the prime minister shows up, is not rewarded for sitting in her living room, though her desire is satisfied. Likewise, a mathematician who desires that his proof be correct is not punished by the mere fact that his proof is not, though this mere fact frustrates his desire. The failings of the desire theory of reward and punishment are, then, just the same as the failings of the learning theory, and could, it seems, be put right with just the same sort of supplementary clause about how, for something to genuinely be a reward or a punishment, there must be some appropriate connection between the reward or punishment and its recipient.

5. Reward and Theories of Desire

The desire theory of reward is thus an excellent candidate theory of reward. So, however, is the learning theory of reward. What is to be done? The question is best approached, I think, by considering the desire theory of reward in the light of the three faces of desire.

Consider first what would be the case if the standard theory of desire were correct. That is, imagine what would follow if motivation were the essence of desire. The desire theory of reward would then become a motivational theory of reward: for P to be a reward for an organism is for the organism to be motivated to bring it about that P. But as was shown earlier, there are a number of objections to any such behavioristic theory of reward. Hence, if the standard theory of desire were the best possible theory of desire, then the desire theory of reward would be false: for P to be a reward for an organism would not be for the organism to desire that P. The learning theory of reward would then be left as the best available theory of reward.

Consider second what would be the case if the hedonic theory of desire were correct, and dispositions to pleasure were the essence of desire. In this case, the desire theory of reward would become a hedonic theory of reward: for P to be a reward for an organism is for the organism to be disposed to feel pleasure upon representing that P. But again, a number of objections have already been raised to any hedonic theory of reward. Hence, if the hedonic theory of desire were the best possible theory of desire, then the desire theory of reward would again be false. Again, the learning theory of reward would be left as the best available theory.

Consider now a third option. Suppose that one were to hold that to desire is to contain an appropriate sort of learning system, so that desiring that P would involve having representations that P contributing to the production of learning signals, of the sort described earlier. If this position were taken, then the desire theory of reward would be the same as the learning theory of reward, for both would hold that for P to be a reward for an organism is for the organism to tend to produce a characteristic learning signal upon representing that P. The objections that have been raised to this theory are relatively technical and readily answered, unlike the objections to motivational and hedonic theories of reward. Even better, this third theoretical option allows one to hold that the two best theories of reward are *both* correct: there is no need to choose.

It seems, then, that no matter how one looks at it, the best theory of reward is the learning theory. And insofar as one takes the desire theory of reward to be an excellent theory of reward, there is reason to hold a reward (i.e., learning) theory of desire. These reasons are hardly decisive. There might be excellent reasons to prefer other theories of desire on other grounds, and indeed there is much, much more to say. But it is worth noting that, even at this early stage, investigating a phenomenon not much described by philosophers, there is already some reason to begin thinking of desire in terms of reward.

3

Pleasure and Displeasure

The structure of chapter 2 was a straightforward one: introduce the everyday notion of reward, supplement it with scientific results, and bring these sources of knowledge together to produce a theory of the phenomenon. That structure will be repeated here, though it may sound a little odd in the present context. Pleasure and displeasure,[1] unlike reward and punishment, are phenomena so familiar that there seems no need for a summary of our everyday knowledge of them. All that is needed for present purposes, one might think, is a simple description of the neural basis for what everyone already knows. Yet things are not so simple. Philosophers have managed to become so confused about the nature of pleasure that they argue about whether it is a distinctive sort of conscious feeling or a style of behavior, and scientists are confused about how best to study it. Even everyday thinking about pleasure and displeasure contains puzzles that everyday thought does not readily solve. A delicate touch will be needed to untie these various intellectual knots. The ultimate result will be a theory of pleasure that makes clear the role of this face of desire.

1. The Folk Psychology of Hedonic Tone

According to common sense, pleasure and displeasure are opposite feelings, found on a continuum that ranges from the unbearably unpleasant, through neutrality, up to ecstatic heights. These feelings have many different causes and many different effects. Both causes and effects are variable interpersonally and intrapersonally, though common sense recognizes some limits to this variability, and it is far from random in nature. Pleasure and displeasure are also held to run over varied time courses, and come to an end during dreamless unconsciousness.

All this is straightforward, but worthy of elaboration. To start with, common sense calls pleasure and displeasure 'feelings' to distinguish them from the five senses. Vision is obviously a sense modality, in that it allows one to sense the (apparently) objective properties of objects around one, and so on for audition and the other senses, but pleasure and displeasure are different. They do not appear to tell us about the objective properties of objects: they appear rather to be purely subjective responses we have to objects. This is the only significant gap common sense puts between hedonic tone and the senses, however. In other respects, pleasure and displeasure are held to be just like experiencing warmth or coldness, seeing bright light or deep gloom, or having other sensory experiences. In particular, pleasure and displeasure are like sensory experiences in that they make a difference to consciousness: there is "something it is like" to be pleased or displeased, to borrow from Nagel (1974). This "something" is like the "something" it is like to see or hear, in that feeling pleased is a qualitatively distinctive conscious event. Some philosophers and scientists have held otherwise (see section 3), but folk psychology is more or less unanimous on this point.

Comparisons to sensations of warmth and coldness, or to seeing light and darkness, are held to be especially apt because feelings of pleasure and displeasure are thought of as opposites. One does not generally feel pleasure and displeasure at the same time: they drive one another out. A man having a good day until he finds that his car has been burgled does not continue to feel pleasure while also feeling sudden displeasure. Rather, the displeasure drives out the pleasure. Likewise, a woman having a lousy day will stop feeling displeasure, at least for a time, if she has a very pleasant experience, such as learning that her research program has received funding. It is sometimes said that the opposite of pleasure is pain, instead of displeasure, but this is not the considered view of common sense. Most people would agree that while all pain involves displeasure, not all displeasure involves literal pain. Though I may be pained when I learn my students are ignorant of key events in Canadian history such as the October crisis, this is not a matter of literally being in pain (unless a headache or a surge of gastric juices into my ulcer is caused by this unfortunate discovery), but it is literally unpleasant to learn such a fact. Pains are just one of many ways in which one may suffer. Hence, the proper counterpart of pleasure is displeasure, not pain.

An interesting minor fact is that pleasure and displeasure, though opposites, are occasionally experienced simultaneously. Especially when one's emotions have been particularly intense over a prolonged time, one can find oneself feeling both pleased and displeased: inclined to laugh and cry simultaneously. It has also been reported to me that the thrill of a roller coaster can involve simultaneous pleasure and displeasure, in the form of literally mixed joy and fear. Such experiences are rare for most people,[2] but poets have seized upon their occurrence in romantic contexts and have made much of sweet sorrow, sweet pain, bittersweet feelings, and the like. Because pleasure and displeasure are opposites, such experiences are always a little odd, but they are nonetheless held by common sense to be real.

Again like sensations of warmth and coldness, or light and darkness, pleasure and displeasure are said to fall on a continuum. There are very slight pleasures, somewhat more intense pleasures, unbridled joy, and so on—and similarly for displeasure. And just as, for any experience of heat, one could always have a more intense experience (though the change in intensity might be slight), so experiences of pleasure and displeasure, however intense, can always be surpassed (perhaps by a vanishingly small margin at the extremes), according to everyday thought. Minimally intense pleasure and minimally intense displeasure meet at a neutral point, itself neither a feeling of pleasure nor of displeasure. This makes hedonic tone more like experiences of warmth and coldness than experiences of light and dark, since the former also has a neutral midpoint whereas the latter does not.

Given that pleasure and displeasure come on a continuum and are opposites, it naturally follows that when pleasure and displeasure clash, the result is something like the addition of positive and negative numbers. If a person feels wonderful, and then has an experience that would typically induce slight displeasure (say, a shoelace breaks), the person is likely to feel only slightly less wonderful than before. If the same person has an experience of a sort typically inducing great sorrow, however, then that person will shift from feeling pleasure to displeasure, though often not as deep displeasure as might have been felt had the person started off with a neutral feeling, or (even worse) a bad mood. But these trends are only trends: as everyone knows, feelings of pleasure and displeasure are more complex than this. Sometimes, bad news not only reduces the pleasure one was feeling but in fact makes the pleasure crumble to dust: one feels even worse than one would have, had one begun the day feeling just average. Similarly, if one has been feeling down for some time, good news that would normally cause pleasure might not have the least effect. It can also happen that pleasure renders one immune to petty concerns, and a former bad mood can be completely relieved simply by a pleasant conversation or a mildly pleasant run of good luck in some trivial domain. So while pleasure and displeasure trade off against one another, everyday observation suggests that this trade-off is often a complex one.

What about the causes and effects of pleasure and displeasure? As already mentioned, common sense holds them to be variable both between people and within a single person over time, though this variation has its limits. Pleasure, it is widely believed, is sometimes felt in response to characteristic sensations such as massage, the scent of warm brie, the sight of graceful movement, and the like, and is other times felt in response to more cognitively sophisticated mental events such as thoughts about the success of one's child in her chosen profession, witnessing an elegant move in a chess match, or hearing a radio advertisement that strikes one as humorously devoid of irony. Thus, there are sensuous sources of pleasure and intellectual sources. Displeasure, like pleasure, is also held to be caused by both simple sensations and complex cognitions: consider the unpleasantness of an overfull bladder, of the sound of very mechanically played swing music, of the thought of paying one's taxes to support an unjust social structure. Physical pain, such as that caused by dropping a heavy piece of lumber on one's finger, is generally taken to be paradigmatic as an unpleasant experience.

Individual variation in more cognitive pleasures is widely believed to be greater than variation in more sensuous pleasures, and similarly for displeasure. Everyone[3] feels displeasure when a bone breaks, a heart attack occurs, or the like, but only a comparative handful of people were crushed when Ireland was eliminated from the World Cup in 2002. Yet even sensuous pleasure and displeasure are known by common sense to admit variation: not everyone enjoys sweets, some people get used to the smell of human excrement, and some people can withstand heat without suffering. I even know a person who finds extreme bodily need for food to be enervating but not actually displeasing: quite an unusual case, but not unbelievable. These variations in causes of sensuous pleasure and displeasure are not widely discussed in everyday contexts, but long training, upbringing, constant exposure, and the like are held to be at least one source of variation. One can become hardened to the cold, to deprivation, to the sound of children screeching, and so on, according to common sense, and one can learn to like bitter greens, the smell of very strong cheeses, very hot baths, and the like. Innate differences are held by common sense to be another source of variation in sources of sensuous pleasure and displeasure: some people suffer in the heat because their "inner thermostats" are just set differently from those of other people, and some children prefer grapefruits to oranges from an early age.

Variation in sources of pleasure and displeasure of a less sensuous, more cognitive nature are dealt with differently by common sense: they are generally attributed to preferences or desires. It is the fact that you wanted Ireland to win, while I was indifferent, that explains why you were displeased by Ireland's elimination while I was not, and so on. From this fact follows an interesting lemma of common sense: that pleasure and displeasure can provide useful information about one's preferences or desires. "What do you want to eat?" asks Tom. "I don't know," Susan answers. "Let me look into the fridge and see." Looking into the fridge allows Susan to survey the options, and whatever induces pleasant interest will be chosen, Susan's pleasure being a better guide to her current preferences than her intellect.[4] Likewise, a person can claim to want a promotion to sales manager, then get it and realize that he didn't want the promotion after all—what he really wanted was simply recognition of his abilities—and his insight into what he wants can be delivered exactly by noting his pleasure in the round of congratulations and displeasure at the prospect of actually taking on the new duties. And in general, a person confused about what she wants is advised to consider the likely options and await the faint anticipatory pleasure or displeasure (not always so faint!) that follows, in order to learn what she wants.

Additional sources of variation in the impact of events upon hedonic tone are factors often called "confidence" and "resignation": in essence, forms of subconscious estimates of likelihood. Two people alike in every way, going on an outing, will be expected to be differently affected by the success of the outing depending upon the expectations they have at the beginning. If both people are normally confident that things will go well, but one has seen heavy clouds presaging rain, and so goes on the outing with low expectations, while the other has seen blue skies, and so expects beautiful weather, then the former will be expected to feel a little less sorrow than the latter if the outing is rained upon. The former person will be displeased, naturally, but, "knowing it was coming," feel that things went "no worse than expected," as might be said. The latter person will be more displeased, for the rain "took him aback"; he will feel let down. Likewise, one is more delighted to get good weather when one had feared bad than when one expected good weather all along. Folk wisdom frequently recommends using this source of variation in order to shield oneself from hedonic shocks: "don't get your hopes up too high" is advice often given to someone in an effort to cushion the person from the displeasure of disappointment, and "appreciate what you've got: you may not have it tomorrow" is a common admonishment to one who is ceasing to take pleasure in something he feels to be certain, but which really is not.

The effects of pleasure and displeasure are just as varied as their causes. Pleased people often sigh, relax, or smile; displeased people often grunt, tense up, or frown. But there are people who register satisfaction with an unhappy-sounding grunt, or who frown at their own enjoyment of something, and people who giggle when deeply uncomfortable with embarrassment. For my own part, I have the unfortunate tendency to a nervous smile when delivering awkward or bad news, but the smile reflects no inner glee. An interesting systematic phenomenon noted by common sense is that some sources of pleasure are consistently soothing or satisfying, while others are exciting and arousing. Orgasm, eating a large meal, resting after a hard day—these are sources of pleasure that, for most people, are linked to a certain laziness. The effect of pleasure in other cases is quite different. A first kiss, news that one has been accepted to the graduate program of one's choice, taking possession of a sporty new car—these are sources of pleasure that are stimulating for most people, inducing jumping for joy, trembling with excitement, urges to act, and so on. In just the same way, sources of displeasure can cause a defeated-feeling lassitude, or they can arouse the will to fight back against the adverse circumstances. These effects are often independent of the actual usefulness of the responses in question. The energy that good news about a graduate school application can provide has no obvious use, just like the energy that bad news about such an application can bring in a person who tends to anger, but an energized state can result nonetheless.

An interesting further phenomenon surrounding pleasure is that common sense recognizes the possibility of "unreal" pleasure. This is not apparent but non-actual pleasure, but rather pleasure that is real but in some sense inappropriate. The pleasure of euphorigenic drugs, including alcohol, is often held to be unreal in this sense, for example, and the same would go for pleasure induced by electrical stimulation of the brain or by psychosurgery or neural insult. The other sort of context in which talk of unreal pleasure comes up is that in which an individual seriously misrepresents her situation and feels pleasure as a result. For instance, there is thought to be something illusory about pleasure felt because one misrepresents a hostile takeover as a mutually beneficial merger. How common sense would justify the notion of an unreal pleasure is far from clear, but the label is applied in both sorts of contexts.

Pleasure and displeasure may last for a short time, as in the unpleasantness of sitting in an awkward position, which disappears almost as soon as one changes posture. It may last for a moderate term, as in the case of the afterglow of sexual pleasure following orgasm, which persists for some time after the initial cause of pleasure. Or it may be felt intermittently for a term of days or weeks, as romantic infatuation and depression are both thought to do. Unconsciousness (of the sort found in dreamless sleep) is generally held to cause pleasure to cease, at least for the duration of the unconscious state, and to likewise give relief from displeasure.[5]

In addition to its confident assertions about pleasure and displeasure, folk psychology also confesses to a certain amount of uncertainty. Two sorts of uncertainty are especially noteworthy. Common sense is not particularly clear on *where*, if anywhere, pleasure and displeasure are felt, or on how *many* sorts of hedonic tone there are. It is only common sense to say that the pain of a toothache is found in one's tooth and jaw, but it would also be absurd to say that the "pain" from a failed romance is literally in one's heart, or anywhere else, and between these cases fall very unclear ones, such as the displeasure felt in smelling rotten meat. Is it literally in the nose? Or is it, like heartache, found nowhere in particular? Or is it found throughout the body? Such questions have no settled, common sense answers. Not unrelated, the question of whether pain is different in kind from heartache in respect of its unpleasantness, or whether the pleasure of a skillful checkmate is different in respect of its pleasantness from the pleasure of a pedicure is also unanswered by common sense. There is enough confusion on these topics to leave room for the philosophers.

2. The Neuroscience of Pleasure

From common sense to neuroscience: our best scientific evidence at present supports the idea that there is a neural seat of pleasure, and an adjacent seat of displeasure, found in a phylogenetically old region of the cerebral cortex known as the *perigenual region* of the *anterior cingulate* cortex (or PGAC, a circumscribed subregion of Brodmann's area 24, found around the "knee," or bend, in the anterior cingulate cortex; see appendix, fig. 2).[6] The thesis that the PGAC is the seat of pleasure and displeasure is not universally accepted, but it has been advanced by a number of scientists (see, e.g., Devinsky et al. 1995; KSJ 2000, ch. 61; Vogt et al. 1992; Whalen et al. 1998), and in this section I will argue that the evidence warrants their assertion.[7]

To begin, it must be made clear that saying there is a neural seat of hedonic tone is not the same as saying that pleasure and displeasure just *are* happenings in neural structures. Whether they are such events, or whether they are, say, functional patterns instantiated by neural structures in humans but potentially instantiated by other structures in other creatures, is a question for another branch of the philosophy of mind, and one that need not be addressed here. The claim being made by our present best scientific evidence is simply that there is a clearly identifiable, localized region of the brain that is the biological realization[8] of hedonic capacities in humans and other animals.

It is also important to be clear that the PGAC is just a small part of the anterior cingulate cortex as a whole, and the anterior cingulate is not functionally homogenous by any means. It includes an important pre-motor region located caudal to the PGAC[9] that is involved in controlling behavior; a structure exerting control over the viscera;[10] and probably other functional subdivisions including one related to attention (Vogt et al. 1992). Thus, not every study examining the anterior cingulate is relevant to drawing conclusions about pleasure and displeasure: attention must be focused upon the perigenual region.

With these clarifications in mind, it is time for the obvious question. What sort of evidence would justify the claim that activity in a discrete region of the brain such as the PGAC is the biological realization of pleasure and displeasure? The best evidence that the PGAC realizes pleasure and displeasure would be evidence that it is the unique structure whose activity is, in a suitably restricted sense, necessary and sufficient for pleasure and displeasure in creatures like us.[11] Consider first sufficiency. It is obvious that there will be many sites in the brain sufficient, in normal organisms, for the production of pleasure. Stimulate my optic nerve in a manner corresponding to the stimulation induced by a painting by Chagall and I will be pleased; stimulate my olfactory center in a manner corresponding to that induced by steaming hot chocolate, and I will be pleased; and so on. Intuitively, what one is seeking is the *last* such location in the chain of neural events sufficient for producing pleasure, but this is tricky. After all, no part of the brain is sufficient for an experience of pleasure if surgically removed from the organism and stimulated in vitro.[12] Sufficiency must be understood only as sufficiency in normal, healthy organisms. As for necessity, it may be understood in a somewhat stricter sense. Even if an individual were to lose all normal sensory and imaginative capacities, it might still be possible for him to experience pleasure and displeasure if some other region of his brain were directly stimulated by chemical or electrical means. Such facts would obviously be relevant to questions of whether or not these sensory and imaginative capacities are the neural basis of pleasure. So what the scientist seeks, in looking for the neural basis of hedonic tone, is a unique discrete structure such that it is the last structure in the normal causal sequence whose activation is sufficient for pleasure and displeasure, and also such that its activation is necessary for pleasure and displeasure.

The obvious methods for testing sufficiency and necessity are invasive, causal studies, in which particular structures in the brain are chemically, electrically, and surgically manipulated. Such studies have, happily, rarely been performed on humans. But humans who can describe their experiences are the best source of information about pleasure and displeasure. The overall quality of information about the neural basis of pleasure is, as a result, poorer than it might be.[13] Still, what evidence does exist appears to strongly support the view that the PGAC plays this role.

Sufficiency

Direct stimulation of a number of regions in the human brain is known to cause pleasure. Stimulation of sub-cortical structures such as the lateral hypothalamus, ventral pallidum, nucleus accumbens, and septum, for example, has been thought to cause pleasure (reviewed in Berridge 2003a, 2003b). But causally downstream of these structures is the PGAC, and stimulation of the PGAC also suffices to cause pleasure and displeasure in human subjects. In studies by Meyer et al. (1973) and Laitinen (1979), stimulation of the cingulum (a bundle of nerves reaching out to the various parts of the cingulate cortex) and the perigenual cingulate itself was found to have a number of effects in human subjects, corresponding to the various functions of the cingulate, including (especially when the PGAC was the specific target) hedonic effects. Some subjects reported displeasure in various forms (fear, agitation, oppression, specific and generalized pain, nausea) while others felt pleasure (including simple pleasure, relaxation, and a sense of well-being).

Necessity

Damage to the PGAC (KSJ 2000, ch. 61) and cingulumotomy (Foltz and White 1962) can cause recipients to report a complete loss in subjective ability to experience displeasure, or any sort of hedonic tone, from either sensuous or more cognitive sources. It might help to recall some of the observations from Foltz and White (1962) quoted in chapter 1. Of their cingulumotomy recipients, they write:

> The patient with a good result simply is not as precipitously reactive to his own environment and his own situation as he was prior to operation. The anguished facies and evidence of suffering are modified markedly. The perception of pain as such does not appear to be modified, but the patient's total reaction to pain and the threat to existence that it represents is modified markedly. Most of the patients stated they continued to have pain but it was "not distressing," "not particularly bothersome," "doesn't worry me anymore," etc.

Such descriptions indicate a radical change in the nature of pain experience, which pain theorists such as Melzack (1973) and philosophers such as Aydede (2000)[14] have interpreted as the feeling of pain losing its unpleasant character while retaining its character as nociception, sensory perception of bodily injury. Also important in showing the unique role of the PGAC is the fact that, while other forms of psychosurgery (such as full frontal lobotomy) are also effective in eliminating the capacity for hedonic experiences, destruction of the PGAC appears to be the most limited procedure that is effective in this regard, and the one that has the least dramatic consequences beyond loss of reported hedonic tone.

Destruction[15] of the PGAC thus appears to be the most limited procedure that eliminates capacities for pleasure and displeasure.

Brain imaging techniques have provided evidence that both pleasure and displeasure cause increased activity in the PGAC, providing further support to the claim that the PGAC is the neural seat of hedonic tone. Beginning with displeasure, a number of pain studies have found that painful stimuli activate the PGAC (Coghill et al. 1999; Craig et al. 1996; Derbeyshire et al. 1998; Mertz et al. 2000; Vogt et al. 1996). There are many, many more studies than these attempting to capture images of the brain's response to painful stimuli,[16] but these studies often fail to distinguish between activation of the caudal anterior cingulate and the PGAC, or have focused upon the caudal anterior cingulate exclusively. Since the caudal anterior cingulate is now believed to be a motor center, and direct stimulation of it has been found to cause no displeasure (Hutchinson et al. 1999), it would be a mistake to draw conclusions about the neural seat of displeasure from studies that do not distinguish between the PGAC and other portions of the anterior cingulate. It has been speculated that, because most pain imaging studies require subjects to remain still while experiencing pain, motor resources are called upon to inhibit avoidance behavior, fidgeting, and so on, and this activates the caudal anterior cingulate, creating a signal correlating with displeasure but not helping determine the neural localization of the feeling. This may well explain why few scientists have noticed the importance of distinguishing sub-regions of the anterior cingulate cortex from one another. Fortunately, these problems are not endemic to all work on the anterior cingulate. Further evidence regarding the neural basis of displeasure comes from studies that induce displeasure without also creating an incentive to avoidance behavior: studies inducing psychologically based displeasure. Shin et al. (2000) found that when subjects experienced guilt (and related emotions such as sadness and shame, all involving displeasure), activity increased in the PGAC. Paying attention to the emotional content (both pleasant and unpleasant) of pictures activates the PGAC as well (Lane et al. 1997), and likewise both pleasant and unpleasant tastes cause increased activity in PGAC (Zald et al. 1998).

Turning now to pleasure, most studies imaging the human brain under pleasure-causing conditions have used drugs to cause the pleasure. Correlations between pleasure and activity in the PGAC have been found in studies on alcohol (Ingvar et al. 1998), cocaine (Breiter et al. 1997), THC (Matthew et al. 1999), MDMA (Gamma et al. 2000), and amphetamines (Vollenweider et al. 1998). Another study, this one looking at pleasure and excitement induced through stories subjectively rated as strongly inducing these feelings, also found activation of PGAC during pleasure (Rauch et al. 1999).

A few studies exist that do not accord with the present thesis. One fMRI[17] study dissociating pain from the anticipation of pain (Ploghaus et al. 1999) found that the anticipation of pain activated a region encompassing the PGAC and other mediofrontal areas, as expected (since anticipation of pain is itself generally unpleasant), but pain itself did not activate the PGAC to a statistically significant degree, though it did activate the caudal anterior cingulate cortex. However, the region of analysis of the anticipation of pain did not differentiate between the rest of the mediofrontal cortex and the PGAC, leaving open the possibility that the PGAC was activated near or below statistical thresholds in both conditions, while the orbitofrontal cortex was only activated, or was much more activated, in anticipation of pain. (Recall, from chapter 2, that the orbitofrontal cortex sends information about known and predicted rewards and punishments to other regions of the brain.) Another study, conducted by Iadarola et al. (1998) using PET,[18] found that the anterior cingulate gyrus was significantly activated by light brushing of the forearm and by injection of capsaicin (the compound that makes chili peppers hot—yes, that really was injected into the forearms of human volunteers!) but not by the allodynia (the pain that non-harmful touching can cause when the touch is to an area that was previously the source of painful stimulation) that followed capsaicin, once the effect of brushing the arm to induce allodynia was factored out. Here, it might be pointed out that allodynia is considerably less painful than capsaicin, and so failure to find significant activation of the PGAC might be the result of a substantially reduced signal. Perhaps most challenging, Porro et al. (1998) found that the temporal profile of the subjectively experienced pain of a painful acid injection (again, human subjects volunteered for this!) correlated with deactivation of the PGAC in an fMRI study, directly contradicting numerous other studies. Likewise, Smith et al. (1999) found that inducing tryptophan depletion to bring on depression in formerly depressed subjects caused a deactivation of the PGAC. How to reconcile these results with the dominant thesis favoring the PGAC is not clear. However, this level of disagreement, even in well-conducted scientific experiments, is far from exceptional, and is not, on its own, powerful evidence against the view under consideration.

It might be argued that the PGAC is activated by any arousing condition, and so its activity merely correlates with pleasure or displeasure without actually realizing hedonic tone. However, this would not explain why certain studies, such as Breiter et al.'s (1997) study on the pleasure produced by cocaine, found strong activation of the PGAC during the arousing "rush" period of the drug's effect, but not during the also arousing "craving" period that follows later. It would also not explain why direct stimulation of the PGAC was found to cause pleasure and displeasure (depending on site of stimulation), rather than feelings or behaviors related to neutral arousal, and it would not explain the loss of hedonic capacities that can follow damage to the PGAC. This style of argument is an important one: taken as a whole, the brain-imaging, neurosurgery, and brain-stimulation studies support much stronger conclusions than any single portion of that evidence taken on its own.

One further line of evidence supports the claim that the PGAC is the neural seat of pleasure and displeasure: no other plausible contender for this role exists within the brain. Most important, the dopamine-releasing reward system discussed in chapter 2 is not a plausible candidate for the neural seat of pleasure.

This reward system, whose core is the output from the VTA/SNpc, is not a ludicrous candidate for the neural seat of pleasure by any means. After all, rewards tend to activate it, and rewards are typical causes of pleasure. Likewise, studies on non-human animals have shown that the VTA/SNpc is a powerful site for self-stimulation (reviewed in Stellar and Stellar 1985), meaning that animals with electrodes planted in the VTA/SNpc, or in areas projecting to the VTA/SNpc such as the medial forebrain bundle, will do whatever it takes to cause these electrodes to stimulate the VTA/SNpc again, sometimes to the exclusion of eating or drinking. It was just these scientific results that led philosopher Carolyn Morillo (1990) to the conclusion that pleasure is seated in these structures. But evidence reviewed in Berridge and Robinson (1998) suggests that the scientific findings are more likely to be explained by the hypothesis that the VTA/SNpc and medial forebrain bundle can indirectly activate the pleasure center than by the hypothesis that either is such a center. For instance, as discussed in chapter 2, Wolfram Schultz and colleagues found that VTA/SNpc activation bursts briefly when an organism first learns that it will get a reward, but then immediately (in less than a second) drops off; most sources of pleasure, however, provide much longer-lasting pleasure than this. If VTA/SNpc firing were the neural basis of pleasure, and not merely an indirect cause, then this discrepancy between the time-course of firing and the time-course of pleasure would be inexplicable. Berridge and Robinson (1998) also report that human and animal experiences of food palatability (measured either by facial expression or self-report) increase with morphine, but morphine administration is not thought to cause VTA/SNpc activity. Benzodiazepines, also thought not to cause VTA/SNpc activity, have similar effects. Finally, Berridge and Robinson (1998) describe a series of experiments in which it was found that rats with massive lesions specific to dopamine releasing neurons (mainly the VTA/SNpc) were still capable of experiencing pleasure in response to sugar and displeasure in response to quinine, as evidenced by the fact that they still displayed the facial responses rats make in response to pleasant and unpleasant tastes in general. As a whole, then, the evidence is strongly against the idea that the VTA/SNpc is the neural seat of hedonic tone.

In a pair of recent reviews (2003a, 2003b), Kent Berridge surveys other prominent candidates for neural centers of pleasure and displeasure and finds most of them wanting as well. Destruction of the orbitofrontal cortex alters emotional response, but nonetheless leaves the full spectrum of hedonic tone available, and so the OFC fails to be necessary to feelings of pleasure and displeasure. Likewise, damage to the amygdala, while blunting or eliminating emotional responses (especially fear responses) to many stimuli, leaves open the possibility of pleasure and displeasure in response to other stimuli. Stimulation of the septum is reputed to be a source of pleasure, but not of displeasure, and in any case it is unclear (according to Berridge) that the results purporting to show this effect in humans are caused by stimulation of the septum. Even if stimulation of the septum can produce pleasure, it can be pointed out that it is generally reported to produce sexual pleasure (Heath 1961, 1963), and sexual pleasure is hardly the whole of human pleasure. Perhaps what has actually been caused is sexual arousal, which in turn is a source of pleasure rather than identical to it.

It should be said that Berridge is also skeptical as to the role of the anterior cingulate cortex in pleasure and displeasure, but here his evidence is somewhat weaker. The region he identifies as cingulate cortex in Berridge (2003b) corresponds to what are now thought to be motor regions of the anterior cingulate rather than affective regions. The PGAC, thus, has not been the center of his attention in reviewing work on the anterior cingulate, and this may have allowed the introduction of some misleading evidence. Berridge's main complaint against the anterior cingulate cortex is that there is a dearth of evidence that it is necessary for pleasure. In particular, there is a study on rats (Bussey, Everitt, and Robbins 1997) showing that rats with damaged anterior cingulate cortices responded as strongly to rewarded stimuli as did control rats. Yet Berridge has been a leader in keeping a very clear distinction between experiments revealing modifications of hedonic tone and experiments affecting motivation. Bussey, Everitt, and Robbins appear to have demonstrated some motivational similarities between lesioned rats and control rats (though there were also striking differences in behavior), but this hardly entails similarities in hedonic tone, and in fact when one attempts to lesion a candidate pleasure center without lesioning the leading candidate for a reward system (the one described in chapter 2), one can expect to see complex results, including reward-based responding, without necessarily observing hedonic responses.

Berridge prefers the hypothesis that the neural realization of what he calls "core 'liking'" is found in the circuit linking the nucleus accumbens, ventral pallidum, and brainstem parabrachial nucleus, all subcortical structures. But according to Berridge, "conscious liking may or may not accompany a given instance of core 'liking'," and he adds that, for his purposes, "it will be enough to identify brain systems that at least cause 'liking'—whether or not accompanied by conscious liking" (2003a, 118). Hence, it is not completely clear that Berridge's target is the same as the target of this section, that is, the neural realization of what people commonly denote by 'pleasure' and 'displeasure'. Berridge's targets are the primitive, deep-brain structures common to many vertebrates that form the biological core processes upon which conscious human pleasure and displeasure depend. Berridge's awareness of the potential discrepancy here between the core processes and the feeling of pleasure itself is what leads him to call his target 'liking', with the quotation marks always scrupulously attached. In fact, given the way Berridge writes about the connection between these core processes and conscious feelings, it appears that he strongly suspects that cortical structures are required for conscious pleasure—a not implausible suspicion, given the importance of cortical structures to consciousness in general.[19] For instance, he describes a neural pathway via which 'liking' could influence "feelings of pleasure that might be instantiated by limbic regions of neocortex" (2003a, 121). The PGAC, it should be noted, is a region of limbic neocortex that is one target of the pathway Berridge mentions.[20] Hence, even if Berridge is right that there is a phylogenetically old core process that underlies feelings of pleasure and displeasure, this need not be incompatible with the view that the feelings themselves are found in somewhat phylogenetically younger structures such as the PGAC.

The evidence that the PGAC is the home of pleasure and displeasure is thus diverse and, while not flawless, impressive. What to make of it is a subject to which we will return.

3. Four Incorrect Theories of Pleasure

With the data of common sense and neuroscience at hand, it is time to find out what pleasure and displeasure really are: to have a useful theory of hedonic tone. There are four answers familiar to philosophers: pleasure and displeasure are modifications of behavioral dispositions and nothing more; they are forms of other sorts of experiences; they are distinctive qualia; and they are players of particular functional roles. This section will argue that each answer is unsatisfactory, and the next will propose an alternative.

Gilbert Ryle (1949, 1954) famously held that pleasure and displeasure are not types of experiences but rather something like modifications of one's dispositions. To engage in an activity with pleasure is to engage in that activity attentively and eagerly, says Ryle, nothing more. The view is hardly exclusive to Ryle: variations on it were widely held by his contemporaries,[21] and a contemporary instance of it is found in Tye (1995). To tell the truth, I have never understood philosophers' capacity to defend the Rylean position. Is it not obvious that pleasure and displeasure are more than styles of behavior? But this is not much of an argument. Therefore, I offer three brief arguments to defend the thesis that pleasure and displeasure are distinctive types of conscious events rather than behavioral styles. An extended defense of this thesis is given by Aydede (2000), and the reader who remains unconvinced is referred to this work.

First, consider instances of intense pleasure (induced by orgasm, peak physical performance resulting in competitive victory, cocaine or heroin, or otherwise) and intense displeasure (induced by toothache, heartache, the death of a loved one, or the like). Such experiences seem to involve a distinct type of experience, pleasure or displeasure, which is made salient by its intensity. I see no reason not to take this interpretation at face value: the burden of proof is on the person who wishes to tell the majority that common sense is misleading us.

Second, common sense suggests that it is possible to feel pleasure and displeasure while dreaming. Sexual dreams and anxiety dreams are especially obvious examples. But if pleasure is a matter of behavioral style or dispositions to behave, then what is to be made of common sense? After all, no actual behavior occurs in normal dreams, and in fact the body's very capacity to move is normally disabled during dreaming (which is why sleepwalking is rare rather than commonplace). If pleasure and displeasure were essentially tied to behavior, it would be impossible for them to occur in dreams.

Third, common sense also suggests that people who are behaviorally disabled are just as capable of feeling pleasure and displeasure as the rest of us. A person unable to control his voluntary muscles, and who has thereby lost the tendency to respond avidly to some stimuli and to shun others, is not ipso facto a person who cannot be made to feel pleasure or to suffer: it would be ferocious cruelty to deliver electrical shocks to a permanently paralyzed person, or to a person with a severe motor-control disorder, says received wisdom, and it is hard to disagree, exactly because we imagine that such shocks would be very unpleasant even though they would not affect tendencies to behave. Recent work in neuroscience concurs for non-humans: recall the rats described in Berridge and Robinson (1998), whose motivational systems were lesioned. Measures of facial reactions showed that rats continued to produce characteristic facial expressions of pleasure in response to sucrose solutions and displeasure in response to quinine solutions, though the rats no longer had any tendency to consume the sugar or avoid the quinine. Rats, like human beings, seem to be capable of the normal range of enjoyment and suffering whether or not they are capable of interesting behavior. A devout Rylean could hold that these facial responses are all there is to pleasure and displeasure in such rats, but this strains credulity to the breaking point.

Ryle (1971, 326–27) seems to be motivated to take the view he does on pleasure largely by the worry that pleasure, if a distinct sort of event in consciousness, must either be something experienc*ed* (a sort of sense datum, accessible to an "inner eye"), which he takes to be inadmissible, or else it must be a type of experience with no distinctive object, which is also intolerable. Likewise, it seems to me that Michael Tye (1995) has a reason to hold pleasure and displeasure to be ways of responding to other experiences only because he is committed to the view that every type of consciousness is an experience *of* something, and he can think of nothing for pleasure or displeasure to be experiences *of*. But Ryle and Tye fail to consider the possibility that pleasure and displeasure are types of experiences that *do* have distinctive objects: that hedonic tone, like vision, "says" that the world is this way or that. This is the approach I propose to take. Such an approach, a *representational* (or, if one prefers, *intentional* or *informational*) approach to pleasure and displeasure, is precisely one that offers a distinctive object for these sorts of experiences, and so addresses Ryle's worry, and Tye's possible worry, by making pleasure and displeasure of a piece with vision and audition. The only intelligible motivation I know for holding a Rylean position, then, is one which I will answer in the next section.

What of the view that pleasure and displeasure are not distinctive events in consciousness but rather ways of having other experiences? This sort of view is less implausible than the Rylean position, since it at least ties pleasure to consciousness, and it also has some distinguished advocates. Perhaps the best version of this theory available at present is that offered by Antonio Damasio (see, e.g., Damasio 1994). According to Damasio, pleasure and displeasure are "particular body landscape[s] that our brains are perceiving" (1994, 263). Exactly what this means is clarified in Damasio's discussion of pain. Pain, according to Damasio, involves both sensation of tissue damage (nociception) and displeasure, which is distinct. "The innocent processing of body change [i.e., nociception] rapidly triggers a wave of additional body-state changes that further deviate the overall body state from the base range. *The state that ensues is an emotion, with a particular profile.* It is from the subsequent body-state deviations that the unpleasant feeling of suffering will be formed" (263, italics in original). Thus, the displeasure component of pain is one's perception of the changes in one's body that follow from being injured. Damasio is not overly specific about which body-state changes one must experience in order to experience displeasure, but details elsewhere suggest that he has in mind things such as elevated pulse rate, tightening of the stomach, sweating, twitching, rapid breathing, loss of blood to the skin, and the like. Damasio has less to say about pleasure, but it too is held to be one's awareness of changes in one's overall body state.[22]

To put Damasio's view in its baldest form, then: to be pleased or displeased is to feel certain clusters of bodily states. The displeasure of fear is the feeling of one's muscles tightening, one's stomach knotting, one's heart pounding, and so on; the displeasure of depression is the feeling of profound lassitude and tiredness, a sinking sensation in one's stomach when activities are contemplated, a slowness of breath and pulse, and the like. The pleasure of orgasm is a feeling of muscular tension peaking and then dropping off, contractions of specific muscles around the genitals, a sudden change from an energized to a lazy state, and so on. Or, if these identifications of types of pleasure and displeasure with types of feeling changes are not quite right, they are at least decent first attempts. These are the sorts of things Damasio holds the various pleasures and pains to be.

Put in this form, Damasio's theory appears almost as implausible as Ryle's. Everyday thought would have it that pleasure and displeasure are distinct types of feelings, not merely collections of experiences of one's bodily states. As a result, the theory runs afoul of the first criticism made of Ryle's theory: that it diverges from common sense without justifying the divergence. In addition to mere implausibility, it can also be pointed out that Damasio's theory appears to get particular cases wrong. Imagine two people about to go skydiving. One is a self-described "adrenaline junkie" who loves similar activities; the other is adrenaline averse, hating most "exciting" activities. As the moment to jump approaches, both people will have powerful adrenal, and so visceral, responses: both will feel their hearts pound, their stomachs tighten, their breathing change, and so on. If both step up and jump in the same way, their experiences of their body landscapes will be quite similar around the time of the jump. Not the same, but in gross outline quite a bit more similar to one another than to the body state of a person sitting quietly with an amusing book and a cup of coffee. On Damasio's theory, the two should have similar hedonic tones, given the similarity of body landscape. Yet one is likely to describe these feelings as "a rush," "the thrill of anticipation," and "elation," while the other is likely to describe them as "a surge of anxiety" and "terror." The difference, it seems to me, is not well explained by the subtle differences in experienced bodily landscape. The difference between the two skydivers is simply the difference in whether one is pleased or displeased by skydiving, or even certain body landscapes. A powerful autonomic response that is enjoyed is described as a thrill. Very similar responses, not enjoyed, are described as fear and trembling.

This brings us to the third and fourth widespread philosophical views of pleasure and displeasure, namely, that pleasure and displeasure are simply qualitatively distinct types of events in consciousness, or that they are events playing particular functional roles (see, e.g., Aydede 2000; Block 1995a,b; Searle 1992 for the former sort of view, and any functionalist for the latter). Common sense concurs to at least some extent with both views. Episodes of pleasure and displeasure have distinctive phenomenologies, most would agree, and they have characteristic effects and causes, and both of these allow them to be distinguished from other events in consciousness.

I do not want to say that either view is completely false. In fact, I think both are importantly right in certain respects. Clearly, nothing would be pleasure unless it had the qualitative character pleasure has for us, no matter what functional role it would play. The "raw feel" of pleasure cannot be left out of any proper theory. More controversially, I am also inclined to the view that nothing can be pleasure unless it plays (or perhaps is supposed to play) a particular role, though I think that this role is not well specified by simply gesturing to the familiar roles played by pleasure within us. But both of these views of pleasure are missing something that is also vital to a proper theory of pleasure. What is lacking in these views of hedonic tone is any room for explaining the familiar facts about pleasure and displeasure. Why is it abnormal to experience both at once? Why do pleasure and displeasure trade off against one another? Why do pleasure and displeasure come in degrees? Why do our desires determine whether a piece of news is pleasing or displeasing? Why do gut-level confidence and resignation make a difference to hedonic tone? Such questions turn out to be very difficult to answer on either view, if either is taken as the last word on pleasure.

Consider the answer offered by the simple functionalist position that pleasure and displeasure are essentially defined by their functional roles. For something to feel like pleasure, for something to *be* pleasure, on this view, is just for it to be a mental thing with an opposite, not normally experienced together with it, which trades off against it, which has certain common causes and other common effects, and so on. Thus, pleasure has all of these roles exactly because it is pleasure: if it had different roles, it would not be pleasure, but something else. Analogously, one could say that someone is a baseball pitcher exactly because she is the person who throws each pitch, stands on the pitcher's mound, and so on: if she were to stand elsewhere on the field and act differently, she would be a shortstop or an outfielder or the like, and not a pitcher.

The functionalist's answer presupposes a controversial view of consciousness that has been attacked elsewhere (e.g., Block 1978; Chalmers 1996), but I would like to raise a complaint that is more specific to the issue at hand. The complaint is that, on this view of pleasure and displeasure, there is no explaining why it is that pleasure plays the role it does in organisms like us. This is an unfortunate feature of the theory. Intuitively, it seems reasonable to ask why pleasure and displeasure trade off against one another, or why it is rare to feel pleasure and displeasure simultaneously, but not impossible. Similarly, prior to any deep theorizing about consciousness, it seems like a sensible philosophical question to ask why pleasure inclines us toward maintaining the feeling, while displeasure inclines us toward ending the feeling. But such questions are ruled out of court by the functional-role theory of pleasure. All it can say in answer is that, had our brains worked differently, feelings other than pleasure and displeasure would have been responsible for these different operations. That is, pleasure has all of these features simply because it is pleasure, and if something had not had every one of these features, it would not have been pleasure. This seems surprisingly little to say. After all, it does not appear obvious that these features of pleasure and displeasure are all equally essential to the very nature of these feelings. All else being equal, a theory with more to say by way of explanation ought to be preferred, if one can be found.

Now consider the answer offered by the view that pleasure and displeasure are essentially defined by their qualitative "feels," by the difference they make to consciousness, and nothing more. It could be held that pleasure and displeasure are opposites just because of the way they feel, and that they trade off against one another as a result. It could also be held that pleasure is, simply by virtue of its feel, motivationally attractive, while displeasure is repulsive, and so on.

The problem for such a view is that the claims about what follows directly from the qualitative character of pleasure just do not hold up. Take the claim that pleasure and displeasure are opposites. Given the common sense observation that it is possible for them to be had at the same moment (in bittersweet moments and the like), in what sense does phenomenology support the view that they are opposites? It seems rather to support only the weaker view that they are distinct. If pleasure and displeasure are only distinct, how does it follow that they must trade off against one another? Given the phenomenology, it seems that pleasure and displeasure do not need to trade off against one another: they could both exist at the same time, each waxing or waning on its own schedule. In the same vein, consider the claim that pleasure and displeasure have their motivational roles entirely in virtue of their qualitative character. This view seems to be dealt a serious blow by the commonplace observation that people can seek out displeasure exactly for its quality as displeasure. People whose self-esteem is so low that they consider it *right* that they suffer, and are thereby motivated to cause themselves suffering, do not appear to derive overall pleasure from their suffering.[23] In what sense, then, can it be held that their displeasure is something motivating avoidance purely by virtue of its qualitative character? Left without answers to such questions, the phenomenological view of pleasure and displeasure is reduced to saying that these feelings just do play the roles they do, and so ends up with arbitrary answers to our questions. It might be thought that the defender of the phenomenological view could just describe the phenomenology of pleasure and displeasure more carefully and so answer these questions, but this is a problematic route for the phenomenological theorist to take. For instance, one could attempt to hold that pleasure and displeasure generally trade off against one another because they are *valenced*, that is, because pleasure is positive and displeasure is negative in quality. But consider what this could mean. It cannot be a mere redescription of the patterns pleasure and displeasure display in trading off against one another (for then it explains nothing) and it cannot be a redescription of the fact that people are drawn to pleasure and repelled by displeasure (then it would not be part of the phenomenological character of pleasure and displeasure). To say that pleasure and displeasure are valenced in quality is, in this context, to say that there is a further way of describing the felt quality of pleasure and displeasure in terms of some independent quality, goodness or badness. And since goodness and badness trade off, so must pleasure and displeasure, at least normally. But to say this is to give up on the pure phenomenological approach and to begin to explain the facts surrounding pleasure and displeasure in terms of the qualities (goodness and badness) to which pleasure and displeasure might putatively relate us. This is to move from a pure phenomenological approach to one closer to representationalism (more on which in a moment).

The phenomenological and functional views of pleasure and displeasure thus present a number of problems. These problems are, perhaps, not as severe as the problems presented by other well-known philosophical accounts of hedonic tone, but they are genuine problems nevertheless, and a theory of hedonic tone without them would have its attractions. It is to the development of such a theory that I now turn.

4. A Representational Theory of Pleasure

Consider, for a moment, vision. It, like hedonic tone, has distinctive phenomenological features, plays a certain functional role and exists in virtue of dedicated neural structures. But it can also be said of vision that it is a tool for giving organisms a representation of the shapes and locations of objects around them, along with a representation of the light-reflecting properties of these objects (Marr 1982). That is, in addition to our ability to think of vision in terms of what it is like to see, and in terms of the neurological means by which we see, we can also think of vision in terms of what it *represents*. Vision involves representing objects in the world as being here or there, red or black, steady or moving, and so on. Thinking of vision as involving representations (or, if one prefers, information or intentional content) has a number of benefits.[24] First, it accords with the common sense observation that vision tells us something about the world, that there is a content to visual experience that we can accept or reject. "My eyes tell me that the two lines bend away from one another, though I know they don't really" and similar expressions give voice to this sort of thought. Second, it lets us say that certain beliefs are or are not justified by virtue of their contents being in logical accord with the contents of experience. The person who apparently sees the milk carton on the counter is, normally, required to believe that the milk carton is on the counter, because to believe otherwise would be to contradict "the evidence of his senses." This presupposes that the senses have contents that can be contradictory to the contents of belief. Third, thinking of vision as involving representations allows us to provide informative and powerful explanations of certain facts about vision. For instance, consider the following:

> The reason that human visual depth perception can be tricked by virtual reality glasses is that the portion of the brain representing depth relies on information about coincidence in the retinal images of the two eyes (among other things), processing such information on the implicit assumption that widespread coincidence in retinal image corresponds to a unique distal cause. Virtual reality glasses provide the eyes with distinct retinal images that happen to systematically coincide, causing a misrepresentation of a common distal cause.

Such an explanation makes good sense only on the assumption that one can talk about representational or informational or intentional contents in the context of human vision. This last consideration, more than any other, has been the primary motivation for neuroscientists to take up talk of representations in the senses, to the extent that they have.

Common sense does not hold that pleasure and displeasure have contents telling us about how things stand in the world: this is at least part of the reason pleasure and displeasure are called 'feelings' rather than 'senses'.[25] Common sense *does*, however, hold that hedonic tone justifies certain beliefs—beliefs about what one wants or does not want—and there *is* a powerful account of the diverse features of hedonic tone that can be given in representational terms. So insofar as there is a case to be made for vision involving representations, there is also a case, if not quite as strong, for holding pleasure and displeasure to involve representations. None of this is to deny a place to the phenomenology of pleasure, or to say that representations can be formed without regard for the functional role that they play. Rather, it is being suggested that such accounts need to be supplemented by a discussion of the representational features of pleasure, just as any complete account of vision needs some discussion of *its* representational character.[26]

If one wanted to give a representational account of pleasure and displeasure, what would one have them represent? The most obvious choice seems to me to be something relating to changes in desire satisfaction and frustration. In representation, there is often a co-occurrence of the representation and the represented, and changes in desire satisfaction and frustration co-occur with distinctive hedonic experiences. By and large, getting what we want pleases us, and being pleased is a sign that things are going our way. Similarly, having our desires frustrated is unpleasant, and being displeased is a sign that things are going against our wishes. Perhaps, then, pleasure and displeasure allow us to perceive whether our desires are being satisfied or not. Here is a first attempt:

Representational Theory of Hedonic Tone (RTHT) 1: To be pleased is (at least) to represent a net increase in desire satisfaction; to be displeased is to represent a net decrease in desire satisfaction. Intensity of pleasure or displeasure represents degree of change in desire satisfaction.

I take net desire satisfaction or frustration to be a function of the satisfaction or frustration of individual desires, with stronger desires being weighted more heavily than weaker desires in the global evaluation. I also take it that net desire satisfaction may increase (i.e., one's desires may be better satisfied, overall, than they were before) or decrease (i.e., be worse satisfied) as a result of events occurring, and a positive or negative change in one's state of desire satisfaction may be greater or lesser.[27]

RTHT1 is a theory with many advantages. Consider first the findings of common sense surveyed in section 1. Common sense holds pleasure and displeasure to be opposites. RTHT1 agrees and can explain: pleasure and displeasure have representational contents that are contraries. Common sense holds pleasure and displeasure to come in degrees, with a neutral point between them. RTHT1 agrees and can explain: the neutral point is a representation of desire satisfaction neither increasing nor decreasing, and hedonic tone comes in a continuous range of intensities because desires can be held with a continuous range of strengths, entailing a continuous range of possible increases or decreases in net desire satisfaction.

RTHT1 can even explain the fact that pleasure and displeasure are not normally experienced together, but can be on occasion. Experiences analogous to simultaneous feelings of pleasure and displeasure can be created by what are known as 'opponent processes'. Though it happens rarely, one can visually experience an object as both moving and stationary—an effect sometimes known as the 'waterfall illusion' because it can be created by staring for a long time at a waterfall and then gazing at the stationary landscape near the waterfall (Frisby 1979). Such an illusion is made possible when mutually exclusive properties are represented by the states of distinct representational structures, rather than by mutually exclusive states of a single representational structure. In such circumstances, design considerations would suggest that the representational structures should be connected so that they will not simultaneously represent the world as evincing an impossible combination of properties (i.e., that they be opponent processes), and indeed this seems to be the case with the representation of motion—under normal conditions. Under unusual conditions, however, we find that the normal controls break down, and experiences with contradictory contents result.

Experience, together with the theory presented so far, suggests that the same sort of illusion can take place in the experience of pleasure and displeasure. Pleasure says that our desires are, on balance, being better satisfied; displeasure says that they are, on balance, more frustrated. Since RTHT1 posits that pleasure and displeasure are two distinct types of representations, and since scientific evidence suggests that they are found in adjacent regions of the perigenual anterior cingulate cortex, we need only go on to hold that these representational structures fallibly inhibit one another in order to accommodate the simultaneous representation of our desires as both satisfied and frustrated. This account does more than fit the phenomenon: it also makes sense of it. Why should it be odd to experience pleasure and displeasure at the same time? Because the two sorts of experiences say contradictory things—their contents are mutually exclusive. Why should it be possible? Because the human psyche is capable of mutually inconsistent pairs of representations, though the brain works to avoid them.

The everyday observation that pleasure and displeasure trade off against one another in something like the manner of positive and negative numbers is also endorsed and explained through RTHT1. Representations of net increases in desire satisfaction can be turned into representations of net decreases if the subject suddenly comes to believe that a powerfully desire-frustrating state of affairs obtains, and likewise a representation of a negative trend in desire satisfaction can be overthrown by becoming aware of a single very deeply desired state of affairs.

Similar progress can be made with the observation that pleasure and displeasure have both intellectual and sensuous sources, for people have both more intellectual and more sensuous desires. Some people want to see brilliant chess played or want to avoid spending time "unproductively"; many people want to be warm and are averse to overfull bladders. These intellectual and sensuous desires naturally translate into intellectual and sensuous sources of pleasure and displeasure.

The ubiquity and apparent innateness of some desires (such as desires to be warm, to be touched gently, to be loved, not to be damp, not to be unlike everyone else, etc.) is the explanation RTHT1 can offer for the corresponding ubiquity and apparent innateness of the corresponding dispositions to pleasure and displeasure. Similarly, the fact that many desires are acquired by experience is held by RTHT1 to explain how there comes to be so much individual variation in what pleases people as adults.

The category of unreal and illusory pleasures is another common-sense phenomenon that can be given theoretical underpinnings within RTHT1. To see this, begin by noting that capacities for pleasure and displeasure exist downstream of other representational capacities: we feel happy when we *seem* to get our way, not simply when we *actually* get our way. Hedonic representations do not have special access to the facts about desire satisfaction, but depend upon other representational systems to say whether or not satisfying or frustrating states of affairs obtain. As representational capacities dependent upon others for their operation, pleasure and displeasure are capable of misrepresentations of two main types: those resulting from failures (or simple non-representation) in other perceptual representation systems, and those resulting from failures intrinsic to the structure producing hedonic representations.

Consider, for instance, the person who is happy that General Electric has purchased his corporation, because he has foolishly concluded that GE shares his corporation's vision of its mission and will help the corporation to achieve it, thanks to GE's superior resources. In fact, GE intends to ruthlessly exploit the company's resources to promote its existing line of products. The naïve employee's pleasure at the situation will be taken by his wiser co-workers to be illusory in a sense. "This is no time to be happy," he might be told. But where is the illusion? In this case, the illusion is in the employee's cognitive system. His happiness is inappropriate, but its inappropriateness derives from no failing on its part: it derives from its dependence upon an error elsewhere in the employee's mind.

A second type of hedonic illusion would seem to stem from the system that produces hedonic representations itself. Consider the sadness that follows the end of a romantic relationship. For a time, the sad individual will be subject to hedonic illusions because the loss will cause the individual to become hedonically insensitive to changes in net desire satisfaction. Friends may rally around the person, demonstrating a degree of loyalty not previously suspected, without ameliorating the displeasure suffusing the grieving person. An unexpected promotion at work may be met with no change of mood as well, even though the promotion is found by the individual to be a significant good. Similarly, a dent or scratch given to the sufferer's car may cause no increase in displeasure. This hedonic insensitivity to changes in how well things are going for the individual is a form of hedonic blindness, on the present account. The fact that we use a language of epistemic failing in such situations—"she just can't take it in," "he isn't seeing things clearly right now"—reminds us that interpreting these phenomena as involving some sort of representational failing accords with common sense.

As for the unreality of pleasures induced through chemical, electrical, or surgical disruption of the brain, the truth behind this thought is demonstrated by RTHT1 by holding that the use of substances such as heroin and cocaine induces a representation of a net increase in desire satisfaction, when in fact no such increase exists (in the simplest case, at least, in which withdrawal symptoms are not an issue, and in which the user has no intrinsic desire for the drug).

That the pleasure generated by euphorigenic drugs genuinely involves some sort of representational error is independently plausible on neurological grounds. As Jon Elster points out in his recent study of emotion and addiction, euphorigenic drugs "hijack" the brain's reward system (1999, 53). Most euphorigenic drugs directly or indirectly stimulate the VTA/SNpc, causing downstream effects on structures such as the PGAC, and it is believed that this is the primary route through which they have their effects on their users (KSJ 2000, ch. 51). As described in chapter 2, the VTA/SNpc is normally stimulated, not by directly infused chemical agents, but by structures carrying information about whether unexpectedly rewarding states of affairs or unexpectedly punishing states of affairs are being represented at present. Hence, in the normal course of affairs, representations of how the world is activate the VTA/SNpc, which in turn leads to pleasure or displeasure. Activation of this system by euphorigenic drugs, that stimulate it at the midpoint of its operation through biologically abnormal means, is indeed a hijacking of the system, and naturally can be expected to lead to misrepresentation. According to RTHT1, the pleasure itself is the site of misrepresentation. Hence the unreality of the pleasures of euphorigenic drugs.[28]

One final noteworthy feature of RTHT1 is that it can endorse and explain the commonsensical idea that pleasure and displeasure sometimes impose epistemic constraints on what can reasonably be believed about what one desires, just as visual experiences can impose constraints on what can reasonably be believed about surrounding light-reflecting surfaces. Everyday thinking holds that a person who is otherwise in normal hedonic conditions (not depressed, not using euphorigenic drugs, etc.) and who finds herself very much enjoying it being the case that P, or very much distressed that it is the case that P, should give some credence to the thought that P satisfies or frustrates some desire(s) of hers, whether or not she believes she has such a desire. A person who has always thought of herself as an unathletic bookworm, but who finds that she gets delight from playing badminton and lifting weights, ought to think that perhaps she desires physical activity more than she knows, for example. According to RTHT1, this is so because her pleasure says that her desires are better satisfied than before, and since this superior desire satisfaction coincides with various forms of physical activity, the conclusion that a desire for physical activity is responsible for the pleasure is reasonable.[29] To ignore her feelings of pleasure and insist that she does not really have any desire related to athletic activity would be akin to denying the evidence of her senses.

The virtues of RTHT1 are thus substantial. With functionalist and phenomenological theories of pleasure, it shares the intuitively plausible claim that episodes of pleasure and displeasure are distinctive types of conscious events. This makes it a more plausible theory than Ryle's behaviorist theory or Damasio's "body-state" theory. RTHT1 improves upon its closest rivals, however, in having the virtues of a representational theory. RTHT1 allows the data of common sense to be given an explanation, something functionalist and phenomenological views struggle with, and RTHT1 also makes sense of the observation that pleasure and displeasure constrain what a reasonable person ought to believe about her desires.

In spite of all these virtues, RTHT1 has at least one serious fault, for it fails to explain one important datum of common sense. Back in section 1, it was noted that one source of variation in pleasure and displeasure comes from confidence and resignation: if a person who desires that P is completely confident that P, then she will tend to be less powerfully pleased by turning out to be right, and more powerfully displeased by turning out to be wrong, than someone who was less certain that P; likewise, a person who is averse to it being the case that P, but who is resigned to it, will tend to feel less displeased if it happens that P, and more pleased if not-P, than someone not so resigned. By invoking only represented net change in desire satisfaction, RTHT1 leaves no room for confidence and resignation to play a role.

A modification of RTHT1 should take care of this problem, however.

RTHT 2: To be pleased is (at least) to represent a net increase in desire satisfaction relative to expectation; to be displeased is to represent a net decrease in desire satisfaction relative to expectation. Intensity of pleasure or displeasure represents degree of change in desire satisfaction relative to expectations.

RTHT2 retains all of the benefits of RTHT1, but also makes room for confidence and resignation to make a difference to hedonic tone. Exactly what difference they make, however, is worthy of further discussion, for it is not completely obvious. After all, a person with a dog phobia can be completely convinced that the dog before him is harmless while nonetheless feeling terrible: why does this confidence not translate into reduced displeasure? Furthermore, being stung by a bee would seem to be unpleasant no matter how convinced one is that the bee is going to sting and one's desires are going to be frustrated. Yet the phenomenon of confidence and resignation making a difference to hedonic tone is a robust one, in need of some account. And it can be added that common sense allows people to become hardened to displeasing stimuli, even to pain, although this has never struck anyone as a matter of confidence or resignation.

A pair of distinctions must be made in order to untangle this mess: the distinction between intellectual expectations and "gut-level" expectations, and the distinction between more intellectual and more sensuous sources of pleasure. First, expectations. Some expectations about what will happen are the product of conscious reasoning, conscious probability calculation, reliance upon authorities for likelihood estimates, and so on. These are paradigms of what I am calling "intellectual expectations." If one talks about what one *believes* to be the likelihood of an event, one is generally talking about one's intellectual expectations. These can be contrasted with what one believes "in one's heart" or "in one's gut" about the likelihood of various things, a likelihood estimate that need not match the estimate one makes "with one's head." As an illustration, think of two people playing roulette, both of whom bet a small amount of money on black, both of whom win. Both have full knowledge of the objective probability of winning (17/36), which is transparent from the structure of the game. At the level of conscious deliberation, both agree about how likely the win was, but one may accept the win practically as a matter of course, being supremely confident in her luck, while the other may be quite surprised, having expected herself "at some level" to have bad luck. These differing expectations, expectations that are sometimes disclaimed at the level of rational deliberation, and that are somewhat independent of rational deliberation in any case, are the sorts of cognitive states I have in mind in talking of "gut-level expectations." Statements such as "Of course I knew she would be late, but somehow it still surprises me" are expressions of the effects of such gut-level expectations. The same sort of phenomenon is found in parents feeling sure that a missing child is alive even while accepting the rationality of holding that there is a great risk that the child is dead, and in people who "can't quite believe" they got the great new job, romantic partner, or piece of financial luck they did. Generally, one's gut-level confidence in a given proposition matches one's consciously held level of confidence, but the fact that these are separate cognitive states is shown by the ease with which they come apart under various familiar conditions.

The second distinction, between sensuous and intellectual sources of pleasure, should already be clear enough from its discussion in section 1. There are feelings of pleasure that stem from sexual activity, emptying one's bladder, smelling freshly brewed coffee, and so on, and feelings of pleasure stemming from contemplation of the vastness of the universe, or the intricacy of a fugue, or even from realizing that a less well funded team has finally beaten the New York Yankees; and similarly for displeasure.

When considering cases, I think the reader will find that pleasure and displeasure tend to vary with confidence and resignation when the confidence and resignation are felt in the "gut" or "heart." Reasoned estimates of likelihood believed with one's "head" sometimes correspond to what is felt in one's gut or heart, but when the two come apart, tendencies to pleasure or displeasure follow the viscera. Examination of cases also reveals that gut-level estimations of likelihood for intellectual pleasure and displeasure are calculated differently from estimations of likelihood for more sensuous pleasure and displeasure.

Consider first more intellectual sources of pleasure and displeasure. The person who had always, in his heart, expected to be denied the job for which he applied is the person who will be less hurt by the bad news than the person, otherwise the same in temperament, desire, and so on, who had believed in his secret heart of hearts that he could not fail to get the job. RTHT2 can explain this phenomenon, so long as its term "expectation" is read as "visceral expectation" or "gut-level expectation." Of course, there are complications in real cases. For instance, people with low confidence in the occurrence of good things are often people who are hurt worst by bad news, while people with high confidence in the occurrence of good things are often people who are most resilient to bad news. But this is because such people tend to be rather different in a large number of ways. People who tend to have low confidence that good things will happen to them are also people who tend to see each negative event as evidence that they are, more than ever, doomed to unhappiness, or as evidence that other bad things will soon happen, while people who tend to be confident that the future bodes well for them do not place such interpretations upon bad news. Naturally, this makes a difference to hedonic tone, but not one that conflicts with RTHT2. Likewise, people who have low confidence in the occurrence of good things often tend to depression, and depression is a condition in which one's hedonic tone is largely unresponsive to one's actual circumstances—a condition of systematic misrepresentation, in other words, akin to numbness in the skin or tinnitus. People who systematically misrepresent deviation from expected desire satisfaction, naturally enough, are not going to have displeasure that is readily predicted by RTHT2. A certain amount of caution is therefore required in comparing everyday cases, looking for the effects of gut-level confidence and resignation. But when this caution is employed, RTHT2 fits the evidence of common sense fairly well—at least when one considers only intellectual pleasure and displeasure.

Pleasure and displeasure stemming from more sensuous sources are somewhat different. It is far from obvious that gut-level expectations make a difference to the pleasure or displeasure caused by a massage or a scratch on one's thumb. Yet there are well-known sources of variability in openness to sensuous pleasure and displeasure that I think are best interpreted in terms of gut-level expectations specific to them. The fact that exposure to various specific forms of hardship can inure one to them, so that one no longer feels displeasure under the same conditions one once did, is widely recognized. Likewise, it was known to the ancient Greeks as well as it is known today that sufficient indulgence in sources of sensuous pleasure leaves one jaded, so that one no longer takes the same pleasure in sensuous stimulation that one once did. Almost equally familiar are the opposing phenomena: people with particularly hard lives are sensuously pleased by what others take for granted, and people with absurdly easy lives are sensuously displeased by what passes unnoticed by others. These phenomena suggest that experience somehow sets a baseline, against which new experiences are measured, which makes a difference to felt pleasure and displeasure. I suggest that this baseline be thought of as a gut-level expectation of sensuous desire satisfaction. But these gut-level expectations are unlike gut-level expectations of more intellectual pleasure and displeasure in that they are much more resistant to change. It takes many more exposures to frigid arctic air, or to the heat of a smelter, to become inured than it takes exposures to a friendly smile from a new colleague before one comes to take it for granted. Yet experience seems to show that such changes can eventually come to one's sensuous pleasure and displeasure.

Talk of two distinct systems of gut-level expectations is rather speculative. Nonetheless, there is evidence to support it. As was shown in chapter 2, the biological reward system begins with inputs about how things stand in the world and ends with the release of a signal that expresses the current deviation from expected reward. Between the input and the output, a calculation must be made of expected rewards. If the argument at the end of chapter 2 was leading in the right direction, and desires are what make things rewards or punishments, then predictions about rewards and punishments entail predictions about desire satisfaction and frustration. Hence, the existence of biological systems predicting rewards and punishments in a manner independent of conscious reasonable judgment will be powerful evidence for the existence of biological systems creating gut-level expectations about desire satisfaction. All that is lacking is evidence that there are two distinct systems, one more concerned with intellectual desires, the other more concerned with sensuous desires. But this is also a reasonable speculation. As I noted in chapter 2, reward signals begin in two very different places: the hypothalamus, which monitors basic states such as blood sugar and hydration, and the cortex, with its higher representational capacities. Though the idea remains rather speculative, it seems plausible to me that there would be two distinct routes to the calculation of expected rewards, and hence two distinct routes to calculation of expected desire satisfaction: one stemming from the "lower" functions of the hypothalamus, the other stemming from the "higher" functions of the cortex.[30]

While the notion of *expected* desire satisfaction is a tangled one, there thus is a way of sorting out the tangle that meets the requirements of common sense, is not biologically implausible, and can be used to improve the match between the claims of RTHT1 and common sense. This is the notion of expected desire satisfaction I will adopt for RTHT2.

To summarize the discussion so far: RTHT2 holds that a feeling of a certain degree of pleasure is a perceptual representation of one's desires being on balance more satisfied, to a corresponding degree, than expected, and an experience of a certain degree of displeasure is a perceptual representation of one's desires being on balance less well satisfied, to a corresponding degree, than expected. The fact that pleasure and displeasure represent our desires allows us to understand the epistemic value of pleasure and displeasure in learning about what we want, and the details of how desire satisfaction and frustration are represented make sense of and systematize many phenomenological facts about pleasure and displeasure. Thus clarified and illustrated, the theory is now ready to face some objections.

5. Objections

A likely objection at this point is that there seems to be pleasure and displeasure not stemming from the satisfaction or frustration of any intrinsic desire. For instance, being stroked or massaged is often pleasurable, even when it is the furthest thing from one's mind. But if one would be pleased were one massaged, then it must normally (statistically or normatively, depending on one's view of representation) be the case, on the present line of thinking, that one wanted to be massaged. Likewise, if being forced to scrub floors with a comatose terrier would be unpleasant for one, then on the present theory it appears that one must have wanted not to be forced to so scrub floors, no matter how far this possibility was from one's mind. These difficulties, however, are not quite as serious as they may initially seem, for the content of these desires needs careful characterization. The fact that one would be displeased if one were forced to scrub floors with a comatose terrier does not entail that one has a lurking desire specifically not to do that sort of thing, even on the present theory: it could be that one's desire is for not doing any of a broad class of things, into which the particular sort of act falls. For instance, one might be averse to maltreating animals or getting dirty, and scrubbing a floor with a terrier might frustrate either desire. Thus, if some sort of event is pleasing or displeasing, the present theory does not require that one has a desire regarding that particular sort of event.

Even if it is accepted that care must be taken in assigning content to the desires whose existence is implied by experiences of pleasure or displeasure, it still may seem that we are left with too many desires. Do we really have desires not to have damaged bodily tissues, desires to ingest certain classes of foods and not ingest others, desires to be massaged, to inhale odors of cedar or sandalwood (however described) but not urine or mold (however described), and so on? That is, do we really have a large class of sensuous desires, one that can explain the many sensuous sources of pleasure that exist? I will argue that the answer is "yes." In common parlance, babies want full stomachs, dry bottoms, cuddling, colorful sights, and soothing sounds, and these basic desires do not vanish as we grow older, though they gain a certain degree of sophistication. Why not, then, say that we have these desires? They are not particularly cognitively complex, of course, but if we are willing to say that babies and many non-human animals have desires (as I presuppose in this work), then inevitably it will prove that there are many desires lacking such sophistication. Furthermore, desires regarding sensuous states would be just the sort of thing one would expect evolution to provide infant human beings, were it capable of doing so—after all, infants have limited conceptual resources, but many sensuous states are reliable indicators of harms or benefits in the environment, and making infants desire some of these (the sound of familiar voices) and averse to others (sharp pricks to the skin) would seem only natural.[31]

One might also add that it is no great innovation to discover desires where none were thought to exist before: though the claim of discovery is always a little suspect, and bears some burden of proof, that burden should not be taken to be one we cannot meet. The fact that a putative desire is having no effect at the moment on one's consciousness, such as a lurking desire that gives one a liking for being massaged, is no reason to deny its existence—we surely desire love, fame, and fortune to the same extent while asleep as while awake, for instance (imagine someone saying "he doesn't care whether I exist or not" about a loved one, simply because the loved one is asleep)—and so the mere fact that one is not thinking of how nice it would be to have a massage need be no reason to conclude that no such desire exists. Likewise, the fact that one would not mention something in a list of one's desires does not show that it does not belong on such a list: perfect introspective access is something we clearly lack for most of our propositional attitudes, desires included.

If the terms 'desire' and 'want' still seem inappropriate when explaining why, for example, certain tastes please and others do not, consider the language of the pro attitudes more generally. We have likes and dislikes, hankerings, tastes, aversions, and preferences. To be told that one would find one has a taste for tom kah kai if one were to sample it is to be told that one is disposed, under normal conditions, to be pleased by eating tom kah kai; so much is uncontroversial. Such a disposition presumably has some ground. Consider, then, the nature of that ground. Tastes (and aversions, preferences, hankerings) can be expressed as tastes for particular states of affairs. Having a taste for tom kah kai is not a matter of being pleased by the existence of the Thai dish, or being pleased when others eat it, but being pleased by a type of state of affairs—one's own tasting of tom kah kai at that instant. In this respect, tastes have something propositional about them. That this something propositional is a mental representation of some sort can be seen from the fact that descriptions of one's taste preferences exhibit intensionality: if I have a taste for black beans and rice, and that is what Pancho

Villa ate before dying, though I know nothing of this connection, then it is just as incorrect or infelicitous to say that I have a taste for what Pancho Villa ate before dying as to say that I have a desire for what Pancho Villa ate before dying. Further, just as in the case of desires, one can seem to get food that is to one's taste without it really being such—for instance, under the influence of certain drugs, even marginally palatable foods can seem very much to one's taste. Desires and whatever grounds our tastes also have substantial functional features in common. Both are poised, under appropriate conditions, to move one to action (to have a second spoonful of Thai soup, for instance), both lead to pleasure or displeasure when particular states of affairs are represented by the organism, both have a legitimate role in practical reasoning, and both can be enlisted in operant conditioning.[32] Given this tremendous wealth of commonalities, why not then identify the ground of a taste with a desire for stimulation of the relevant sort?

One might wish to deny that tastes involve the concepts articulated in language, while desires essentially do, and this cannot be dismissed out of hand. Yet, at the same time, such an objection strikes me as more of a terminological dispute than a dispute of genuine interest. Even if we distinguish desires from tastes, if it turns out that they have essentially the same roles in our mental economy, the sole difference being whatever it is distinguishing perceptual content from belief content, then such a distinction seems to be as much terminological as substantive. I am not one who would hold that any desire must have a content of the fully conceptual, as opposed to non-conceptual, sort (if this distinction is even legitimate), but for those philosophers who prefer to use the word 'desire' in this way, I would suggest that this book must be understood to be a work on the nature of desires *and tastes*, which I collectively call 'desires'. The philosopher wishing to make the distinction is welcome to do so, as is the philosopher wishing to distinguish "true desires" from wishes, say, but the distinction distinguishes amongst phenomena that are more similar to one another than differing, and that form a unified group for most psychological purposes, and so I will continue to deal with them without drawing the distinction.

One more point should be raised, this stemming from the neuroscience of pleasure. At least some sources of sensuous pleasure, such as particular smells and tastes, are processed in regions of the brain very close to the reward-processing region of the OFC and send projections there (Rolls 2000). If chapter 2 was correct, then such projections to OFC are probably what constitute these smells and tastes as rewards. But if chapter 2 was correct, then exactly similar connections to OFC are probably used to constitute complex states of affairs such as the approval of one's peers, or the timely launch of a space shuttle, as rewards. That is, as rewards, smelling violets and getting a new bicycle are on a biological par. In the case of getting a new bicycle, it is natural to hold that it is a reward because one wants a new bicycle. Given that the biological underpinnings are very much the same in the case of smelling violets, why not once again say that the person for whom this is a reward is a person who desires to inhale such scents? And once this has been said, there is no bar to saying that the pleasure felt as a result of inhaling such a scent represents an improvement in desire satisfaction.

A powerful argument is still available to the critic. Suppose that the critic accepts, as just argued, that the grounds of our tastes (aversions, etc.) for various forms of immediate sensory stimulation are similar in structure to our standing desires. The critic may then pose a difficult choice. Tastes are the sort of thing that tempt one to say "I want it because it pleases," while for desires "it pleases because I want it" is the natural order of explanation. If the similarities between desires and other pro attitudes are so great, then one order of explanation must triumph over the other. My claim has been as follows: most of us enjoy, say, chocolate because most of us have a standing desire for a broad class of taste experiences into which the taste of chocolate falls (and of which the taste of good chocolate is the perfect exemplar, perhaps!), just as we enjoy knowing that our loved ones are flourishing because we desire that they flourish. The alternative available to the critic is to argue that we desire not only chocolate because it pleases but also the welfare of our loved ones because that also pleases. If correct, this would refute the thesis of this chapter, for one cannot make use of the concept of pleasure in saying what it is to be a desire, if one also wishes to appeal to the concept of a desire in explaining what pleasure is—ontological circularity looms. In short, if we are to treat the relation of pleasure to all pro attitudes equally, we are forced to choose between a counter-intuitive thesis about tastes and psychological hedonism. Given such a choice, I favor the unlikely conclusions about tastes—I am far more certain that I would willingly care for my father in his old age for his sake, and not for the sake of my own pleasure or avoided displeasure, than that I do not have desires for all sorts of sensuous states. Given that desires and the grounds of tastes are so similar, a decision is called for, and the decision to call the grounds of our tastes, aversions, and so on 'desires' seems best.

These considerations are not decisive, admittedly, but they add some further measure of plausibility to the picture being painted of pleasure and displeasure, and further measures of plausibility will have to suffice. One final point needs to be made, and then other objections will be considered.

Even if we grant that pleasure is not the only intrinsically desired end, it surely is one end that is often desired intrinsically. Sometimes, I want to have fun, and am pretty open to what other ends I pursue so long as I will have fun pursuing them. Or sometimes I want to eat something that tastes good and am pretty open to what I eat so long as it will bring pleasure. According to the present theory, the content of an experience of pleasure is that one's intrinsic desires are being better satisfied than expected; what then to say when the pertinent desire is for pleasure? There is a hint of circularity here, but only a hint; what actually exists is not circularity but hierarchy (recalling a similar hierarchy from chapter 2). To seek pleasure is to seek, not simple improvement over expected net desire satisfaction, but the *representation* of such improvement. Suppose one goes looking for pleasure, finds it in playing a good game of pool, and is pleased to get it.

Then one represents an improvement over expectations in net desire satisfaction in being pleased, and (if one does not misrepresent) one does so because one's desires are, on balance, being better satisfied. One desire, for pleasure, is not satisfied until the pleasure begins, and so this desire cannot be the one to trigger the representation of superior desire satisfaction. That first desire to be satisfied would be the desire to play pool well (in this example) or some other desire (such as to show off to one's friends or to be dextrous) that is satisfied by good pool playing. That desire's satisfaction leads one to represent improved desire satisfaction and so to being pleased. Being pleased satisfies one's further desire to be pleased, and so one represents one's desires as satisfied to an even greater degree—one enjoys having a good time, and has a better time for it. (Compare this with the phenomenon of not noticing one is having fun, and so missing out on some of the fun one might have had, or the phenomenon of having a good time but finding it objectionable to do so in that context, and so not enjoying oneself as much as one might.) There is nothing in the present theory that forbids intrinsic desires for pleasure or aversions to displeasure, so long as these desires are not taken to be the only sort that exists.

There is quite a different objection I want to take up concerning the anticipation and recollection of desire satisfaction and frustration, and the related phenomenon of daydreaming. It often happens that the mere anticipation or recollection of desire satisfaction or frustration is pleasant or unpleasant, even when it is quite evident that actual satisfaction or frustration is still some time in the future or the past. Likewise, daydreaming can be very pleasant, even when one does not really think that the daydreamed scenario will ever be realized (and not merely in an intellectual fashion; one may pleasantly fantasize about winning a Booker Prize while knowing in one's heart that one will never even start a novel). How can the present theory accommodate these forms of pleasure and displeasure, holding as it does that they stem from represented deviations from predicted net desire satisfaction or frustration, and not from representation of merely possible changes?

One important point to make is that we may have present desires regarding these things: for example, we may presently desire that our desires will, in the future, be satisfied, and so believing that our desires will be satisfied in the future may also satisfy desires now. Indeed, to the extent that we now care about our future, the pleasure and horror of anticipation will be fully justified.[33] Likewise, a person may desire to exercise her imagination, or that it be conceivable that she receive a literary prize, or that she always recall a certain special day, or similar such things. Thus, anticipation, recollection, and daydreaming may all directly satisfy desires. This is certainly not the only mechanism by which these processes modify hedonic tone, however.

Another, equally important explanation of how recollection and daydreaming (and some cases of anticipation) can lead to pleasure or displeasure assimilates this fact to the fact that misrepresentation of the world can cause pleasure and displeasure, though there are special subtleties involved. Consider what is involved in anticipation, dread, reminiscence, daydreaming, and the like. One uses one's imagination, or even engages in overt behavior, calling to mind the desire-satisfying or desire-frustrating scenario. One visualizes relaxing on the beach, or hears in one's "inner ear" the applause of the crowd—or its humiliating laughter. Those with good olfactory imaginations can actually "smell" the home-cooked bread before it is begun, and the memory of a lover's kiss may recall a tingle to the lips. Likewise, in imagining, one may alter one's bearing, tighten or relax particular muscles, make gestures, mumble phrases and otherwise mime, re-create or "pre-create" some event. These are voluntary behaviors, both inner and outer, and we can hardly fool ourselves with them into thinking that the imagined scenario is really happening. In this sense, they involve no misrepresentation on the part of the person. Yet I would suggest that, to the extent that they evoke hedonic responses, they have fooled some internal mental system, just as the visual system may be fooled by optical illusion-producing designs even though the person is not misled. Kosslyn (1994) tells us that many of the same cortical areas involved in perception are used in imagination. If so, then it should be no surprise that voluntary stimulation of the perceptual system should lead the brain to respond, to some degree, as though perception were occurring—after all, the neural activation created by the imaginative process is going to try to follow the channels it usually follows, even if the fact that one is voluntarily producing this stimulation changes the context in which this activation flows. Just as one can cause one's heart to race by imagining a frightening scenario vividly or cause one's muscles to tense by imagining vigorous activity, so, I would suggest, one can cause internal systems to misrepresent desire satisfaction or frustration by imagining scenarios that would be satisfying or frustrating, and so experience pleasure or displeasure. To the extent that one is not for a moment fooled by one's imagination, one can expect the pleasure or displeasure to be weaker, for not being fooled is at least partly a matter of one's voluntary stimulation of one's sensory system being imperfect, and this imperfection has weakened "downstream" effects as a natural consequence. To the extent that one's imaginative state approaches a reverie or method acting, however, one may expect a concomitant increase in emotional impact, for the imaginative state comes closer to fooling, not just a limited selection of neural subsystems, but oneself.

Finally, there are the puzzles raised by common sense that must be addressed. Where, if anywhere, is pleasure located? And how many sorts of experiences make up pleasure and displeasure?

First, the location of pleasure and displeasure. One might think RTHT2 should recognize pleasure and displeasure as having locations, at least on some occasions, as common sense does (pleasure is in the genitals during orgasm, displeasure is in a wound during pain, and so on).[34] This would certainly be a problem for RTHT2 if the demand were reasonable. However, I think close phenomenological attention will reveal that pleasure and displeasure are not themselves localized in such cases: it is their sources that are. One is aware of the location of a pleasant touch, but when the touch ends, the pleasure may continue without either being found in the touched body part or being forced to relocate itself. Likewise, the unpleasantness of a scraped knee can disappear without anything seeming different about one's *knee*, as is shown by the results of cingulumotomies for pain control and the like (discussed earlier). Once again, hedonic tone seems not to be localized so much as to have a very salient source. And the non-localization of more intellectual pleasure and displeasure is obvious upon examination. That pleasure and displeasure are not localized makes them an oddity among the senses, but since their contents are that one's desires are on balance better or worse satisfied relative to expectations, their having felt locations would be even odder.

Second, and more challengingly: How many sorts of experiences make up pleasure and displeasure? More carefully, it can be asked whether pleasure and displeasure are what might be called 'natural phenomenological kinds', or whether they are heterogeneous groupings of diverse experiential phenomena. The person raising this sort of question typically has in mind the dissimilitude of having an orgasm, on the one hand, and enjoying a play by Brecht, on the other—or, equivalently, the vast gulf between finding oneself displeased with a child's hygiene and quaking with fear at the prospect of summary execution. Pleasure and displeasure appear in so many forms, it is sometimes thought, that there is nothing in common to all of them which can be called 'pleasure' or 'displeasure' and treated as a discrete entity. This is a puzzle raised, not as a result of arcane prior philosophical commitments, but as a straightforward result of noting that different experiences of pleasure and displeasure are genuinely very different.

The worry that pleasure and displeasure might not be a unified phenomenon is not wholly unreasonable phenomenologically, but it is ultimately unwarranted. Three possible sources of this worry come to mind: the fact that pleasure and displeasure are different from one another (call this 'valence incomparability'), the fact that some forms of pleasure and displeasure seem not to admit of comparison as greater than, equal to, or less than other forms (call this 'quantitative incomparability'), and the fact that the total character of some (un)pleasant experiences is so different from the total character of other (un)pleasant experiences (call this 'qualitative incomparability').

I will answer each in turn, beginning with the first and most readily answered worry—that pleasure and displeasure are not unified types of experiences because they differ from one another, and so should be thought of as being at least two distinct types of experiences, one with positive valence and the other with negative. This is, of course, true in a perfectly good sense, but it is no impediment to holding pleasure and displeasure to also be unified types of experiences in another, equally good sense. Just as experiences of warmth and cold are one sort of experience,[35] so it can be said that experiences of a range of pleasure and displeasure make up one kind of experience. No one, I take it, is inclined to deny that experiences of temperature are of a kind because they come in two types, experiences of warmth and of coldness, and hedonic tone should be no different. Displeasure is instantly recognized as the counterpart of pleasure, just as cold is instantly recognized as the counterpart of warmth, and this would not be the case unless there were some obvious phenomenological relation between them, in addition to whatever differences there are. Valence incomparability is not really incomparability after all.

Perhaps the troubling phenomenology is not that hedonic tone comes in positive and negative types, but that they are not always quantitatively comparable. How, one might ask, can one compare the degree of pleasure of knowing one is loved to the degree of pleasure one gets from sinking into a hot bath? But think of the feeling of freezing at a bus stop in January in Winnipeg, say, and of having an ice cube pressed to one's belly while sunbathing in July, and you will probably find it hard (as I do) to imagine the two experiences in a way that makes their felt coldness just the same. Yet this would hardly convince anyone that there are really many different feelings, different in kind, which we lump together under the word 'cold'. The fact that it can be hard to compare types of experiences in respect of their variation along some quantitative dimension is common to many classes of experiences, and not unique to pleasure and displeasure. As a result, it can hardly be sufficient grounds for holding pleasure and displeasure to be disunified phenomena. Furthermore, it is clear that, however many hard cases of quantitative comparison there might be, there are many more easy cases. For any (un)pleasant experience one has had, one can always (as a matter of empirical fact) recall many (un)pleasant experiences that were intuitively very different sorts of experiences, and yet were clearly either more or less (un)pleasant. I find it hard to compare the displeasure I experienced sledding into a brick wall to the displeasure I experienced the day my best friends ridiculed me, but I can compare them both quite readily to the displeasure I experienced eating a very inferior crème caramel (that displeasure was less) and to the displeasure I suffered upon learning of a death in the family (that was greater). Once again, it seems that the difficulties of quantitative comparisons reveal nothing very deep about the nature of hedonic tone. Comparing the redness of paint swatches or the pitch of various sounds presents all the same problems, which just goes to show how insignificant such problems are to a theory of hedonic tone.

As for the third worry, it certainly must be granted that, say, feeling cheerful because it is a sunny day and savoring the sublime elegance of Creation are different total feelings, with different qualitative characters, but I would resist the conclusion that they are such because they involve qualitatively different types of pleasure. Compare the total experience one has while hearing a teething baby cry at a certain pitch to the total experience one has while hearing a recording of a mass sung by the Vienna Boys' Choir when the choir hits the exact same pitch. There is a world of qualitative differences between the two experiences, and yet there is no temptation to attribute the difference to a difference in the sort of pitch experienced. Rather, the difference is clearly due to volume, timbre, context, pleasure, one's experience of one's bodily response to both experiences, and so on. Without special motivation to do otherwise, there seems every reason to treat the hedonic case in just the same way. One could also wonder what it would be like to have the exact experience of enjoying the sublimeness of Creation except for the hedonic component, substituting instead the hedonic component of being cheerful on a sunny day. Holding feelings of energy, of the viscera, of muscle tone, of having particular thoughts, and so on constant, would there really be a way of enjoying the sublimeness of Creation with sunny-day pleasure rather than the usual sublime-Creation pleasure? I cannot imagine it myself.

Finally, the results of studies on the PGAC further confirm that pleasure and displeasure are unified phenomena. Studies on displeasure identify the PGAC as a displeasure center whether they use disgusting images (Lane et al. 1997), pain (Coghill et al. 1999) or guilt (Shin et al. 2000), and studies on pleasure similarly stimulate the PGAC whether through alcohol (Ingvar et al. 1998) or fond memories of competitive victory (Rauch et al. 1999). Though one could resist such evidence if one had excellent reasons to think that pleasure and displeasure are deeply disunified (one could use such evidence to show that the PGAC must not be a dis/pleasure center), in the absence of such reasons the scientific data provide yet another confirmation of the view being presented here.

6. Pleasure and Theories of Desire

If RTHT2 is correct, then no hedonic theory of desire can be correct. Any hedonic theory of desire holds that to be a desire is to be a thing which is X, where X is some property involving pleasure and displeasure. A few possible variants of the theory were mentioned in chapter 1, but whatever form a hedonic theory of desire might take, it will hold that pleasure and displeasure are part of the ontological ground of desire: desires are made of pleasure and displeasure, which are more basic ontological entities, though not necessarily maximally basic entities.

Given this, it is clear that no hedonic theory of desire can accept that pleasure and displeasure represent an organism's own desires. For a representation of X is less ontologically basic than an X: if pleasure represents desire, then it must be possible to say what desire is without mentioning pleasure, while it will be impossible to explain pleasure without mentioning desire. This finding is a simple one, and yet it deals a very serious blow to the hedonic theory of desire.

On the other hand, the standard theory of desire and the reward theory of desire are both left as viable theories. If pleasure represents changes in desire satisfaction, and desire satisfaction amounts to the obtaining of states of affairs the organism was inclined to bring about, that is all well and good. Likewise if desire satisfaction amounts to the obtaining of states of affairs constituted by the organism as rewards. In either case, there will be no ontological circularity in the nature of pleasure or desire.

There is one point of interest to note here, however. As described earlier, the PGAC receives input from the reward system, which appears to be a normal proximal cause of pleasure. And the reward system releases a signal carrying information about the difference between expected and actual reward. If the reward theory of desire is correct, then the reward system's signal also carries information about the difference between expected and actual desire satisfaction. So the capacity of the PGAC to represent changes in expected desire satisfaction is straightforward. On the other hand, if the motivational theory of desire is correct, then the PGAC must somehow be drawing conclusions about the attainment of states of affairs the organism was motivated to obtain based upon information about the difference between expected and actual reward. This is not impossible, since in many cases rewards are things an organism is motivated to obtain, and things the organism is motivated to obtain are rewards for it. Reward information is thus indirect information about the obtaining of states of affairs the organism is moved to bring about. Yet this would seem to be an odd way of arranging to represent change in desire satisfaction. If the present chapter has been right, then, the hedonic theory of desire is in serious trouble, and the standard theory of desire raises an odd puzzle. Only the reward theory of desire escapes unscathed. Once again, the consideration is not decisive by any means. Yet once again, it is certainly of interest.

4

The Production and Prevention of Movement

The last face of desire remaining to be considered in detail is its motivational face. Human bodies move, and fail to move, in all sorts of ways. Limbs extend, facial expressions freeze, eyes focus, veins throb, feet trip, poses are held, steps are taken, and we all turn around Earth's axis. Likewise, human bodies move, and fail to move, for all sorts of reasons. I fell because I was pushed, your arms moved like that because you are double-jointed, he reached for the coffee because he planned to offer it to a friend, she did nothing because she was afraid the tiger might notice her. And somewhere, in all of this, lie the movements we make because of our desires.

Among the explanations given for bodily movements, it is natural to distinguish between those motivated by some consideration found in the mind of the person moving and those caused by external forces, muscle spasms and other non-mental entities. Likewise, moments of stillness can be divided into those stemming from psychological inhibition against moving and those stemming from physical restraint, unconsciousness, and so on. Correspondingly, it is common to divide bodily movements and non-movements into those which are *actions* and those which are not. The actions are the movements stemming from internal psychological motivation or inhibition, while the non-actions are movements otherwise produced, roughly speaking.

The natural thing to do at this point, given the previous two chapters, would be to construct a theory of action, with the goal of shedding light on how action relates to desire. After all, in chapter 2, the goal was to give insight into how desires are related to rewards, and the method was to develop a theory of reward. In chapter 3, the goal was to give insight into how desires are related to pleasure, and the method was to develop a theory of pleasure. But developing a theory of action is too large a task, because it involves settling too many questions tangential to the needs of a philosopher who seeks a theory of desire. Existing theories of action debate whether actions are bodily movements caused by mental events,[1] mental events fit to cause bodily movements,[2] or the combination of the mental causes and the bodily effects.[3] They debate whether actions always result from *trying* to act.[4] They debate whether all actions are autonomous.[5] And so on. These issues are important for a full theory of action, but they are irrelevant to the philosopher whose real interest is in desire.

Without at least an implicit theory of action, however, it is also not possible to explain how action relates to desire, for any such explanation would presuppose some theory or other. So neither the ultimate goal of this chapter, nor its method, can exactly parallel those of the previous two chapters. Yet it is still important to explore action in some sense, as the motivational face of desire is the most prominent and public face of desire, and the face most favored by theorists at present.

Less controversial than action is bodily movement. Where an action begins or ends might be subject to dispute, but bodily movements are a more straightforward subject matter. My arm moves from my lap to my coffee cup, and whether this is an action, the result of an action, or a component of an action makes no difference to the fact of its movement. So perhaps this chapter would do well to restrict itself to considering the nature of bodily movement. As a theoretical topic, however, bodily movement as such is philosophically uninteresting: there is no theory of movement around Earth's axis or during a coughing fit that will shed any light upon desire. So this chapter will have to strike out in a new direction. Rather than giving a theory of action and allowing it to illuminate desire, I will present a summary of what is believed about the production of bodily movement by the mind, a summary of how motivation and inhibition get our bodies out of bed and engaged in the varied activities of life. This will not be a full account by any means: not enough is known at present to fully explain even a simple action in neurological terms. Yet enough is known to give us a sense of what sorts of causal influence various mental states have upon bodily movement. With this information in hand, it will be possible to draw some conclusions about the standard, hedonic, and reward theories of desire. We will have to forgo the opportunity to gain insights into the nature of action, but we will also be spared the effort, and perhaps this is all for the best.

1. Mind, Brain, and Motivation

According to common sense, one can be moved by desiring ends, thinking of consequences, having goals, making plans, being filled with emotion, sensing opportunities, perceiving risks, being aware of the situation, needing something, wanting something, wishing for it. And on one could go: the turns of phrase denoting sources of motivation and inhibition are almost endless. In this chapter, however, I would like to focus on just five: trying, having a prior intention, being rewarded, being pleased, and desiring. Focusing on these five will be challenging enough, and quite sufficiently revealing for present purposes. As usual, I will consider both what is thought about these phenomena by people of common sense and what neuroscientists have to say about them. That neuroscientists have anything at all to say about the motivating effects of trying, prior intention, and the like might take many scientists themselves by surprise, as the scientists seem reluctant to interpret their findings in psychological terms. There is very little talk of desiring, intending, trying, habit, or anything else recognizably mental in the field: neuroscientists typically prefer to talk of "motor representations" and "commands" (Jeannerod 1997, 51) or, most commonly, "causes of movement." Yet the evidence of neuroscience nonetheless will shed light upon these everyday notions.

Trying

Take trying first. Common sense holds that trying to do something is a fairly common cause of doing it. "You won't know if you can do it until you try" is a common saying, and we enjoin people to "give it a try." One can also try not to do things: try not to move, not to breathe, not to embarrass oneself, and so on. Trying to do something does not guarantee success, holds common sense. One can try to win an Olympic medal and fail, and, when very young, or very drunk, one can try to stand and fail. Trying does not even guarantee that some relevant activity will take place in one's musculature: a person who is paralyzed can try desperately to make some motion to convey that he is nonetheless conscious, for example, without succeeding in stirring a single muscle. And, more trivially, if one is trying to stay still—for instance, to maintain a bored, impassive expression—then success will result in an absence of movement, naturally enough.

Some philosophers hold that trying is one component of the production of every action, while others claim that trying exists only when the success or failure of the action is in real doubt. Everyday thought appears to favor neither view. If I perform a trivially simple action, such as taking a book down from my shelf, then it would not occur to the person of common sense to say that I tried to take it down, but the same person would reject the assertion that I did *not* try to take the book down.

When it comes to the neuroscience of trying, the first point to make is to admit to very limited knowledge. People can try to do a tremendous number of things: sit and stand, make ice cream, pacify angry colleagues, and so on, but contemporary neuroscience lacks the capacity to explain most of these things. Trying to make ice cream, for example: such an endeavor might begin with casting about in one's mind for likely sources of information, or an attempt to recall a recipe: neuroscience has very limited resources for explaining how such information retrieval is voluntarily directed. At some point, a plan must be formed for making the ice cream step by step, and each step must be carried out at its appropriate time. Again, neuroscience is at a loss to explain how this is organized within the brain. When it comes to explaining how one tries to open the freezer door, though, or how one tries to whisk, neuroscience comes into its own. The explanation of trying in general is too much, but trying to make *simple bodily movements* is another matter: here, neuroscience has an impressive, though still limited, depth of knowledge. To the extent that one tries to make one's simple bodily movements, there is a rich story to be had here.

The *motor cortex* (appendix, fig. 2) is the core of the neuroscientific account of trying. The motor cortex takes input principally from other, higher level motor control structures, and sends its output principally to the spinal cord, thereby controlling the skeletal muscles and so movement. It is the bottom layer of a rough motor control hierarchy, and its instructions to the body are correspondingly simple: to flex a single finger, to kick a leg, and so on. As the bottom layer, the motor cortex performs a vital function, and complete bilateral[6] loss of motor cortex results in total paralysis (KSJ 2000, ch. 38). Different patterns of activity in the motor cortex command different movements, each with a specific direction and force.

Interestingly, the type of movements that the motor cortex commands the body to perform correspond to what Arthur Danto (1963, 1965) calls "basic actions" and Donald Davidson (1980, ch. 3) calls "primitive actions." These are actions which one performs directly, without needing to perform some other action as an intermediate step. In this terminology, typing the word "owl" is not a basic action, since it is something I do by means of first typing the letter *o*, then *w*, then *l*. But moving the third finger of my right hand out and downward, thus striking the *o* key, *is* a basic action. My movement is something I do directly, and not by means of doing anything else. Of course, various things must happen in my body in order for the movement to come about, but none of these things is something that I would say I *do*. The category of basic actions is based entirely upon the felt experience of acting and our everyday descriptions of it, but it is striking that the commands issued by the motor cortex are (at least, according to the best current scientific accounts) commands for movements that correspond to basic actions. The correspondence between the two suggests, though of course does not prove, that activity in the motor cortex merits some sort of psychological description, such as trying to bring about this or that basic bodily movement.

Other structures directly implicated in trying to move one's body are the *supplementary motor area*, or SMA, and the motor region of the *anterior cingulate cortex*, or AC (see appendix, fig. 2). The SMA and motor AC work largely through their activation of the motor cortex, though they send signals directly to the spinal cord as well. They play upon the motor cortex as if it were a keyboard, whose patterns of activation produce single notes and chords of bodily movements. The SMA and motor AC are able to organize the single notes and chords into what one could think of as simple themes and chord progressions, though not complete compositions: they are only intermediate levels in the motor control hierarchy, and like the motor cortex, they in turn are played by other regions of the brain. There is no center in the SMA or motor AC whose stimulation would cause one to find a telephone and order a pizza, for instance. Instead, activation of these centers causes movements such as lip smacking, simple vocalization, coordinated limb and trunk movement, strumming movements, and more (Devinsky, Morrell, and Vogt 1995; Fried et al. 1991; Talairach et al. 1973). Electrical stimulation of the motor AC has been reported to cause "an irresistible urge to grasp something" and the appropriate movements in a woman with epilepsy (Kremer et al. 2001), and epilepsy focused in the motor AC has been known to cause obsessive-compulsive symptoms (Levin and Duchowny 1991). If trying is psychologically real and a common cause of bodily movement, then trying to make strumming movements, to make simple utterances, to grasp objects, and the like are mental states realized, at least in part, by activity in the SMA and motor AC.[7]

Further evidence that the SMA and motor AC are important to trying comes from the fact that widespread damage to the motor AC, together with damage to the adjacent SMA, is known to cause *akinetic mutism*. In this fascinating condition, sufferers make no voluntary movements or vocalizations, not as a result of straightforward paralysis, but because they can no longer initiate actions. Individuals recovering from akinetic mutism have reported that while immobile they had no thoughts and attempted no actions. One subject reported she had been mute because "I really had nothing to say" (Damasio 1994, 73).[8]

Although obviously relevant to understanding trying, it is not clear exactly what such findings entail. It is tempting to hold that, given the phenomenon of akinetic mutism, activity in the motor AC and SMA is at least necessary for trying: after all, isolated damage affecting these areas eliminates both behavioral evidence of trying and subjective experience of trying. It is also tempting to hold that such activity is sufficient for trying, given that electrical stimulation of the motor AC has been found able to cause a felt irresistible urge to grab something. Yet there are many objections that could be raised. Most simply, one could put forward the alternate hypothesis that the motor AC does not originate episodes of trying, but is a necessary waystation both for their execution and for consciousness of them. This hypothesis about motor AC function is consistent with existing evidence, but it entails that motor AC activity is neither necessary nor sufficient for trying. The existence of such alternative explanations for motor AC and SMA function should make it plain that it would be premature to leap to conclusions about these neural structures framed in everyday language. Nonetheless, the information we have at present is certainly suggestive.

One other structure linked to trying has been neglected so far in this discussion, but its role, though biologically very important, appears philosophically less substantial. This is the visuomotor region of the parietal cortex. At least in the case of humans and other primates, signals reaching the motor cortex from this structure are believed to come in the form of information useful for performing visually guided movements, especially reaching and grasping (Jeannerod 1997). The visuomotor centers of the parietal lobe receive information from the parts of the brain dedicated to tactile and visual processing, and send their own impulses on to the motor cortex in a manner that is vital for accurate visually guided reaching and grasping movements. Thus, when one tries to reach out to or grasp a particular object, or even when one contemplates doing so, the visuomotor centers of the parietal lobe become engaged. However, it seems that this activity is not necessary for reaching or grasping per se. Individuals with lesions of the visuomotor centers of the parietal lobe are still able to make these motions. Rather, these neural structures are required for precise and accurate reaching and grasping motions: they are required if the arm and hand are to be flawlessly and effortlessly guided to their target by sight. Because these structures add only precision to things one can try to do whether or not one is particularly precise, they seem to add little of specifically philosophical interest.

Prior Intent

A second source of motivation and inhibition to which I want to draw attention is *prior intent*. Sometimes, motivation or inhibition strikes one without prior deliberation upon the matter: I see my father and am suddenly motivated to give him a hug, though I had not planned it, or I am inhibited from saying anything about his new haircut, though I had not planned to avoid that topic of conversation. On other occasions, however, motivation and inhibition are the product of intentions formed prior to the moment of (in)action. Having heard from my sister that the haircut is not flattering, I have resolved to suppress any urge to comment upon it, and when I see the haircut, I have the urge to comment, but my resolution is activated and the urge suppressed. Or, having considered that we would both enjoy more open displays of affection, I have resolved to hug my father when we next meet, and when we meet, I am thereby moved to give him a hug.

According to common sense, prior intent is typically formed consciously, stored unconsciously, and executed consciously. That is, one typically forms the intention to do or not do something as part of a process of conscious reasoning about what to do, and the feeling that one has settled upon a future course of action is the indication that one has actually formed the intention. The intention then resides somewhere in one's unconscious mind for some length of time— perhaps minutes, perhaps years—until the time to carry out the intention is at hand. Then the intention returns to consciousness, and one is aware that one still intends to do or not do the act in question. Finally, one acts upon one's intention. This account of what is typical is *only* an account of what is typical, however, and there are many variations possible at each stage, according to everyday thought. For instance, intentions can be forgotten because of distraction or the passage of too much time, and so cease to exist without ever being executed. How *exactly* intentions are formed or carried out is a subject about which common sense has little to say. The normal circumstances of their formation and execution are familiar, but not the precise mechanism. Is the formation of an intention itself something one can intend? Is it typically a motivated behavior, or is it something that just happens? Common sense is not a clear guide to such matters. Are intentions always executed through the invocation of trying? Again, there is no widely agreed-upon answer.

A phenomenon very much like conscious, short-term prior intention has been studied in depth by neuroscientists, and depends crucially and selectively upon the proper functioning of the motor regions of the *pre-frontal cortex*, or motor *PFC* (see Goldman-Rakic 1987, 1998 for reviews; see also appendix, fig. 2). The motor PFC stands above the SMA and motor AC at the top of the motor hierarchy, and sends input to them. It, in turn, receives input from many regions of the brain, especially those concerned with representing how things stand in the world. It is thus poised to issue the most complex, context-sensitive motor commands of any motor region of the cortex. What distinguishes the motor commands issued by the motor PFC from the motor commands issued by the SMA or motor AC is not complexity, however. Rather, it is the apparent fact that the commands issued by the former are conditional instructions for future movement. Commands issued by the SMA or motor AC say "Do this!" but activity in the motor PFC is more complex: it holds the capacity to tell the SMA or motor AC to give the order "Do this!"—holding it until some condition has been met. The motor PFC thus appears to give commands of the form "When condition C is met, do this!" This, to at least a first approximation, is the character of a prior intention to do something when the appropriate moment comes.

There are, however, two paradigmatic ways in which one can be moved by a prior intention, and movement produced by the motor PFC corresponds neatly to only one.[9] In the simplest, one decides to do something at some appropriate juncture in the near future, and waits expectantly until the moment arrives to perform the intended action. If I stand in front of a washing machine that is just finishing a wash cycle, intending to open the lid as soon as the machine stops spinning my laundry, I have an intention of this simple sort. Other intentions, the ones that are formed, then ignored, then activated some time later, are more complex, as they involve a storage period. This is the sort of intention I form if I put some laundry in the washing machine and then go back to my apartment and set a timer, intending that I will move the laundry from washer to dryer when the timer rings. Having formed the intention and set the timer, I then cease to think of my intention, and am not in any particular state of readiness to execute it. Instead, I go back to reading a book or grading papers, and only recall my intention when I hear the ring of the timer.

The motor prefrontal cortex appears crucial for the simpler sort of acting on prior intentions. Studies on monkeys have been particularly illuminating in this regard. Typical experiments have trained monkeys to perform tasks such as reaching to a given location, selecting one of two covered food trays or directing eye movements in a given direction, and then monitored the activity of dozens to hundreds of neurons within the motor regions of pre-frontal cortex (KSJ 2000, ch. 38). Under these conditions, it has been found that when the monkeys have been trained to respond immediately to their cues, the pre-frontal cortex is not involved. The pre-frontal cortex only becomes involved when the monkeys receive cues that require a *delayed* response. When a delayed response is required, select groups of motor PFC neurons (a distinct group for each sort of response) become active, and remain active until the time comes for the response to be made. Once the response commences, the neurons cease firing. That is, when the monkey learns what it must do to get a desired reward, specific groups of neurons commence firing, and continue to fire during the delay until the monkey can act, at which point they cease firing. If the relevant neurons have been damaged, the monkeys are selectively impaired in their ability to execute appropriate action after delay. Declarative memory remains intact, as does the ability to respond immediately to stimulation (even in very complex ways), but the ability to see what must be done and hold that thought until the time comes to do it—that ability specifically is destroyed.[10] Similarly, if the motor PFC neurons stop firing before the waiting period is over, then the monkeys do not generally perform the appropriate action once the waiting period ends: they act as though they have forgotten what they were going to do. One natural interpretation of these results is that when the monkeys are cued, they form the intention to reach here, select that food tray, gaze there or the like, and that this intention persists until it is executed or forgotten.

The evidence that the motor PFC is the home of immediate prior intentions is not perfect, however. Human beings with injuries to the PFC display a whole range of disabilities, some of which sit well with the notion of damage to the capacity to maintain intentions over delays, but others of which seem quite distinct. Of course, brain damage is very rarely a precise phenomenon affecting a single functional region of the brain, but there is room for uncertainty here. Further, other regions of PFC appear to be involved in other forms of "working memory," as neuroscientists generally call it, which look quite unlike prior intention (Goldman-Rakic 1987, 1998). For instance, a region of PFC is thought to be involved in maintaining an 'articulatory loop', used when one silently rehearses, say, a phone number over and over before calling it. A corresponding visual loop is also thought to exist. Such structures might be useful for carrying out prior intentions (to call the number one is rehearsing, for instance) but would have to be distinguished from them. Their existence raises the question of whether the neural activity in motor PFC that looks so much like immediate prior intention might not have some other interpretation also, more along the lines of mental rehearsal of a possible action, which would be distinct from prior intention and more in keeping with functions elsewhere in pre-frontal cortex.

With these reservations registered, it can still be said that if any region of the brain is likely to be the home of immediate prior intentions, the motor PFC is it. Matters are rather less clear, however, when one considers other, more complex sorts of intentions that involve the long-term retention of plans, and their execution hours to years after their initial formation. As it happens, no neural structure actively fires at an elevated rate in a high school student who intends to pursue a career as a dental hygienist from the time she forms her intention until the time she gets her first job: the mechanism for sustaining such an intention is thus unlike the mechanism used for short-term prior intent. Unfortunately, exactly how long-term intentions are stored and acted upon is beyond the ken of modern neuroscience, and so nothing more can be added to the topic of prior intention along these lines.

Reward and Punishment

Going on, awareness of possible or actual reward or punishment is a third source of motivation and inhibition. People are motivated to attain rewards, and are inhibited from foregoing them. Likewise, they are inhibited from being punished, and motivated to avoid punishment. This was all described in chapter 2, and is quite straightforward so far as everyday thought is concerned. "Stop that squirming, young man, or I will give you such a smack!" has been a powerful source of inhibition for many a boy, and is just as familiar as the more positively motivational "If you'll help me mix the cake you can lick the beaters when we've finished."

As was also described in chapter 2, rewards and punishments are also commonly thought to have indirect, long-term effects upon behavior through unconscious learning. A child who has trouble sitting still at the dinner table loses the urge to squirm after a long process of rewards for sitting still and punishments for squirming, and so on for the many other sorts of behavioral tendencies one can inculcate in children through reward and punishment. This sort of habit learning is not held to end in childhood, though the habits learned later in life through patterns of reward and punishment are not generally taught by an authority figure, but taught "by life itself," or by a conscious effort of will, or perhaps unconsciously by the behavioral tendencies of those around the individual forming the habit. Examples include the habits (good and bad) one forms as a car driver, habitual manners of washing and dressing, and workday habits such as lunching at a particular deli or clearing out one's accumulated e-mail before doing other things. Common sense also includes smoking as a habit (along with other addictive drug behavior), though it allows for complications here.

In order to discuss how the neural realizer of reward causes movement, it will be convenient to begin by reminding the reader of the structure of the biological reward system. Recall from chapter 2 that the reward system begins with the capacity to represent the obtaining of certain states of affairs, a capacity found in cortical sensory and cognitive systems, and in the hypothalamus. The cortical representations send signals to the orbitofrontal cortex, or OFC, which, in turn, sends signals to the basal ganglia—where signals are sent by the hypothalamus as well. Within the basal ganglia, computations of the difference between expected and actual reward are made, and the result is released as a reward signal via two dopamine-releasing structures, the VTA and SNpc. This reward signal reaches a number of targets, cortical and subcortical, and has a number of effects, though its primary effect is to drive a particular form of learning.

Now that we have reached the subject of motivation, the motivational effects of VTA/SNpc signals can be stressed. Output from the VTA/SNpc affects two sorts of targets with motivational implications: cortical targets responsible for trying and prior intent, and sub-cortical targets in the basal ganglia.

The cortical targets of the VTA/SNpc include the just-described motor anterior cingulate and motor pre-frontal cortex (KSJ 2000, chs. 19 and 45; Crino et al. 1993). The motivational role of dopamine in the motor AC remains unclear, but a little more is known about its motivational use in the motor PFC. Experiments in which the dopamine-releasing cells of the VTA projecting to the motor PFC were destroyed found that this impaired monkeys' abilities to keep a prior intention in mind long enough to execute it after a delay (KSJ 2000, ch. 19). This effect was found to be an immediate one. That is, it did not depend on repeated training events and the long-term effects of dopamine reward signals upon neural connection strengths. Rather, the dopamine reward signal was of direct use in maintaining each given motor intention over time. It has been suggested (Durstewitz et al. 1999) that the primary role of dopamine in the motor PFC is precisely to stabilize its goal-serving motor intentions against interference by other possible motor intentions that would be counter-productive. That is, information about expected reward is used to keep people and other animals like us focused upon our reward-directed intentions, to prevent us forgetting them or going off to do something else before carrying them out. Dopamine released by the VTA to cortical structures may have other immediate motor effects as well, but they have not been studied in any depth as of yet.

Better studied are the effects of dopamine reward signals upon sub-cortical targets in the basal ganglia. While some structures in the basal ganglia are involved in computing and producing a reward signal, as chapter 2 indicated, others are involved in the control of movement, and these are profoundly influenced by reward information. These movement-controlling structures of the basal ganglia are the motor *striatum*,[11] the *globus pallidus*,[12] and the *substantia nigra pars reticulata* (appendix, fig. 1).[13] The striatum receives input from nearly the entire cortex, including all higher representational capacities and all movement-production systems. It also receives reward input from the SNpc, and input from the dorsal raphe nucleus about punishment (if, as chapter 2 speculated, that is the DRN's role). Motor output from the striatum ultimately[14] reaches the globus pallidus and substantia nigra pars reticulata, and these structures powerfully influence[15] all the cortical motor systems: the motor cortex,[16] the SMA, the motor AC, and the motor PFC (KSJ 2000, ch. 43; Mink 1996). Thus, the effects of reward signals (and, presumably, punishment signals) are ultimately influential upon the likely loci of trying and prior intention.

Experimental investigation of the effects of dopamine (the chemical, recall, released by SNpc neurons carrying reward information) upon the motor regions of the striatum has confirmed the importance of reward information to movement. It appears that such dopamine has a "focusing" effect. One important group of neurons in the striatum tend to be inactive, but can be brought close to activation by multiple inputs arriving from cortical regions all at the same time. When dopamine is released upon these neurons, those that are far from activation have their activity further suppressed, while neurons already close to activation have their activity aided by the arrival of dopamine. The net effect is that action-producing tendencies coming through these striatal neurons are enhanced by dopamine when already strong, but suppressed by dopamine when weak (Mink 1996, 2001; Nicola 2000). That is, some actions are made more likely because one is in a context that one associates with the performance of that action, and if the context also produces a reward signal in one, such actions are made more likely still.

There are many more and less subtle demonstrations of the power of reward information to control movement. For instance, in a recent experiment Lauwereyns et al. (2002) monitored the activity of individual neurons in the striatums of two monkeys. These neurons were found both to reflect information about expected reward and to influence the speed with which the monkeys moved in order to obtain the reward: they created a "response bias" toward the action alternative that would produce a reward. Here we have reward information causing neural activity that enhances reward-attaining action. Another example comes from Volkow et al. (1999), in which former cocaine abusers received two injections of a cocaine-like drug. Subjects who reported feeling strong urges to use cocaine had enhanced activation of the motor striatum, while those who did not report such urges did not. Because cocaine-like drugs all act directly upon dopamine transmission, effectively enhancing the reward signal, this experiment also shows the links between reward, motivation, and the motor striatum.

The effect of the reward system upon motivation and inhibition can also be seen if one looks at the consequences of neural damage along the reward system. For instance, damage to the OFC is known to severely disturb normal behavior, in a manner that reflects the role of the OFC in reward (and punishment). Deprived of a well-functioning OFC, people tend to make decisions against their apparent interests, to not learn from their mistakes—even when they are aware that they are making mistakes—and to allow immediate consequences to determine their actions, regardless of intellectually foreseen outcomes (Bechara et al. 1994; Damasio 1994). They do not lose any deliberative capacity, but rather the capacity to be moved to act in light of their deliberations, especially insofar as this involves weighing future costs and benefits. This incapacity is particularly clearly revealed in a well-known study (Bechara et al. 1994). Researchers administered a series of tests to three groups of people: normal controls, subjects with brain damage to the OFC, and subjects with other sorts of brain damage. In these tests, experimental subjects were presented with four decks of cards, and asked to make a total of 100 choices from between these decks, trying to optimize the amount of play money received. Each deck had its own per-card payoff and its own schedule of additional penalties, both of which were revealed to subjects only through play. Two of the decks had high payoffs but even higher penalties, while the other two decks had lower payoffs but even lower penalties, making these latter the only profitable decks from which to select in the long run. No deck had an easily determined payoff structure: subjects were required to rely on their "gut instincts," instincts the OFC is thought to mediate (Damasio 1994; Elliott et al. 2000). It was found that subjects with OFC injuries tended to select from the apparently better-paying but ultimately money-losing decks, while normal subjects and subjects with other forms of brain damage soon learned to select predominantly from the lower-paying but safer decks. Loss of OFC function apparently prevented sufferers from acting upon information about likely rewards and punishments.

The overall power of the reward signal upon movement is perhaps most dramatically illustrated by Parkinson disease and its chemically induced analogues. In Parkinson disease, sufferers lose a very large percentage of the dopamine-releasing cells in the SNpc, cells that project principally to movement-controlling regions in the basal ganglia (KSJ 2000, ch. 43). The result of this loss of reward information is familiar to many: tremor, reduced muscular power, slowness of movement and, in the most extreme cases, absence of spontaneous movement and rigidity. In chemically induced versions of the disease, the destruction of dopamine-releasing neurons is almost complete, and the symptoms are always profound, with sufferers and experimental animals showing a complete absence of voluntary movement (Berridge and Robinson 1998; Langston and Palfreman 1995). Importantly, the dearth of spontaneous movement in sufferers of severe Parkinson disease is a direct effect of the loss of reward signal. Without the reward signal from the SNpc reaching the motor striatum, the motor striatum has a diminished or completely impaired capacity for influencing the production of movement. By default, the motor systems of the basal ganglia powerfully inhibit movement, damping down possible causes of movement in the cortical motor areas. This inhibition is selectively released in response to input to the motor striatum, especially reward input from the SNpc (Mink 1996, 2001). Hence, without reward signals, the motor system of the basal ganglia "thinks" that there is no good reason to release its inhibition of cortical motor systems, and spontaneous action is completely suppressed.

As for punishment, without confidence in the identity of a neural punishment signal it is awkward to ask what role the hypothesized punishment signal has upon the neural levers of motivation and inhibition. If it turns out that serotonin released by the DRN carries a punishment signal, however, then the findings on serotonin's effect upon movement will certainly match expectations, for this effect is powerful and in keeping with what one would expect from a punishment signal. As indicated in chapter 2, increased serotonin levels have been found to increase behavioral inhibition (Engleman et al. 1995), and decreased serotonin levels have been found to decrease inhibition (Higgins et al. 1988; Thiébot and Soubrié 1982; for a review, see Soubrié 1986). It is also interesting in this regard to note the work of Howell et al. (1997), in which it was found that drugs manipulating serotonin could counteract the effects of a drug manipulating dopamine, inhibiting behavior that the dopamine-manipulating drug had stimulated.

Any discussion of the neuroscience of reward and punishment must inevitably lead to a discussion of operant conditioning as well. Dopamine plays a significant role in changing long-term activity dispositions in the striatum (Grove et al. 1995; Suzuki et al. 2001). Given that dopamine carries reward information and changes neural connections elsewhere in the brain in the manner expected of a reward signal (as discussed in chapter 2), it would seem inevitable that dopamine release in the motor striatum implements some form of operant conditioning. In my opinion, this effect has not, as yet, been clearly observed. However, the number of studies claiming to distinguish between a "habit-learning" system in the motor striatum and other forms of learning based elsewhere in the brain is impressive. A number of these studies were already discussed in chapter 2. These were studies in which human subjects with Parkinson disease (hence with impaired reward input to the motor striatum) were unable to learn to perform a trial-and-error learning task, though subjects with anterograde amnesia were unimpaired (Knowlton et al. 1996) and studies on rats in which apparent stimulus-response learning in the motor striatum was distinguished from fact learning elsewhere in the brain (Packard and Teather 1997, 1999; Packard and McGaugh 1992; Packard and White 1991; White 1996, 1997). Given these studies, it is hard to see how else their findings can be explained than by the existence of a habit-learning system in the motor striatum, driven by reward and punishment signals.

The significance of these studies in everyday terms is that they are the best vindication to date of the common sense idea that reward and punishment inculcate unconscious habits. Consciousness of reward and punishment possibilities makes an enormous difference to behavior, certainly. But the findings on implicit or habit learning in the motor striatum go on to give support to the folk idea that rewards and punishments leave behind behavior tendencies that influence us whether we recall their origins or not. If it appears to a parent that rewards and punishments have, over time, slowly taught a child to sit still even when bored, or to say "please" and "thank you," or to always lay the blame on a sibling when something has been broken, then to the extent that this appearance is correct, the parent has observed changes being made in the long-term dispositions of neurons in the motor striatum, changes wrought by reward and punishment signals, it seems. What goes for children goes for adults as well: if, as an adult, I have unconsciously learned to avoid certain arguments because of the rewards and punishments associated with doing so, or if rewards and punishments have unconsciously taught me to always pat my pockets for my keys before leaving the office, then the best explanation available at present is that this habit-learning has been mediated by long-term change in the motor striatum.

On the subject of habit learning, a brief digression should be made to discuss the *cerebellum* (appendix, fig. 1), for it is also involved in forms of learning quite distinct from declarative learning: forms more allied to habit learning, yet needing to be distinguished from them. The primary function of the cerebellum is, apparently, to co-ordinate sequences of movements that other regions of the brain have selected. It does this by learning to emit signals to the motor centers that correct for potential conflicts between the individual movements being sequenced (KSJ 2000, ch. 42). Because of the job performed by the cerebellum, individuals with damaged cerebellums are still able to move, but they move awkwardly. They have a tendency to oscillate between overshooting and undershooting limb movements, they have difficulty maintaining balance, and they are often forced to pause after each isolated movement before going on to the next movement in a sequence. These individuals have "forgotten," and cannot "relearn," how to act smoothly and gracefully.

Putting the terms 'forgotten' and 'relearn' in scare-quotes signifies that these are not failures of declarative memory: there is no failure of knowledge-that in individuals with damage to the cerebellum.[17] Rather, there is a failure of knowledge-how, of procedural, skill-based knowledge and learning. Such learning might be mistaken for reward-driven habit learning, but this is not correct. The cerebellum's learning is driven, it seems, mostly by information about the discrepancy between the intended outcome of a movement and the actual outcome. The cerebellum is self-modifying in a manner that leads it to minimize these differences, to the extent that it can, by modulating the commands issued by the motor cortex and SMA, and by sending commands to the skeletal muscles through brain-stem nerve centers: reward and punishment appear not to enter into the matter. So the cerebellum is engaged in some forms of skill learning, but it learns based on internal representations of intended outcomes, rather than on the basis of rewards and punishments brought about by actions already performed. It is thus of minimal relevance to present discussions, and appears here only in order to avoid possible confusion.

Pleasure and Displeasure

Pleasure and displeasure (especially pain) form a fourth phenomenon widely held to be capable of moving us to action or inaction. If I burn my hand on a hot stove element and am thus moved to pull my hand away, I am moved by the pain I feel, according to everyday thinking. And if I am reluctant to get out of the warm swimming pool and walk through the frigid air leading to the showers, that is probably because the pleasure I now feel and the suffering I anticipate are conspiring to keep me in place. Pleasure and displeasure are motivating in proportion to their intensity, but even when intense they can generally be overridden when the cause is sufficiently good—or if one is sufficiently irrational.

Many undergraduates, and a handful of philosophers, endorse *psychological hedonism*, the claim that the only ultimate source of motivation or inhibition is the quest for pleasure (and flight from displeasure). But common sense itself is highly pluralistic about motivation and inhibition, and does not share this reductionistic enthusiasm. That said, common sense does consider pleasure and displeasure to be powerful and common sources of motivation.

One interesting feature of pleasure and displeasure is that, even when intense, they can have varying motivational effects. As discussed in chapter 3, there are sources of pleasure that are exciting and invigorating: these leave one jumping up and down with enthusiasm, bursting with energy, ready to tackle the world; there are also sources of pleasure that are soothing and relaxing: they encourage one to wallow in the moment, to rest content. The pleasure of winning a prize in a lottery is typically of the former sort, while the pleasure of a massage is of the latter sort. Some sources of pleasure, like sexual activity, contain both: foreplay and direct sexual contact are often found to be stimulating, arousing, energizing, and so on, while orgasm is found to be a source of contentment and relaxation. The same can be said for sources of displeasure. As a result, the exact connection between hedonic tone and motivation is far from clear to everyday thought.

It is something of a surprise to find that neuroscience has documented very few strong links between pleasure and motivation. Recall from chapter 3 that the neural seat of pleasure and displeasure is found in the perigenual region of the anterior cingulate, or PGAC. Recalling also that there is a very important motor region in the anterior cingulate, the reader might naturally have drawn the conclusion that pleasure and displeasure have a powerful influence over motivation through dense connections between these two regions. However, such connections are sparse (Devinsky, Morrell, and Vogt 1995), and it appears that the influence of pleasure and displeasure upon motivation is generally more indirect.

The anatomical findings are supported by the existence of individuals with surgical or accidental damage restricted to the PGAC, who remain functional and goal-directed. Recall the findings of Foltz and White (1962), described in chapter 1, upon patients receiving cingulumotomies. In their words, "It must be accepted that these patients are changed persons after the cingulumotomy, but the change is indeed subtle." Patients no longer capable of being "distressed" or "bothered" by their experiences are found to be "less precipitously reactive" to their environment, but this decline in reactivity does not strip them of the ability to go about their lives autonomously, engaging in diverse activities. Compare this degree of behavioral change to that found in individuals whose reward systems are lesioned, either partially (as with the loss of the OFC) or totally (as with loss of all dopamine-releasing neurons in severe Parkinson disease).

Further weakness in the link between pleasure and motivation is demonstrated by a series of experiments conducted by Kent Berridge and colleagues, in which motivation is manipulated without manipulating pleasure or displeasure. The Berridge and Robinson (1998) survey article mentioned earlier and in chapter 3, which described the devastating effect upon movement of chemical lesions to the reward system, also attempted to measure the hedonic impact of these same lesions. Measurements of facial reactions to food[18] indicated that the capacity for pleasure remained intact in the experimental animals. The apparent conclusion: that insofar as pleasure has influence upon movement, this influence is mediated by the dopamine-releasing system and does not stem directly from the pleasure itself.

Another, subtler experiment conducted by Wyvell and Berridge (2000) also points to the same conclusion. In this latter experiment, rats were trained to press one of two levers for sugar pellets, and independently allowed to learn that a light indicated that sugar pellets were freely available. Then the same rats were allowed access to the levers again, sometimes with the light on, sometimes with it off, but this time no pellets were dispensed, however much the rats might push either lever. Under these conditions, rats would push both levers for a while, though they favored the lever previously associated with the release of sugar pellets. Adding minute quantities of amphetamine to the nucleus accumbens of these rats (amphetamine being a drug that mimics reward signals in the nucleus accumbens) proved to powerfully increase their motivation to push the lever previously associated with sugar pellets, so long as the sugar-associated light was also on. Yet taste-reactivity measures found that the rats thus manipulated had no changes in their hedonic dispositions. They did not like the taste of sugar better as a result of the amphetamine stimulation. On the contrary, there was a slight suggestion that, if anything had changed, they found it slightly less pleasing. They had thus become powerfully motivated to do something they had only been modestly motivated to do previously, and this change in motivated behavior was independent of changes in hedonic tone.

One other study, this by Berridge and Valenstein (1991), is especially worth mentioning. In this study, once more, a dissociation between pleasure and motivation was observed. Berridge and Valenstein investigated a well-known neuroscientific phenomenon, that of eager eating in rats receiving electrical stimulation of the lateral hypothalamus. It had generally been assumed that such eating was the product of powerful pleasure provided to the rat by stimulation of the lateral hypothalamus, for such stimulation was known to be something rats would generally work to cause in themselves. However, by observing rat facial reactions, Berridge and Valenstein came to the opposite conclusion: their rats were eating eagerly in spite of *dis*liking their food. They were eating, but simultaneously making gapes, tongue movements and head shakes characteristic of rats consuming very bitter, disliked substances. The experimental manipulation of the rats was somehow powerfully motivating the rats to eat, but this motivation flew in the face of pronounced displeasure on the rat's part in eating.

In spite of all these studies, no neuroscientist claims that pleasure and displeasure have no influence at all upon motivation. No doubt there is some route or other from pleasure to action. For instance, activity in the PGAC no doubt influences the movement centers of the basal ganglia directly, just as almost all cortical centers do, and no doubt contributes to the release of reward or punishment signals, which (as we have seen) strongly influence motivation. Furthermore, the PGAC may send some of its output to centers such as the motor PFC and motor striatum which, in turn, influence motivation more powerfully. That is, pleasure and displeasure may have effects upon motivation through the same channels that the other sense modalities use to exert influence upon motivation. But there appears to be little room for pleasure and displeasure to exert a particularly privileged form of control over motivation.

Desire

Finally, motivation and inhibition are supplied by *desiring*. If I want to see the world, that might motivate me to visit Cuba. It might also inhibit me from spending all my money on fine French chocolate. And, in fact, common sense generally holds that if there is motivation or inhibition to be explained, desires are a good place to turn. If I am motivated to visit Cuba, surely it is because I want to, and if I refrain from buying the best chocolate money can buy, it is surely because I do not want to spend my money that way. Common sense thus links desire and motivation very tightly together, which is a considerable part of the appeal of the standard theory of desire (as discussed in chapter 1).

Just as desiring moves us to act, it also moves us to try, and to form intentions, according to everyday thought. "What are you doing?" asks mother. "Trying to make my eyes cross," comes the answer from daughter. Mother's next natural question will be, "Why are you trying to do *that*?" She will demand, though perhaps not expect, an answer in terms of desires: in terms of what the child wants to accomplish. Similarly, it is expected that if Helena intends to travel to Regina, there will be something she wants to do by carrying out her intention.

Common sense reserves a prominent place for desire in its explanations of motivation and inhibition, but it once again displays its aversion to reductionism, holding that desire is not the only source of motivation or inhibition. If I promise to call the dentist at nine o'clock, it might be the last thing I want to do, yet I might call her anyway, says common sense. If I put on my casual shoes on the way to a formal affair, it might be out of sheer habit, and not out of a desire to dress down. If I sit down and plan to take one route to the airport, and then later change my mind, I might still end up taking the first, intended route, even though I don't want to go that way any longer, simply because I "was on autopilot" and carried out my prior intention. If I am in a war, I might want to run away from the heavy machine gun fire, but be inhibited from doing so because of my training. Common sense sees such examples as genuine exceptions to the main pattern, but relative rarities: the main pattern is the *main* pattern, after all.

What does neuroscience say about desire and motivation? There are, at present, three candidate answers. Arbitrating between the three candidate answers is not a task to be performed in a paragraph or two; it will be the topic of the next section. Even then, matters will not be fully resolved until the end of this work, for when the very nature of desire is under discussion, the connection between desire and motion cannot be definitively described in an independent fashion. But we are now at the point at which a reasonably fair assessment can be made of the main theories linking desire and motivation.

2. Three Theories

The previous section has provided a wealth of data upon which to draw. Now the time has come for theoretical conclusions. This section considers the various advantages and disadvantages presented by the standard theory of desire, the hedonic theory, and the reward theory as theories explaining how desires motivate.

The Standard Theory of Desire

The theory of desire best able to explain movement would seem to be the standard theory. Common sense holds that behind most motivated behavior (and inhibition of behavior) lies an intrinsic desire that would appear to be served by the behavior. What simpler and more elegant explanation of this fact could there be than to hold that to desire simply *is* to be motivated?

Unfortunately for the standard theory, there is a serious problem that arises once one looks into the details of movement production. The problem does not amount to outright refutation, but it should certainly give the standard theorist pause. The problem is simply that there are complex psychological causes of well-organized movement that appear not to be desires.

Back in chapter 1, I suggested that trying and intending, though tending to cause the realization of their contents, might not be reducible to desiring. I also suggested that certain attitudes, such as the thought of stuttering, tend to cause the realization of their contents without involving desires that their contents be realized. Both sorts of examples threatened to show that motivation to bring it about that *P* does not suffice for desiring that *P*. The objection from trying and intending is not one I will pursue here, for it requires substantive discussion about the precise nature of trying and intending, and this would take us far afield. But the objection from movements brought about in the absence of any pro-attitude whatsoever is simpler to treat, and in fact can be given a proper discussion now that we have a reasonable understanding of how bodily movements are produced.

Consider the phenomenon of Tourette syndrome. Tourette syndrome is a disorder in which the sufferer is subject to frequent tics, which consist in "rapid, recurrent, non-rhythmic, stereotyped motor movement[s] or vocalisation[s]."[19] That is, a person with Tourette syndrome will rapidly and repeatedly touch nearby objects or people, bark, grunt, cough, or utter whole words, twitch, blink, mimic others' facial expressions, throw objects, or engage in other, similar behaviors in an intermittent fashion while awake.[20] The popular image of a person with Tourette syndrome is of a person who has uncontrollable urges to shout "shit!" or "fuck!" in public. While this is a rather crude image, it is not invention: such tics are not uncommon. The subjective experience of Tourette syndrome is typically an experience of having muscular tension, or an urge, which the Tourettic individual finds unpleasant, and which he or she knows can be relieved by ticcing. These urges are sometimes brought on by thoughts or sensations the individual has, sometimes by no apparent stimulus. The individual then either tics "voluntarily" (subjectively choosing to tic in order to relieve the urge) or "involuntarily" (subjectively being overwhelmed by the urge and forced to tic). Ticcing that feels voluntary in response to the felt abnormal urge is apparently common among Tourettic individuals, but typically a voluntary refusal to tic will cause the felt tension or urge to build until it is intolerable, or until it bursts out on its own, and so there is a limit to how voluntary one can consider such movements to be (Cohen and Leckman 1992; Leckman et al. 1993).

Particularly interesting at present are instances in which Tourettic individuals have a thought with the content that *P*, perhaps one of saying "shit!" in some context, and come to have a Tourettic urge to bring it about that *P* as a result. Prima facie, such instances present counterexamples to the standard theory's claim that to desire is to be moved (perhaps by a representation that *P*) to bring it about that *P*, for they apparently present instances in which individuals are moved, in a very basic way, to say "shit!" without desiring to do so, or having *any* pro attitude toward saying "shit!" which might serve as an ultimate justification for doing so. Phenomenologically, it is true that Tourettic individuals often feel that they tic as a means to an end, the end of discharging a troublesome urge. But on other occasions, they experience the urge as causing them to act in spite of themselves, and there is no apparent instrumentality to the tic on such occasions. Furthermore, it seems implausible that the urge to say "shit!" or similar urges are manifestations of intrinsic desires to say "shit!" on the part of Tourettic individuals. Generally, this is exactly what they desire not to do, but are moved to do anyway. Tics of this sort are thus like episodes of stuttering brought on by the thought that one is going to stutter: they pose an apparent counterexample to the standard theory of desire.

It remains open for the defender of the standard theory to dismiss the phenomenology and say that the production of tics, stuttering and the like, though mysterious, will ultimately prove to be explicable in terms of desires, thus saving the theory. This argumentative option has so far remained open precisely because philosophers have remained ignorant of how such movements are produced. The best existing theory of Tourette syndrome, however, suggests a powerful case against the standard theory.

Responsibility for Tourette syndrome appears to lie with a biological disorder of the motor striatum (Mink 2001; Peterson et al. 1998). The exact problem in the motor striatum remains to be determined, but its outlines are clear. The basal ganglia, by default, suppress possible motor instructions, unless powerful input is received simultaneously from cortical and sub-cortical sources, both of which contribute to the same action. The basal ganglia then selectively release inhibition against that action. But in Tourette syndrome, the motor striatum does not play its role within the basal ganglia successfully, and motor instructions that would normally be suppressed manage to be promoted to actions without the normal confluence of cortical and sub-cortical input. That is, representations of the world, that normally give rise to all sorts of weak movement tendencies suppressed by the basal ganglia, instead give rise to movement tendencies that are not suppressed, which build and build until the Tourettic individual practically explodes with the urge to perform the tic. Thinking that a particularly unattractive piece of pottery is "a piece of shit" may cause weak activity in the motor system preparatory for expressing such a thought in normal people, preparatory activity so weak that it is suppressed by default; in a Tourettic individual who says "shit!" as a tic, this weak activity might not be so readily suppressed, and become a powerful urge to say "shit!"

If this account of Tourette syndrome is correct, it poses a further problem for the standard theorist who holds that real desires are, somehow, involved in Tourettic urges. Tourettic individuals have urges, true enough, but these urges are different in kind from other motivating urges people have. Normal motivation is a two-factor process, with input about the state of the world and input about reward meeting in the motor striatum, and activity in the motor striatum selecting from among possible movements. The mechanism by which urges to tic are produced appears to ignore reward information, and the Tourettic individual's striatum does not freely select from among possible movements: during an urge to tic, one possible movement is constantly thrust upon the action-selection mechanism, sometimes bursting through to cause movement in spite of the individual's best efforts. This difference in kind between normal motivation and Tourettic motivation strongly suggests that the term 'desire' cannot be appropriate for the source of both. Desires should form a coherent psychological kind, but the neural details reveal what phenomenology suggests, that Tourettic urges and normal desires are very different. Yet, because Tourettic individuals can sometimes be moved to bring it about that P by entertaining the thought that P, the standard theory appears required to say that Tourettic individuals intrinsically desire to perform their tics. This seems a serious fault of the theory.

It is open to the standard theorist to respond by holding that desiring is not being motivated in any old way, but being motivated in a very specific way: being motivated to bring it about that P via reward or punishment information. Such a theory of desire is no longer a pure motivational theory of desire, however, but a combined motivational/reward theory, and so does not so much save the standard theory as transform it into something else. The advantages and disadvantages of such hybrid theories are taken up in chapter 6. For the moment, it will suffice to note that they do not save the standard theory as such from the criticism leveled against it.

The Hedonic Theory of Desire

As we saw in chapter 1, the most promising form for a hedonic theory of desire is something like the view that to desire that P is to be disposed to pleasure if it seems to be the case that P. What connection is there between the ground of this disposition in normal human beings and the ground of motivated movement? At first glance, it appears that there is very little connection. If activity of the biological reward system is the normal cause of pleasure, then the ground of a disposition to be pleased involves the reward system. In particular, it will involve the portion of the reward system running from representation of the world, through to the production of a reward signal, through to the production of pleasure. But this portion of the reward system and its connection to felt pleasure and displeasure is not the portion that influences movement. It is connections from the reward system to the motor striatum (which is not itself connected to the PGAC) and to the motor PFC and motor AC that have a direct impact upon movement, and it is the long-term changes wrought by these connections that have an indirect impact upon movement. The pathway from reward to pleasure is a different pathway. So the ground of dispositions to pleasure will itself have no impact upon movement, not even indirectly.

Yet pleasure itself, as opposed to its immediate biological trigger, clearly has some sort of effect upon movement, as do thoughts of pleasure. If pleasure is the nature of desire, then this will have to be enough of a connection between movement and desire. It will have to be enough that desire, through instances of pleasure, contributes to the production of a reward signal, and so contributes to movement. Or it will have to be enough that desire has some modest influence upon activity in the motor AC, with aversions reining in some commands the motor AC might issue, and appetitive desires pushing other commands to the fore. Or it will have to be enough that desires sometimes contribute to the context-setting signal sent to the motor striatum, to which the reward signal is added to produce movement. Or, if the hedonic theorist is lucky, all three roles will be played by desires in producing movement.

Even if desire plays all three of these roles, however, it will still be the case that desire plays a very undistinguished role in movement production. If the hedonic theory is correct, then desire is on a par with representations of sweet tastes, representations of tissue damage, representations of readily available money, and so on. For all of these representations, like pleasure itself, have the capacity to influence movement through sending their output to the reward system and to the motor striatum. It is true that these representations do not, as pleasure may, have the capacity to influence activity in the motor AC directly, and the motor AC is clearly very important to the initiation of movements. But since whatever direct connection exists between the PGAC and the motor AC appears to be weak, there remains relatively little to distinguish movements made on the basis of desire from those made on some other basis. The experiments of Kent Berridge and his colleagues confirm this: pleasure and displeasure can readily be outweighed by other influences upon motivation in experimental contexts. If pleasure is the essence of desire, then desire is a weak motivational force indeed. Furthermore, if the hedonic theory is correct, desires only play a role in motivation when people are pleased or displeased. When people are neither pleased nor displeased, desires are motivationally idle. Phenomenologically, however, a neutral hedonic tone seems not uncommon, and quite compatible with ongoing action. When I shave in the morning, for instance, I am not typically aware of any particular pleasure or displeasure, yet I am moved to shave nonetheless, moving my body in quite complex ways. If this phenomenology is accurate, then it is not uncommon to be in a state in which one's movements are indifferent to one's desires.

Desires are widely thought to be the cause of most normal actions. The hedonic theory of desire, however, is forced to give desire a much more diminished role in its account of action production. This, I think, is a serious blow against the hedonic theory. It might be true that there are important psychological sources of everyday motivation other than desire. Perhaps moral considerations are such sources. But when one is moved to act by the availability of something sweet, or by the opportunity to earn five dollars, one expects to hear that one has been motivated by one's desires, not by some special, distinct phenomenon. The hedonic theory, however, appears forced to claim that representations of such opportunities motivate in the same way that desires motivate, while being distinct from desires. This is a very odd claim to be forced to make, to say the least.

The Reward Theory of Desire

The reward theory of desire proves to be the most promising of the three for explaining motivation and inhibition. To show this, I will begin by describing the mechanism linking reward to motivation in detail, then go on to show how this mechanism lacks the flaws of the standard and hedonic theories, mentioning further virtues along the way.

If reward is the essence of desire, then desire moves us via reward and, presumably, punishment signals. Initially, there are representations of the world as hot or cold, having a surface here, a footfall there, containing a person saying "you may be seated," or the like. The output of these representations converges on the motor PFC, which, in turn, excites other structures lower in the motor hierarchy (the motor AC, SMA, and motor cortex). But these excitations on their own do not lead to movement. They simply create possibilities for movement. Before movement can happen, these same representations of the world must send their input to two more destinations: the motor striatum and the reward system. The reward system uses this input to determine if the environment contains a better than expected reward, an expected reward, or a worse than expected reward: to determine how well the organism's intrinsic desires are being satisfied, according to this theory. Having done so, it releases its own signal to the motor striatum and selected cortical targets (in particular, the motor PFC and motor AC). Information about how things stand and about reward (which, on the reward theory of desire, amounts to information about desire satisfaction) meets in the motor striatum, which then uses this input, along with its existing intrinsic connections, to determine which possible movements to release from ongoing inhibition. Released from inhibition, the cortical motor centers issue commands to the body, and the movement is made. Thus, is if reward is the essence of desire, then desire moves us through determining what is a reward, and so determining what input will be sent by the reward system to the motor striatum, tipping the balance in favor of this movement or that.

Desire also gets an opportunity to influence movement through habit, if reward is the essence of desire. Having intrinsic desires opens one to neural learning driven by reward and punishment signals in the brain, and one form of such learning is habit learning. Such habit learning is at least part of what makes given inputs to the motor striatum lead to given outputs, on at least some occasions, and perhaps on every occasion (though this is probably too Skinnerian to be true). Desires are thus involved both in determining what input the motor striatum receives (by determining the reward signal) and in determining what output a given input will produce from the motor striatum (by modifying the motor striatum's intrinsic properties). This role for desire in controlling movement indirectly, by controlling what input will lead to what output, was the main role envisioned for desire in the work of Fred Dretske (1988), who stands out as the lone philosopher to have championed reward as an important aspect of desire.

Against the standard theory of desire, the reward theory has the virtue of not counting every goal-directed urge as a desire. Tourettic urges, in particular, appear not to depend upon deviant input from the reward system (Mink 2001), and so do not stem from deviant desires, according to the reward theory.

Against the hedonic theory of desire, the reward theory has a virtue at the same point the hedonic theory has its greatest fault. If the hedonic theory of desire is correct, then desires and representations of money, say, motivate similarly and independently. But the motivational force of representations of money is not independent of the motivational force of reward signals, but is *mediated* by the motivational force of reward signals. And, Tourettic impulses and the like aside, every representational capacity (including pleasure and displeasure) has its motivational force mediated in just the same way. If reward is the essence of desire, then the fact that both representations of money and pleasure lead to reward signals entails that both money and pleasure are desired, and so the unique link between desire and motivation is kept, whereas it is lost by the hedonic theory. It can also be noted that while the loss of hedonic capacities only partially impairs motivation, the loss of reward input to the motor striatum causes the most severe symptom of Parkinson disease, total loss of voluntary movement. A neural system can hardly have a more powerful influence upon motivation! This loss of voluntary movement is just what one would expect when desires are severed from their action-producing role.

It can also be pointed out that, while the hedonic theory struggles to explain how desire can influence motivation even while no pleasure or displeasure is being felt, the reward theory has no such struggle to explain how desire can influence motivation in the absence of a positive or negative reward signal. Parkinson disease demonstrates that even a neutral reward signal, indicating that desire fulfillment is as expected, is a substantial contribution to movement production.

Finally, an interesting feature of the reward theory is that it connects to the familiar philosophical claim that goal-directed movement is normally the product of some belief-like cognitive state and desire, while modifying it. According to the reward theory, there are two distinct types of information reaching the motor striatum, releasing possible movements. The first sort of input is information about how things stand in the world: perceptual representations, higher order representations, information about the movements one is making at present, and the like. The second is information about one's desires. These two streams of information must meet in order for movement production to go on normally in the brain, according to the reward theory. If the reader was already well-disposed to the philosophical claim—as many philosophers and others have thought since antiquity—this is a virtue. If not, it is at least a challenge: for it is plain that the reward signal is a crucial part of normal action production, and if that signal does not bear information about what an individual intrinsically desires, then it bears information about something else, and the philosopher who doubts that beliefs generally meet desires in the production of movement will have to say what it is that beliefs *do* meet, in the guise of reward information, if not desires.

Summary

Once again, it appears that the reward theory of desire emerges as the strongest of the three theories under consideration. Though as usual the considerations advanced are not decisive, they are, also as usual, substantial on their own.

5

Desire and Aversion

The time has come to stop enumerating faces of desire. Desires are connected in many ways to many different phenomena, each with some claim to being called a face, and if philosophy were physiognomy, I would not be stopping at three. But there are only two historically important candidates for the nature of desire, and only one new contender on offer, and three is an elegant number. And in any case, the time has come to gain some perspective on all the detail and present a unifying framework.

Desire's best-known face, motivation, seems to stem from the brain's reward system. Desire's other well-known face, pleasure, seems to represent the activity of the reward system. And desire's neglected face, reward, is constituted by the activity of the reward system. Consideration of each face has suggested that reward is the primary face of desire. The time has thus come to produce a detailed theory. Such a theory was given the briefest sketch in chapter 1; in this chapter, that sketch is fleshed out in full.

1. The Nature of Desire

There being no time like the present, this chapter begins with a statement of a reward theory of desire.

> **Reward Theory of Desire (RTD):** To have an intrinsic (positive) desire that P is to use the capacity to perceptually or cognitively represent that P to constitute P as a reward. To be averse to it being the case that P is to use the capacity to perceptually or cognitively represent that P to constitute P as a punishment.
>
> RTD has many features, all of which will bear explanation, and this section will make them clear.

To begin: as always, this is a theory of intrinsic desire. That is, it is a theory of what it is to desire, say, that my father be happy, that my favorite team win the tournament, that I not smell the odors from the cat litter, and so on: to desire things for their own sakes. It is not a theory of what it is to desire things merely as a means to some end, not a theory of desiring to take the bus today in order to benefit the environment, say, or of desiring to smell the cat litter in order to determine how urgently it needs cleaning. Later I will have a little to say about instrumental desire, but it is not the aim of RTD to say what instrumental desire is. Intrinsic desire will be desire enough.

Also as usual, the term 'desire' is meant in a broad but not limitlessly broad sense, encompassing things naturally thought of as wishes, wants, goals, desires, ends, and so on, but not intentions, plans, episodes of trying, or beliefs about what is good. In particular, 'desire' is meant to include wishes about how the past might have been as well as desires for the present and future, and to include sensuous along with intellectual goals.

Beyond these obvious starting points, the most salient feature of RTD is that it distinguishes between (positive) desires and (negative) aversions. The terms are not ideal—natural language is not particularly precise at this point—but the phenomena they are meant to designate are real enough. Both are forms of what philosophers generally call 'desire', but they are theoretically distinguished from one another in that (positive) desire opens one to being rewarded if the content is satisfied, while (negative) aversion opens one to being punished if the content is satisfied. In making this distinction, RTD follows a distinction made by common sense, though neglected by philosophers (perhaps because the terminology in which it is expressed is so imprecise). As argued in chapter 1, being averse to something—say, to Adam's lateness—is not the same as having a positive desire or appetite for its contrary—say, that Adam be on time. A person who positively desires Adam's timeliness is prone to delight when he is unexpectedly on time, while a person who is simply averse to Adam's lateness will more typically be relieved, not delighted, by such events. Aversion sets one up for anxiety or relief; positive desire makes possible joy or disappointment. RTD not only incorporates but also helps to explain the distinction, for a parallel and underpinning distinction exists in the nature of reward. Theories of reward distinguish between a positive reward (an intuitive reward), a negative reward (a non-occurrence of an expected punishment), a positive punishment (an intuitive punishment), and a negative punishment (a non-occurrence of an expected reward). Biologically, the same distinctions can be drawn: Wolfram Schultz and his colleagues have observed the VTA/SNpc release both positive reward signals (increased dopamine in response to an intuitive reward) and negative punishment signals (decreased dopamine in response to the failure of an expected reward to appear). Positive punishment and negative reward would involve a distinct mechanism, using a different chemical signal.[1] Because reward and salient absence of reward trigger one biological system, while punishment and salient absence of punishment are expected to trigger a different one, they can have different phenomenological and behavioral effects, thus giving rise to the everyday distinction between types of desires.

Going on, RTD invokes the notion of perceptual or cognitive representations. It is from these representations, or, more carefully, these representational capacities, that desires get their contents. A desire that justice be served is an entity that involves, as a part, the capacity to perceptually or cognitively represent that justice is being served, and it is from the content of this representation that the desire acquires its content. These representational contents may run the gamut from representations that my mouth contains a very salty substance through representations that a face is before me at a certain location in space and on to representations that it is impossible to travel faster than the speed of light. That is, the representations involved in desire, and so the contents of desires, may, according to RTD, be of any degree of abstraction or concreteness, and found anywhere from basic perceptual systems to the most abstract reasoning centers the human brain has to offer.

An advantage RTD receives from having desire contents derived from perceptual and cognitive contents is that it explains one interesting symmetry, and another asymmetry, between desires and perception/cognition. The symmetry is the fact that the possible contents of my perceptions and beliefs are identical to the possible contents of my desires. Whatever I can perceive or conceive, I can want, and whatever I can want, I can perceive or conceive. If the contents of beliefs and desires were independent, this would be a somewhat mysterious fact. But given RTD, this fact can be derived from the nature of desire. The asymmetry explained by RTD is the fact that, while we can comfortably imagine a creature able to conceive but not desire (a "thinking machine" or a purely contemplative god, say), we cannot equally imagine a creature able to desire but not conceive. Intuition rebels at the latter: if the creature could not conceive of justice, say, what would enable its desire to be a desire specifically for *justice*? If RTD is right, then perhaps mental representation can exist in the absence of desire (if, as might seem reasonable, mental representation can exist in the absence of reward and punishment signals), but desire cannot exist in the absence of mental representation.

It might be worrying that RTD does not allow for objectless desires. Objectless longing is a not unfamiliar experience: must it be dismissed by RTD? In a sense it must, just as it must be dismissed by other familiar philosophical theories of desire. All desires are desires that *P* according to these theories, and so if objectless longing is to be construed as a desire that *P* for no *P* at all, there can be no such thing. But RTD allows for objectless desires in at least two weaker senses of the phrase. There can be desires whose effects are felt, either by the restlessness they create or by the felt dissatisfaction they produce, whose contents are unknown to us.[2] These are apparently objectless desires, desires whose objects are obscure to us. Then there can be feelings of dissatisfaction produced in the absence of any apparently unsatisfied desire: illusory displeasure, making one feel as though one's desires are less well satisfied though one has not received any new information about desire satisfaction that would justify such a feeling. In this case, the objectlessness is real but it is not the desire that is objectless, but the feeling. These could be called 'objectless apparent desires'. Between these two phenomena, RTD can account for everything common sense takes so-called objectless desires to amount to.

The fact that desires include perceptual and cognitive representations as proper parts is likely to strike many as confusing. Does this mean that every time one perceives a pie one also desires it? Does it mean that one cannot desire the well-being of a child without thinking of that child's well-being? No. According to the theory, desires need not involve tokened representations, need not involve actual episodes of representing pies or well-being. Rather, to desire is to be so organized that tokened representations of pie or well-being, if they occur, will contribute to the production of reward signals. The desire exists whether the representations are being tokened or not. This is why RTD requires a link between representational *capacities* and reward signals, rather than a link between occurrent representations and reward signals. Thus it is also possible for RTD to explain the commonplace fact that people who are asleep, anesthetized, and the like still have desires. Although such people may not be representing anything at the moment, they are all constructed so that, were they to represent certain states of affairs, this representation would contribute to the production of a reward or punishment signal.

It should be said that the term 'representation' itself is not meant with great seriousness. RTD is not committed to the view of mental representation found in the works of, say, Dretske (1988, 1995), Fodor (1990, 1998), or Millikan (1984, 1993). All that is required for something to be counted as a perceptual or cognitive representation, so far as RTD is concerned, is that it be a content-bearing thing, making up some perceptual or cognitive attitude, localized in or distributed through some perceptual or cognitive center of the brain, capable of passing output to the reward system. These minimal requirements are not completely empty, note: the accounts of the mind given by Brandom (1994) and Sellars (1963), for example, are not compatible with RTD, for they do not allow one to see perceptual episodes or beliefs as located in the brain or as causally interacting with the brain's reward system. But philosophers who hold that the brain's perceptual systems involve genuine mental contents while preferring not to call such contents 'representations', for example, are welcome to make their preferred terminological adjustments to RTD; this much is a matter of indifference to the theory.

The feature of RTD in most need of explanation is what it is to constitute something as a reward or a punishment, but fortunately chapter 2 has already prepared the ground. To summarize: to constitute something as a reward or a punishment is to use a representation of it to drive the production of a reward or punishment signal. Reward and punishment signals, in turn, are to be understood in terms of learning theory. A reward signal is an event that causes a characteristic, mathematically describable form of learning, and a punishment signal is an event that causes an opposing form of learning. And, as explained in chapter 2, this is learning in a very specific sense: it is a change in the connectivities of units that are themselves describable at an appropriately abstract level. These units are neurons in the case of creatures like us, and their form of connection is very specific to their biological character, but nothing in the nature of learning theory forbids the existence of very different, even inorganic, units playing the roles that neurons play in us. Hence, if something is a causal system that is mathematically describable as instantiating contingency-based learning, then it is the site of such learning. The events that trigger one form of causal change, modeled as one form of learning (strengthened connectivities), are the reward signals; the events triggering the opposing form of causal change (weakened connectivities) are the punishment signals. If there are representational events that characteristically contribute to the production of the reward-signal-type causal events, then the represented states of affairs are rewards; if there are representational events that contribute to punishment-signal-type causal events, then the states of affairs represented are punishments.[3]

Given the way that constituting something as a reward or punishment has been treated, certain questions remain unanswered. For instance, suppose that a physical system could be modeled as implementing reward-based learning but not punishment-based learning, or vice versa. Would that system count as implementing contingency-based learning, and so as constituting states of affairs as rewards or punishments? I see no reason in principle to say no. There could be creatures who had only (positive) desires and no aversions. There could also be creatures (oh, unhappy creatures!) who had only aversions, but no (positive) desires. Such creatures would have phenomenological and behavioral lives quite different from our own, and no doubt would be worse fitted for life in our sort of environment than we are. But conceptually there seems to be no bar to the idea of having one sort of desire without the other, and mathematically there seems no bar to the idea of grouping a select family of distinct but related learning algorithms under the heading of contingency-based learning.

A rather different set of questions about constituting things as rewards or punishments has also been left open. I have given a functional-role account of what it is to constitute something as a reward or punishment. So long as a causal system is well modeled by the mathematics of contingency-based learning theory, that causal system counts as emitting reward and punishment signals. This invites questions about how precisely the causal system must fit the mathematical model in order to count as implementing learning. Suppose that there is a not-quite-perfect fit between causal system and model: what then? What about a worse but still recognizable fit? Suppose that typically there is a perfect fit between the two, but that when the causal system gets roaring drunk there is a less perfect fit between them. Suppose that a causal system fitting the model perfectly were changed, one atom at a time, into a causal system bearing no relation to the model of contingency-based learning. At what point would it cease to be a learning system?

These are hard questions. Some, such as the last question, may be based upon an unreasonable demand that the property of desiring that *P* be somehow more precise than the property of being bald, or the property of being a heap of sand. (Or perhaps the unreasonable demand is that a philosopher of mind solve the problem of vagueness en passant.) But the others seem to merit some sort of answer. Unfortunately, I am no more able to solve the technical problems of functional-role theories for the case of desire in particular than other philosophers have been able to solve these problems for functional-role theories of mentality in general. I can only say that my intent was that a physical system need not be an exact fit to a learning algorithm in order to count as a learning system: it need only be close *enough*. And the border between a physical system that learns and one that does not is one I expect to be like the border between heaps and non-heaps, whatever exactly that border looks like. This is not much of an answer, admittedly, but I am afraid that I see no way to do better. In section 2 I will return to a very specific instance of these sorts of questions and give a more concrete answer; this will have to suffice in place of general principles.

Some philosophers will be tempted to replace my causal-role theory of reward learning, and so of (an essential component of) desire, with a teleological-role theory. Millikan's (1984, 1993) account of pro attitudes, for instance, takes just such a position. According to Millikan, to be an "imperative icon," as she calls the pro attitudes, is not to be a content-bearer playing a certain causal role, but to be a content-bearer the uptake of which has the biological function of playing a certain role. Following suit, one could hold a version of RTD that replaces causal roles with biological functions.

> **RTD***: To have an intrinsic (positive) desire that *P* is to embed the capacity to perceptually or cognitively represent that *P* in a system, the biological function of which is to constitute *P* as a reward. To be averse to it being the case that *P* is to embed the capacity to perceptually or cognitively represent that *P* in a system, the biological function of which is to constitute *P* as a punishment.

RTD* may have certain virtues over RTD regarding issues of demarcation. For instance, in situations in which a learning system is temporarily prevented from executing its learning algorithm (say, by the introduction of some reward-blocking chemical agent to the system), it remains clear that the learning system retains its biological function, even though it is prevented from fulfilling it. My heart, after all, has the function of pumping my blood even when I am having a heart attack: that is what makes a heart attack a failure of function (or so teleological philosophers of mind will argue). Since it does seem plausible that a brief interruption in the operation of my desires does not briefly rid me of my desires, but only interferes with their operation, the fact that RTD* allows this conclusion is a point in its favor. However, RTD* also reaches less intuitive conclusions when one considers extreme failures of functionality. A heart as full of holes as a sponge still has the function of pumping blood, on the usual Millikanian-style accounts of function, but it cannot pump blood at all. This may be all right for hearts, but is it really true that a person who has nothing inside her ever performing the proper role of desires, and so can never be moved to act, never be moved to feel, never react to anything as a reward or punishment, nonetheless has desires? This strikes me as less plausible, even if the individual contains (non-functional) neural structures in representational and reward centers of the brain of the sort normally creating desires. Even though the neural structures might exist, and have the function of producing desire-constituting reward signals, if they are not producing the reward signals or any of the symptoms of those signals, it seems more reasonable to me to deny that a desire exists at all. My suspicion is that RTD is probably superior to RTD*, but no more will be made of this judgment in this work. If the reader prefers RTD*, that will make no difference in what is to come.

One final point of explication is required. According to RTD, a desire exists when there is (or is supposed to be) a stable connection between a representational capacity and a reward system, and the desire exists as long as the connection does. These connections appear to be fairly stable sorts of things. Does it then follow that desires continue to exist even when satisfied? Can this possibly be right? What, after all, is a desire except a *lack* of some sort, which disappears once satisfied?

The reward theory of desire rejects the idea that desires are like holes, disappearing once filled. When a desire is satisfied, feelings of dissatisfaction are likely to disappear, and motivational urges may also disappear. But neither of these is the desire itself. Consider, for example, my desire that I live a fairly decent life: an intrinsic desire, suppose. Upon my deathbed, it is clear to me that I have accomplished my goal. My life has indeed been decent, and my desire has been satisfied—already, note, before the time of death. Nothing I can do now in the hours remaining to me will change the overall decency of my life, not even if I quarrel cruelly with my children and pinch the nurse's bottom, for my past behavior has essentially guaranteed that I cannot, with the time remaining to me, bring my life's average decency below what I hoped it would be. Having clearly satisfied my desire, will it now be the case that I cease to have this desire? Certainly, any anxiety I might have had about the overall shape of my desire will be eliminated, if my feelings are appropriate to the occasion, and I will not be motivated by my desire to do one or two last good deeds in order to fix up the final balance sheet. But if I actually cease to have my desire to lead an overall decent life, how will the knowledge of my decently lived life comfort me upon my deathbed? What pleasure will there be for me in contemplating this aspect of my life, if it no longer satisfies any desire I have? What will motivate me to dwell upon this aspect of my life? What will motivate me to tot up the sum once again, just for the pleasure of seeing it confirmed that I have lived well? These sorts of considerations seem to show that, while satisfied intrinsic desires may not act upon us in the way unsatisfied desires do, they continue to act upon us nonetheless.

Less melodramatically, one might instead mention a desire that one's child attend the same college that one attended years ago. Such a desire might be satisfied at a particular time, but the evidence that one continues to have that desire persists even once it is satisfied: there is the fact that one is motivated to bring the topic up, the fact that one takes continued pleasure in it, and so on. It is true that, in everyday conversation, one does not say "I want my daughter to have attended Harvard; thank goodness she did." But one can admit to still caring about whether or not the daughter went to Harvard, and this appears to amount to the same thing. Likewise, people continue to care, intrinsically, about what German citizens did during the Second World War; wish, intrinsically, that the Vancouver Canucks had won the Stanley Cup; regret, intrinsically, the manner of Nietzsche's death; and so on—none of which make sense in the absence of the attitude I have been calling 'desire'—though these matters are all over and done with.

With the various muddles surrounding the notion of implementing contingency-based learning at least made manifest, if not actually resolved, RTD has been rendered as clear as it is likely to get. But no doubt the reader will be left with a thousand questions about the consequences of holding RTD. What does RTD mean for measuring desire strength? For the relationship of desires to consciousness? For the acquisition of desires? For direction of fit? And so on. Answering such questions is the work of the next section.

2. Everyday Desire

So far as the reward theory of desire is concerned, all that is required for the existence of a desire is a suitable representational capacity disposed to contribute to the production of a reward signal. A creature need have no feelings in order to desire, need have no ability to move, need not have stronger or weaker desires—need not have much of what we would recognize as desires, in fact. In this respect, the reward theory of desire is just like the standard theory. Both claim that there is a slim, elegant, economical account of what desires *are*, and so are left in need of a further, supplementary story in order to say what human desires are like in everyday life. A philosophical theory of desire is only required to describe the nature of desire, but no theory will be very credible unless it explains the rich, complex, lived experience of desire, and this goes for the reward theory as much as it did for the standard theory. Accordingly, this section presents what I think is the most plausible set of positions available to a reward theorist on the metaphysically inessential, but very important, features of human desires.

Desire Strength

What does desire strength amount to, on the reward theory? If to desire is to constitute a state of affairs as a reward or punishment, then a strong desire is one that constitutes a state of affairs as a substantial reward or punishment, whereas a weak desire would constitute the same state of affairs as a minimal reward or punishment. If contingency-based learning in a given organism is not incredibly crude, then some representations will normally contribute to very powerful learning signals—signals with great power to change neural connections—while other representations will have much less influence over the learning process. The strength of a desire will thus come to the relative power of the desire to change neural connections (all else being equal), and so modify its owner's mind.

Desire strength is normally thought of quite differently. Standard theorists generally think of it in terms of strength of disposition to behave, as described in chapter 1. But if the reward theory of desire is correct, then having a powerful disposition to action is just a natural consequence of having a powerful desire, and is not constitutive of it. Under the reward theory, strong desires cause powerful behavioral tendencies in human beings because, all else being equal, they generate powerful reward signals, and powerful reward signals have a powerful impact upon the motor striatum, and the motor striatum, in turn, has a powerful impact upon movement. It is thus to be expected that strong desires will have more influence over movement than weak desires, all else being equal, though of course only in creatures whose movements are directed by their desires. In creatures with desires but no capacities for movement, or creatures whose movements are directed independently of their desires, desire strength will be visible only through reward-driven learning, and perhaps through the representation of desire satisfaction in pleasure.

The separation of strength of desire from motivational force of desire allows for weaker desires having disproportionate motivational success against competing stronger desires. Contentiously, one could say that it makes room for irrational action, but I would prefer not to be drawn into a discussion of either rationality or action, and so will restrict myself simply to speaking of motivational efficacy disproportionate to strength. Borrowing an example from Michael Bratman (1999, ch.4), imagine that I am deliberating about how to spend my evening. Before dinner, I consider the amount of beer I want to drink that evening and the amount of philosophy I want to read, and the option I settle on, which is maximally desire-satisfying at the time, is to drink one beer with dinner and then read philosophy. But at dinner, I find myself more motivated to drink a second beer (which will prevent me from doing useful philosophical work that evening) than to stop at one and read philosophy.[4] Does it follow that my desires have changed, so that my intrinsic desires would now be better served by drinking the second beer?[5] The scenario is particularly interesting to Bratman because he imagines facing the same choice every evening, and every evening feeling the same way both before dinner and after the first beer, and so drinking the second beer, never reading philosophy in the evenings, and so seeming to be both rational at each moment and yet self-defeating. The reward theory of desire can offer at least two different possible explanations of such phenomena, without holding the implausible view that my intrinsic desires are in constant flux.

In the simpler explanation of the scenario, what is true is not that my desires change in strength, but that my occurrent representations change. Before dinner I clearly represent the features of both scenarios that are relevant to my intrinsic desires, both beer-related and philosophy-related, and so they contribute to productions of reward signals in proportion to their real strengths, and under these circumstances I am moved to have a single beer and then read philosophy. Acting on this motivation, I have the first beer. But, after one beer, my imagination becomes more focused upon beer. My attention is drawn to the relaxing qualities of beer, its pleasantly complex flavor, and so on, and is drawn away from the book I am to read, my philosophical aspirations, my looming tenure decision, and the like. That is, I clearly represent the intrinsically desired features of having a second beer, but because of the way my attention has shifted, I do not represent the intrinsically desired features of working tonight, or represent fewer of them, or represent them only infrequently, in between much longer representations of the features of a two-beer evening I find appealing. When this happens, then the stronger desire (or set of desires), which would be served by stopping at one beer and spending the evening writing philosophy, has less impact upon reward-signal production than it otherwise would. Because I do not adequately represent the features of a one-beer-and-philosophy evening I intrinsically desire, my philosophy-directed desires do not have an opportunity to contribute to reward or punishment signals, and so do not have an opportunity to contribute to movement. At the same time, the weaker desire (or set of desires), served by having the second beer, has the maximum impact it is capable of having. My thoughts initially contemplated both beer and philosophy equally, but because of the vagaries of attention (perhaps because attention is drawn by more salient stimuli, and the beer is right here, in front of me), they have shifted to greater contemplation of beer, and so thoughts of more beer influence movement production out of proportion to their strength, and carry the day. Or perhaps I have ceased to represent the desire-satisfying features of reading philosophy this evening, and represent reading philosophy as merely depriving myself of beer. Everyone, I take it, has made foolish decisions in this way: one thinks so much about some lesser good[6] (or evil), and so little about some greater good (or evil), that one responds to the lesser when a truly prudent person would respond to the greater instead. The sort of people who, worried about holding a successful wedding reception, can become so fixated upon finding the perfect centerpiece for each table that they do not represent to themselves the problems of feeding the guests, and so leave themselves only one afternoon to arrange all of the catering, are equally good examples of this sort of motivational trap.

In the more complex version of Bratman's scenario, the philosophically attractive features of a one-beer evening do not slip from my mind. After my first beer, I face my decision squarely once again—drink another, or commence writing philosophy—and all the familiar advantages and disadvantages of each option return to mind.[7] Even in this scenario, the reward theory has the resources to explain how one might be moved to change decisions without one's desires changing strength. For it might be the case that, although my representations do not change, my subjective, gut-level estimate of the likelihood of their satisfaction has changed. Recall from chapter 2 that reward signals are determined not only by strengths of desires and tokenings of their representational contents but also by subjective, unconscious estimates of the likelihoods of desire satisfaction. Stronger reward signals are produced, all else being equal, when an organism learns that a desire is very likely to be satisfied, and weaker signals are produced, all else being equal, when it learns that a desire is less likely to be satisfied. With this in mind, consider my situation before any drinking has begun. At that moment, I attach a certain unconscious likelihood to certain desire-satisfying states of affairs if I go ahead and drink two beers. Given that beer is generally pleasant and relaxing, and that it generally increases my sociability, and that these things straightforwardly satisfy intrinsic desires I have, the likelihood of these desires paying off is high, should I drink two beers. I also attach a certain likelihood to other states of affairs, ones that would contribute to satisfying philosophical desires, if I have one beer and then write. Given that I am unlikely to finish a book in one night, and that making progress on reading a book is something that happens over a longer time, and that its contribution to satisfying my most general philosophical desires (to spend time philosophizing, to examine certain issues deeply) is somewhat tenuous, the progress I expect to make on satisfying my philosophical desires is not very impressive, even if I should spend tonight writing. In Bratman's scenario, I weigh these two possible courses of action and accurately find the one-beer-plus-philosophy scenario expected to be most desire-satisfying: my intrinsic philosophical desires are so strong that even weak progress on them would be better than none, when weighed against likely but not certain satisfaction of lesser desires. So far so good. Now consider my situation after having consumed a single beer. I am enjoying a certain amount of pleasure, relaxation, and so on: states satisfying intrinsic desires I have. (After all, if having the first beer had not been so relaxing, or if I had fretted about finishing my reading, or if it had turned out only unappealing beer was available, I would not be facing a dilemma.) Now, after the first beer, it is quite certain that these desired states of affairs will cease quite soon if I stop drinking and begin reading philosophy, and it is quite certain they will be prolonged if I have a second beer. Their likelihood of satisfaction, in my gut-level estimation, has gone up. If I stop drinking now, I give up on what looks like a sure thing. At the same time, my subjective estimate of the progress I am likely to make tonight on satisfying my philosophical desires has not increased. (Again note: if it had—if, say, a brilliant idea had struck me over dinner—I would not be having this dilemma. I would be eager to set to work.) Now, weighing the two options, taking the sure thing seems the better course of action: I can always do philosophy tomorrow, after all. Thus, although my desires have not changed in strength, I have changed motivational direction. And perhaps I am right to do so. Given that having beer is working out so well, and given that philosophical progress is slow, perhaps it would be in keeping with my desires to have the beer tonight after all. Since the uncertainty about the beer has been resolved in favor of the beer, while the uncertainty about philosophizing has not been resolved, it may be in keeping with combined desire strength and likelihood of satisfaction to stick to the sure thing. In this more complex scenario, desire strength does not change, but the action that is most desire-responsive does.

One might worry, with Bratman, that if it really is in keeping with my desires to have the second beer tonight, that it will be appropriate to do so every night—and then I will never read philosophy in the evenings, and my philosophy will suffer, and overall my desires will not have been best served, and all in a way I foresaw from the outset. However, this is mistaken. For after a week of pleasant but philosophically empty evenings, my subjective, gut-level estimates of how much progress I would make on my philosophical desires by a night of philosophizing are themselves likely to change. Deadlines are looming: a night of work put in now, after delay, clearly *will* make a difference to meeting the deadline, and so in turn make a difference to my philosophical success, to my professional success, and so on. Even if deadlines do not loom (though, really, when would that be?), I am still likely to change my gut-level estimates of how much a night of philosophy is likely to contribute to desire-satisfaction as time goes by. I may have a desire for a highly intellectual life, for example, and by not working in the evenings, I may find that the extent to which I lead a highly intellectual life is perceptibly declining, so that I am now clearly leading a less intellectual life than I want to. The likelihood that I would make progress on satisfying this desire was low back when I worked every evening and always forswore the second beer: one more evening of work was not clearly needed to satisfy this desire. But now that I spend my evenings with bottle in hand, my desire to lead a highly intellectual life is suffering, and an evening full of philosophy would probably mark a clear improvement. With my gut-level estimates of the degree to which a night of philosophy would contribute to desire satisfactions thus changed, I will (all else being equal) be moved to philosophize rather than drink, even after the first beer. I am sure the reader can think of other, similar changes in estimates of likely desire satisfaction that would take place as one allowed precious time to slip away from one. Thus, in the more complex version of Bratman's scenario, the long-term behavior that will be proportionately responsive to all my desires will be to sometimes drink more beer in the evening, and sometimes philosophize, depending on how well each activity can be expected to turn out and how well my each of my standing desires is being served.

The simple and the complex scenarios are not the only conceivable ways of reading Bratman's story, but I think they are two very psychologically realistic ways of reading it, and on both the reward theory has something interesting to say about how one's motivation can fluctuate while one's desires remain constant. The extent to which this commends the theory will be judged by the reader in proportion to how illuminating she finds the accounts, but I think that the very fine-grained psychological description of such examples, encouraged by knowing the biological underpinnings of the psychology, is a tremendous advantage.

Other routes to acting on desires in a way disproportionate to their strength are also conceivable, on the reward theory. For a final example, consider that one pattern of behavior may frequently have been rewarded in the past, and that sort of behavior have a strong tendency to be carried out, even without the assistance of a very strong reward signal, while another sort of behavior may have rarely been carried out, or rarely rewarded when carried out, and so have a weaker tendency to be acted upon given an equally strong reward signal. That is, habit and other, milder expressions of the effects of past reward and punishment, can be sources of disproportionate motivational force, and lack of habit can be a disproportionate motivational impediment. For my own part, I experience such forms of irrationality all too often. Presented with an obviously superior but fairly unfamiliar new method for achieving some goal, I have a strong tendency to stick to the old ways. Unaccustomed to using e-mail to back up files, for example, I nonetheless find myself in a situation in which this is clearly the course of action best satisfying my intrinsic desires. But what do I do? I dither. Somehow, the motivation to connect to the Internet and spend thirty seconds protecting very precious files is absent, and the task seems on the other side of a very high motivational barrier: I feel as though I must struggle with myself in order to do the obviously sensible thing. With nagging from my friend Nomy spurring me on (representations of ridicule rather than foreseen benefits apparently doing most of the motivational work), I do the deed and find it, as I knew I would, painless and easy. The resources of the standard theory to explain such stories in a plausible manner are limited. It must, it seems, postulate some intrinsic desire served by not backing up the files, and postulate that this desire was very strong on the occasion described, for it almost governed my movements. Yet I am not actually averse to novelty, and I do not intrinsically value doing things in the same old way all the time. Rather, I, like most people, am a creature of habit, and am moved to run in familiar channels in part simply because they are channels, and they tend to carry me along unless strong reward or punishment signals interfere.

Still on the subject of apparent and actual desire strength, a very different way of looking at desire strength is the phenomenological approach: desires are strong in proportion to how powerfully one feels them. This is the sort of view one expects from the hedonic theory of desire, but it has its roots in common sense just as much as the standard theory's interpretation of strength does. What would a love song be without the singer's burning and yearning to attest to the strength of his desire? The response of the reward theory here parallels its response to the standard theory. Desires are normal causes of strong and weak feelings, principally through their representation in pleasure. But there is room for desire strength to be misrepresented by feelings, and furthermore there is more to feelings than strength of desire even when nothing is being misrepresented. Recall the suggestion from chapter 3 that pleasure and displeasure represent deviations from net *expected* desire satisfaction, so long as one understands 'expectation' here in the gut-level, unconscious manner posited by learning theory. If this is correct, then a strong desire can be satisfied without any substantial emotional flicker, so long as one felt completely assured that the desire would be satisfied. Likewise, a weaker desire can still cause a surge of emotion if its satisfaction was unexpected. Thus, the emotional impact of getting a $50 check from an unheard-of organization recognizing outstanding members of the Kenyan-Canadian community may be delightful, leaving one cheerful all day, while the fact that one's child survived another day of school unharmed may not even register on one's emotional horizons, in spite of the fact that the latter is much, much more desire-satisfying. Even in straightforward cases, then, strength of feeling is not a reliable guide to strength of desire. Furthermore, strength of feeling can be manipulated independently of desire strength in manners inducing misrepresentation. Being tipsy can make one's feelings of worry disappear without causing one to cease to be averse to tenure decisions, mortgage payments, and so on, as everyone knows: people get tipsy to forget their cares, not to eliminate them.

Consciousness and Desire

Talking about felt strength of desire naturally leads to saying a little more about the ways in which desires have an impact upon our conscious lives more generally. There is more to their impact than just pleasure and displeasure, after all. There are also felt urges to act, for example. These urges are indicative of desires—insofar as they are—because desires are causally influential in behavior, and so in feelings of being on the verge of action. But because these urges are fairly far removed from desires themselves, there is plenty of room, once again, for a disconnection between the symptom and the desire. People with Tourette syndrome, for example, feel all sorts of urges produced directly as a result of their biological disorder, rather than as a result of a desire.

Some felt urges to act take us by surprise and strike us as inexplicable. Here stands Kristín on her balcony, looking down the eleven stories to the ground below. She feels a vague urge to jump off, an urge that frightens her a little. Yet it would be so easy: just climb over the railing and sail downwards. The only bad part would be landing, of course, for Kristín does not feel suicidal in the least. The urge to jump, though, is growing, and now is really alarming. Kristín steps away from the balcony, and the urge slowly disappears. Kristín's Sartrean vertigo, though stronger than average, is hardly unique to her. How is it to be explained? From within the standard theory, it would seem that one would have to postulate a powerful desire: to jump, to soar, or to die, presumably, since only a limited number of desires would be served by jumping from that height. But each hypothesis faces severe challenges. In particular, why is it that none of these desires has any felt efficacy, or any behavioral efficacy, away from the balcony edge? Kristín skis and snowboards, and so if she had intrinsic desires to soar or jump she would have many opportunities to act on them, or at least feel their pull, but does not delight in jumps in either sport. Nor does she exhibit signs of a death wish. The fact that the felt urge strikes her only when she peers over the edge seems significant.

The reward theory of desire can step in with a possible explanation of the phenomenology. Felt urges, as described in chapter 4, stem from the formation of activity in the motor centers of the cortex. This activity is initiated by one's perceptions, which promote all sorts of movement possibilities. The basal ganglia inhibit all these possibilities by default, but can selectively release this inhibition (Mink 1996, 2001). And Tourette syndrome vividly shows that, if activity in the motor center is only partially inhibited, it continues to be felt as an urge. The application of these facts to Kristín's case is speculative, but plausible, and in particular I think it is substantially more plausible than any similar explanation a standard theorist might offer. I suggest that one thing distinguishing Kristín from other people with much weaker senses of Sartrean vertigo is that, when she perceives a height from which she could leap, this inspires leaping-appropriate activity in her cortical motor systems. Perhaps this is a result of her love of birds or imagining what it would be like to fly. Whatever its precise origin, this connection between perception and motor activity is not a desire, according to the reward theory. But it poses a possible action, which the basal ganglia by default suppress. Since jumping from a height is not habitual to her, she does not leap unthinkingly, and since it would be massively desire-frustrating, no reward signal appears to release this possible action from inhibition and cause her to jump. Kristín remains on the balcony in part because she is not in the habit of leaping off heights (unsurprisingly!) and in part because of her strong desires not to die or be harmed. As Kristín continues to peer over the edge, however, her perception continues to promote jumping as a possible action, and while this possibility is held in check, it becomes felt as an urge, they way that a Tourettic individual feels an action possibility held in check as an urge. Aware of the urge, Kristín becomes aware of the consequences of acting on it, producing a punishment signal which is both felt by her and inhibits her from jumping. She feels fear and, while she does not jump, she continues to feel the movement possibility in her. It occurs to her that she should leave the balcony, and this, plus her desires for safety, aversion to harm, and so on move her to back away. As she ceases to perceive the leap-affording edge of the balcony or imagine the possibility it affords, that representation weakens and ceases, and so ceases to promote jumping as possible action (were Kristín Tourettic, perhaps this cessation would not happen). The felt urge to jump disappears, and Kristín feels better, though shaken. If this speculative account is correct in outline, then it can explain how Kristín can feel this bizarre urge even though it is massively contrary to her desires to act upon it. Normal people, like people with Tourette syndrome, can feel strong urges without having substantial desires behind them.

Perhaps the most interesting way in which desires affect consciousness, according to the reward theory, is in directing conscious deliberation. The motor output system of the basal ganglia does not control motor output alone. It also has a powerful influence upon higher cognitive processes such as conscious deliberation. Conscious deliberation requires the activity of non-motor regions of the pre-frontal cortex, and this activity, like activity in the motor PFC, is under the influence of the basal ganglia, and hence, ultimately, desires. Thus, we should expect that the voluntary, goal-directed aspects of deliberation—what to deliberate upon, whether to continue on one intellectual task or to switch tasks, whether to stop deliberating upon arriving at an answer or whether to seek an alternate answer—will all be influenced by our desires, just as our bodily movements are.

Acquiring and Losing Desires

Further topics that should be addressed are the acquisition of new intrinsic desires and the loss of existing desires. Human infants appear to be born with a large stock of intrinsic desires, as described in chapter 3. They desire food and water, warmth, dry skin, human contact, and so on. Likewise, they are generally averse to powerful stimulation in any sense modality, and to certain specific sensory experiences such as experiences of bitterness and nociception. From this basic stock of desires, new desires are acquired, until as adults they have intrinsic desires for and aversions to a panoply of things. Some of these acquired intrinsic desires, such as an aversion to visual cliffs, appear to come with maturation, but most appear to be fairly sensitive to environmental context. I desire *my* father's well-being more than *your* father's well-being through the historical accident of having been raised by my father, and not by yours. Similarly for my intrinsic preferences for various sorts of tastes and smells (surely I would now desire Chinese desserts if only I had grown up with them, though in fact I am averse to them), intrinsic desires for the success of particular sporting teams and the acclaim of particular nations, and so on. Of course, the influence of the environment over the development of intrinsic desire should not be exaggerated: there are very few environments that lead to people desiring extremely bitter flavors, or desiring social ostracism, or being averse to maintaining adequate blood sugar. Tastes and more cognitive desires, though flexible, are not limitlessly flexible any more than the brain upon which they depend for their existence is limitlessly flexible.

In addition to gaining new intrinsic desires, we can also lose them. It appears very difficult to lose the most basic desires with which one is born, such as desires for nourishment, warmth, and the like, but most other desires can be lost under appropriate circumstances. My childhood desire for very sweet tastes and my aversion to bitter tastes both seem to have disappeared, or at least to have substantially changed in content, as is common as people age. And we all know of instances in which intrinsic desires of a more cognitive nature have disappeared: people who once collected stamps may cease to find the hobby appealing, people who once were in love can cease to desire one another's well-being, and so on.

How does the reward theory explain what we know about the acquisition of new intrinsic desires and their loss? In principle, there should be no problem. At birth, there are existing connections between some perceptual structures (cognitive structures not yet being well formed) and the reward system, such that perceiving this or that contributes to a reward or punishment signal of this or that magnitude, all else being equal. Other perceptual and cognitive structures also send outputs to the reward system, but at birth these connections are not efficacious in contributing to reward signals. As the organism experiences its world, some perceptual or cognitive representations, not yet contributing to reward signals, will routinely be tokened in a way that coincides with other representations that *are* contributing to reward signals. Because of the coincidence of output from these representations to the reward system with the release of a reward signal, the connections between the representations and the reward system will become strengthened, until the connections are efficacious at producing reward signals on their own. Thus a new desire is born. This in-principle story is a version of a standard story told by behaviorists: states of affairs regularly associated with primary reinforcers become independently reinforcing themselves. Or, in the language I advocate, states of affairs regularly associated with intrinsically desired states of affairs tend to become intrinsically desired themselves. Born a self-centered baby, I come to desire my mother's presence because I associate her with things I antecedently desire, such as food, warmth, and human contact, but once the association is formed, I desire her presence even when I am fed, warm, and recently cuddled. Starting cub scouts as an unconvinced seven-year-old, I come to care about the cub scout pack itself because I associate it with things such as game playing, camaraderie, and recognition of individual achievement. As discussed in chapter 2, common sense parenting lore reveals that this sort of learning has many complexities, but in its crude outlines, it should not be a problem for the reward theory to explain the acquisition of new desires. A similar story applies to the loss of intrinsic desires. It may happen that a representational capacity is well connected to the reward system, constituting its content as a reward, and yet it regularly happens that when that representation is tokened, other representations are also tokened that cause a punishment, rather than reward, signal to be released. Or perhaps neural connections degrade over time by default, and it suffices that a reward signal is not released. Either way, the connection between representation and reward becomes weakened, until eventually no efficacious connection is left at all. Initially desiring the well-being of Brett, and thinking him a friend, I nonetheless find myself betrayed by him on one occasion, insulted by him on several, and ignored by him often, and in the end I find that there is no vestige of friendship left: I have become indifferent to his fate, no longer desiring his well-being or company as once I did.

So much for the principle. What empirical support is there for it? The work of Edmund Rolls and colleagues upon the orbitofrontal cortex is important here.[8] As discussed in chapter 2, neurons in the OFC fire in response to stimuli one would, intuitively, call rewards. They also fire in response to other stimuli that, intuitively, are not rewards but that predict rewards. Thus, perceiving a rewarding taste will activate a given set of OFC neurons, and regularly perceiving an arbitrary fractal image just before being given a rewarding taste experience will activate a different set of OFC neurons. Rolls and colleagues have found that OFC neurons can readily "learn" to fire in response to stimuli they did not previously respond to, once the stimulus is associated with an existing reward. They have also found that these same neurons readily learn not to fire in response to the stimulus anymore, once the stimulus ceases to be associated with the reward. Because these activity patterns are acquired and lost in a way that corresponds directly to how well they predict other rewards, it seems implausible to think of them as implementing anything other than predicted satisfaction of other, existing desires. However, nothing in the existing literature impugns the idea that these temporary connections might be strengthened until the point at which they could survive autonomously, able to contribute to reward or punishment signals even if no longer reliably associated with other rewards or punishments. Perhaps, if the connection between the representation and the reward system were to be strengthened again and again, over a period of days, weeks, months, or years, by association with multiple types of wanted states of affairs, a durable connection would be formed. If so, then the formation of new intrinsic desires would be brought about in the theoretically prescribed manner. Likewise, nothing impugns the idea that once formed, these connections can be eroded by a long-term version of the process Rolls and colleagues have observed acting over very short time periods. So there is theoretical principle, and there are the beginnings of empirical demonstration. One final relevant empirical observation is that money is known to activate the OFC in human subjects (Thut et al. 1997). Obviously, there is no inborn connection between representations of money and the reward system, so the connection is learned. And clearly it was not learned for the first time during the experiment. So there would appear to be a learned, stable association between representations of acquiring money and contributions to reward signals. All that is lacking is evidence that dopamine reward signals brought this connection about, but given what chapter 2 revealed about the action of dopamine, this evidence should not be lacking for long.[9] There is less empirical evidence relevant to normal loss of intrinsic desire, but happily there is no barrier in principle to acquiring such evidence, so we may still hope for the relevant studies to be undertaken in the future.

A complication comes to mind if one considers the phenomenology of watching sporting contests. Imagine that Brenda is watching a match between two teams she really knows nothing about. Perhaps she is watching Italy play France in volleyball at the Olympic Games. Not being particularly connected to Italy, France, or volleyball, Brenda may nevertheless find herself cheering for one team or the other. Sometimes this is the result of some clear antecedent desire: she has not forgiven the French for their last, monstrous entry into the Eurovision song contest, and desires their defeat as a result. But on other occasions, one simply picks a team to root for on more or less arbitrary grounds. The Italians serve an ace, and Brenda decides to cheer for them because the serve was impressive. Or she likes their colors. Or they happen to be serving, so cheering for them means cheering for the team that, right now, has a chance to score a point. Such arbitrary attachments, formed on arbitrary grounds, have a way of sustaining themselves for the duration of a match, and even beyond. If the Italians go on to be pummeled by a clearly superior French team, and the Italian who served the ace never comes close to replicating the feat, Brenda is likely to find herself sticking to her losing cause, hoping they will find a way to win. To all appearances, for the duration of the match she is likely to act and emote in a way suggesting that she intrinsically desires the victory of the Italian team. Two weeks afterward, though, she is likely to have forgotten who she cheered for and who won. What can the reward theory say about such phenomena?

The phenomenon is interesting first because it appears to be an example of the creation of a new intrinsic desire in a very short time. But it also brings us back to questions raised earlier about how stable a new intrinsic desire must be in order to count as a genuine intrinsic desire. For the phenomenon invites two responses. One response is to say that Brenda really does intrinsically desire the Italian team's victory, even if this desire is quick to form and quick to disappear, and so the reward theory needs an explanation of how intrinsic desires can be formed and abandoned so quickly. The other response is to say that exactly because the apparent desire is formed and abandoned so quickly, it was never an intrinsic desire after all, and so the reward theory need not explain it as such. Pretheoretically, there are virtues to both positions. In favor of the claim that Brenda intrinsically desires Italy's victory one can cite her cheering and disappointment, the feelings she has, and the apparent non-instrumentality of her support. While she may have decided to commit to one team instrumentally, in order to make the match more exciting, having committed, she is stuck.[10] If the match would be more exciting were she cheering for the French, it is too late to switch: her cheering for the Italian team is not a tool she is freely wielding to manipulate her emotions in an entertaining way, but something she is now stuck with, at least for a short time. Against the claim of intrinsic desire is the fact that Brenda would deny that she really cares who wins, and the fact that once she has forgotten the events (which happens quickly enough) she shows no sign of having cared.

I find the pre-theoretic considerations in favor of saying that Brenda forms a genuine intrinsic desire more compelling. Of course, her intrinsic desire does not seem particularly strong. As we have seen, the strong feelings her desire produces while she watches Italy play France are no particular indication of the strength of her desire, and in fact they are probably more linked to her having few antecedent expectations regarding the play of the Italian team than anything else. And equally obviously, her desire does not seem particularly stable. Given the familiar phenomenology of such desires, Brenda will probably continue to favor the Italian volleyball team to some extent after the match ends, but probably a week or two will be enough to erase all overt signs of this preference. Covert signs may last longer—studies have often shown the existence or persistence of preferences of which we were unaware (think back to the study by Johnsrude et al. [1999], described in chapter 2)—but soon enough there will be no real ground for attributing an intrinsic desire anymore. Yet for all the weakness and transience of Brenda's desire, it still has all the most obvious marks of a true intrinsic desire. Having elected to cheer for Italy, she soon finds herself in the grip of a concern she cannot voluntarily shake off. She can ignore her new desire, turn away from the game, pretend to find it a bore, but if she began the match in the way all watchers of sports know from experience, then she will still care who wins, and if she later learns that Italy lost, she will be moved emotionally to some small extent, and perhaps even (as sports fans everywhere) blame herself for not having cheered them on, even though she was watching the match on television.

Because of these considerations, I suspect that the reward theory must not put an excessive value on the stability of the connection between a representation and a reward signal in giving a theory of desire. The sorts of transient connections described by Rolls and colleagues, lasting a few minutes in a laboratory, seem insufficient to create anything robust enough to earn the name of desire, but connections only modestly more stable, such as those supporting the existence of Brenda's concern for Italian volleyball, seem to pass muster. Cases like Brenda's seem to set a minimum lower bound on the stability of desires: any connection between representation and reward that achieves this level of stability is stable enough to constitute a desire, all else being equal.

Fleeting Desires

In a related vein, it should be asked what the reward theory has to say about the notion of *fleeting* desires. I walk down the street and I see a beautiful new car, and I am possessed by a fleeting desire to own such a car. Or I spot cheesecake on the menu and have a fleeting desire to order it, before noticing that I can also have mango ice cream. Or I am squirted with water by a nephew, and have a brief desire to find a squirt gun and squirt him back before I realize that I can get the garden hose instead. If desires are required to have a certain amount of stability, what becomes of fleeting desires? The answer of the reward theory must be that fleeting desires are never intrinsic desires lasting for a matter of seconds. They are rather fleeting feelings of desiring, caused in a variety of ways. Inspection of the details of fleeting desires bears this out, I think.

Consider first a fleeting desire to own a car of this sort or to order a dessert of that sort. Typically, these will be instrumental desires. I intrinsically desire the admiration of others, efficient transportation, episodes of curve-hugging driving, or the like, and these desires would be satisfied by owning the car I see. I intrinsically desire taste experiences of certain sorts, and this desire would be satisfied by placing a certain order. As a result of having these long-standing intrinsic desires, I experience a fleeting feeling. When I represent myself behind the wheel of the sporty roadster, a small reward signal is released and I feel a little thrill of excitement; when I represent myself eating the cheesecake, I have a similar experience. But then I cease to represent this state of affairs, because it is unrealistic (the car) or because I am drawn to some other state of affairs (the dessert), and the feeling my intrinsic desire caused in me disappears. Furthermore, the desire does not go on to control my attention, imagery, or overt behavior in any way. Other representations and other desires take over my affective and behavioral life, and so I say that I experienced a fleeting desire. More accurate would be to say that I experienced a standing desire fleetingly.

Slightly different is the case of the fleeting desire for a squirt gun. In this case, again, there is a stable intrinsic desire—for play, perhaps, or to have a good relationship with my nephew—but in this case the stable intrinsic desire has its effects felt both in the fleeting desire for a squirt gun and in the slightly longer-lasting desire for the hose. What happens here is that I continue to feel the effects of a single intrinsic desire, but my choice of means to satisfy that desire rapidly changes. At first, getting my own squirt gun leaps to mind as the best means to engage in this sort of play, or to bond with my nephew. My desire causes certain thoughts and certain motor instructions to be prepared: I begin to head for a squirt gun, thinking about how best to use it. But soon enough a better idea leaps to mind: turn the hose on the boy! The same desire now causes a shift in experiences, with new deliberations and new felt urges to action. In this case, the first, fleeting feeling of an urge for a squirt gun does reflect a fleeting desire, but it is a fleeting *instrumental* desire, not a fleeting intrinsic desire, and so is not covered under the present theory. Both the urge for a squirt gun and the urge for the hose, as well as my pleasure at this play, are feelings deriving from my intrinsic desire. But this latter desire is not fleeting, nor is it fleetingly felt (its effects are felt for quite a few minutes, as I busily soak my nephew), and so it hardly qualifies as a fleeting intrinsic desire in any sense.

Fleeting urges to do things one does not actually desire to do in any sense (such as Kristín's urge to leap from the balcony) might also be called 'fleeting desires' by some people, but the reason to deny them the status of intrinsic desires has already been sufficiently discussed, and need not be repeated.

A final candidate class of fleeting desires worth considering is that exemplified by hunger or thirst. An hour ago, I had what seemed a perfectly normal intrinsic desire that I eat; now, it seems that I do not intrinsically desire to eat. In fact, I no longer have any non-instrumental attitude toward that meal. Instrumentally I remain glad I had it, of course—I would not be alert and energetic if I had gone without food for too long—but it was not such a memorable meal that I can look back and say "I'll long be glad I had that particular meal." So hunger, thirst, and related desires would seem to present examples of true fleeting intrinsic desires. What can the reward theory say in response?

If we look at the neuroscience of hunger, it seems that there are two main features relevant to present purposes. The first is that we must begin with the hypothalamus. As mentioned in chapter 2, the hypothalamus monitors a variety of bodily conditions such as blood sugar, temperature, salt levels, and so on. The second is that output from the hypothalamus links its representations of these conditions to the operation of the reward system. This connection is a stable one, of the sort the reward theory leads one to expect. Note, though, that it is not a stable connection between representations of food ingestion and reward, or between seeking out warm places, or drinks, and reward. Rather, it is a stable connection between representations of homeostatic balance and reward. Deviations from homeostasis contribute to drops in reward signals, or to boosted punishment signals, while returns to homeostasis contribute to opposite effects.

From the perspective of the reward theory, the desires based in the hypothalamus of the sort just described are not intrinsic desires to eat or drink, but intrinsic desires for constant levels of nourishment, constant body temperature, constant salt levels, and so on.[11] I see no reason to disagree. Consider what conclusions follow. If the reward theory is right to interpret the desires realized in the hypothalamus in this way, then it must turn out that the desire to eat at a particular time, or to drink water, and so on, is not an intrinsic desire but an instrumental one. The underlying intrinsic desire that creates the felt displeasure of lack, and that puts motivational force behind impulses to acquire food, is an intrinsic desire for something like constant blood sugar.[12] This intrinsic desire, being ill-satisfied at a given moment, sends output to the reward signal causing one to instrumentally seek out some means of raising blood sugar: food, generally, though if a patient in a hospital intensive care ward feels hungry he might also ask a nurse for a more nourishing intravenous drip. Eating satisfies the desire for the moment, and so the instrumentality of eating disappears: to continue eating would be to overshoot homeostasis, again frustrating one's intrinsic desire. With the disappearance of the instrumentality of eating, one says one's hunger has disappeared. So it has, in the sense that one no longer has a desire that can be satisfied by eating. But in another sense, it has not, in that one remains a creature that cares about its level of nourishment. All of this seems in sufficient accord with common sense. No particular dictate of common sense is rejected, and while quite a bit that goes beyond common sense has been added, these additions are both biologically justified and philosophically supported by the general virtues of the reward theory. Given these considerations, there seems no harm and substantial theoretical unity to holding that the satisfaction of one's hunger does not extinguish the intrinsic desire that gave rise to the feeling of hunger.

A perfectly detailed and subtle account of the desires surrounding food would have much to add to the crude account just developed, for our intrinsic desire for adequate nourishment hardly exhausts our food-related desires. I have intrinsic desires to have certain taste experiences be a part of my gustatory life (it would be desire-frustrating for me to go for a long time without eating good chocolate, for instance), and these desires shape my dining experiences in complex ways that have nothing to do with nourishment. I also have an intrinsic aversion to artificiality in food even when I cannot perceive it directly (snobbery or overexcited environmentalism, perhaps, but it is an aversion I have all the same). Then there is the manner in which food is presented, ideas of "high" and "low" cuisine, the enjoyment of food known to be expensive, and so on. But I see no particular difficulty in holding that these other desires are also stable desires rather than fleeting ones.

Instrumental Desires

Having appealed so often to the distinction between instrumental and intrinsic desires, I want at last to say something systematic about it. The intuitive distinction is clear enough, and RTD gives a clear statement about the reward theory of intrinsic desire. What, then, is the reward theory's account of instrumental desire? In order to give an answer, we must first get a clearer view of the phenomenon of instrumental desire.

Here sits Nathaniel. He is a physicist, and he intrinsically desires to engage in physics research. He is aware that if he operates his computer *so*, he will get a display of the output being produced by the experimental apparatus he is using. He is also aware that, if he gets this display, he can make progress in conducting physics research. But it certainly need not be true that Nathaniel has an instrumental desire to see the display. Perhaps he is busy playing a computer game instead, and is repressing no impulse to shift to work. Perhaps, just now, work would be an unpleasant chore. In these circumstances, we would normally deny that Nathaniel wants to shift from playing his game to looking at the experimental results. So it seems that something being an available means to an intrinsically desired end does not suffice to make something instrumentally desired. All the same, it does not seem necessary that Nathaniel actually cease playing the game and shift over to the experimental results in order to have an instrumental desire to do so. If he were to be torn between the two activities, to the extent of having one finger poised to strike a key that will switch him from computer game to experimental results, the finger hovering uncertainly as he wrestles with his inner dilemma, it would be natural enough to say that Nathaniel wants the game to be displayed (instrumentally, to play) and that he also wants the experimental results to be displayed (instrumentally, to work). Because of his conflicting intrinsic desires, he has formed conflicting instrumental desires, and both exist, though only one can be acted upon.

Hence, intrinsic desires can generate instrumental desires, even though these desires are not acted upon. But, as was suggested a moment ago, one does not generate instrumental desires merely by virtue of having intrinsic desires to which they would be appropriate. Something more has to happen. What this something more might be may become clearer if we consider a few more examples. Suppose Nathaniel has an inner conflict, but of a less dramatic nature. He is enjoying his computer game but the itch to return to research is coming on. He says to himself, "Well, I'll just finish playing the current scenario, and then I'll work," and he feels content with this decision. Under these conditions, it seems most natural to say that Nathaniel does not have conflicting instrumental desires. He does not, at this very moment, want both to view the game and to view the experimental output. Rather, right now his instrumental desire is a complex desire that he finish play, then shift to research. This example appears to show that the generation of an instrumental desire comes about through deciding to take some course of action, but it would be hasty to accept this appearance without qualification. Consider one more example, just like the previous one except that Nathaniel's exercise of saying to himself, "Well, I'll just finish . . ." is empty: after saying it, he is really no more inclined to carry out his resolution than he was before. The computer game retains its mesmerizing grip upon him, and when he finishes the current scenario he just continues playing another. Under these conditions, it seems much harder to say that Nathaniel instrumentally desires to switch displays after completing play. He appears to endorse forming such an instrumental desire, but not actually to form it as a result.

These cases suggest that something must happen in order to generate instrumental desires, that this something can generate conflicting instrumental desires, that this something can generate instrumental desires for immediate action or for future, conditional action, and that this something is not merely the taking of a positive attitude toward that future action or superficially deciding to engage in it: the something must bring about a state with real motivational weight, even if that motivational weight is outweighed by something else. In the brain, it is clear what meets these criteria: the activation of the structures in motor cortex, SMA, motor AC, and motor PFC. As argued in chapter 4, these are the structures that underlie trying and intending. They are structures not activated merely by intrinsically desiring: turning a desire into motor activation is a complex process. They are structures that can generate conflicting motor commands, requiring the basal ganglia to select one of the competing options as the motor command that will actually be executed. They are structures that generate commands both for immediate movement (the motor cortex, SMA and motor AC) and for future movement conditional on this or that occurrence (the motor PFC). And they are structures that, when activated, carry real motivational weight, issuing commands to the body, even if these commands are countermanded by other neural structures.

At this point, a number of radical conclusions suggest themselves. If instrumental desires are found in the same neural structures housing intentions and episodes of trying, then perhaps there are no instrumental desires after all: perhaps instrumentally desiring can be reduced without residue to intending and trying. Or perhaps the opposite reduction can be performed, and we can dispense with intending and trying and retain only instrumental desires in our ontology. Or perhaps all these mental states are really aspects of some as-yet unnamed mental state encompassing them all. Such radical philosophical fantasies are pleasant, and may ultimately have something to them, but they face serious obstacles as well. Recall that Nathaniel had two conflicting instrumental desires but only acted upon one: he was certainly not trying or intending to do both. This seems to show that one can instrumentally desire that *P* without intending or trying to bring it about that *P*. Recall also Mele's (1990) example of the person who is offered money if she will try to do something, and who tries to do it, without having any desire to actually succeed (as success is not required for payment, only effort). This seems to show that one can try to bring it about that *P* without having any instrumental desire that *P*. Such examples seem to question the possibility of any quick reduction in the number of pro attitudes. On the other hand, it remains interesting that these attitudes are so closely linked. The reward theory need not resolve exactly how they are linked, fortunately. Making these links clearer goes far enough, I think, toward discharging the theory's obligation to say something more specific about the difference between intrinsic and instrumental desires.

Direction of Fit

Finally, a very different, very technical philosophical topic: direction of fit. What does it amount to, on the reward theory? One might ask what it amounts to in any case, for direction of fit is far from the clearest notion employed in the philosophy of mind. Everyone can agree that there are some mental states capable of being true or false, inaccurate, veridical, or the like, but not fulfilled, frustrated, executed, or impeded, and that there are other mental states for which the opposite is true. Mental states with the former qualities have the belief-like direction of fit, while mental states with the latter qualities have the desire-like direction of fit. What is controversial is what makes it true that a mental state has a given direction of fit. Do desires have the desire-like direction of fit because they tend to modify the world so as to realize their contents?[13] Because a rational person changes the world, and not his desires, if his desires are not satisfied?[14] Because they perform their biological function by changing the world to satisfy them?[15] Here controversy reigns.

Without a resolution of the controversy, it is impossible to show conclusively that the reward theory of desire can demonstrate that desires have the desire-like direction of fit. And I certainly do not intend to resolve the controversy here. As second best, though, I will highlight those features that the reward theory attributes to desire which are relevant to direction of fit. Whichever theory of direction of fit proves best, the reward theory will have to accommodate it with the resources I describe, or admit that, according to it, desires lack the desire-like direction of fit.

Some philosophers of mind make little or nothing of the notion of direction of fit in their philosophical writings.[16] To them, it might seem absurd to worry about whether or not the reward theory of desire allows the correct direction of fit to be attributed to desires. I cannot agree. The basic fact described by 'direction of fit' is that beliefs can be true but not fulfilled, while desires can be fulfilled but not true. This is a fact that I do not expect to go away. Furthermore, it is a fact that I do not expect to be irreducible. There must be something about the nature of belief, and something about truth, that makes the two fit together; there must be something about the nature of desires and fulfillment, similarly, making them a natural match. A full theory of all four should make it conceptually clear why they pair up the way they do. Given this, it will certainly not do to have a theory of desire that ignores direction of fit completely, for it might turn out that, according to the theory, desires have the features suited for truth but not for satisfaction, and this would prove quite a disaster. I will thus press on with the best sketch I can of the links between the reward theory of desire and direction of fit.

According to the reward theory, desires do not motivate in of themselves: their connection to motivation is only an accident of evolution. If having a desire-like direction of fit requires moving an organism to bring about a state of affairs (the desired end itself, or the forming of an intention to take the necessary means to the end, say), then the reward theory cannot explain why it is necessarily true that desires have the desire-like direction of fit. As has been argued throughout this work, however, the motivational theory of desire is implausible on independent grounds, and it is clear that motivational theories of direction of fit are implausible on some of the same grounds. What becomes of the direction of fit of wishes that the past be different or that the laws of nature be otherwise, if direction of fit requires motivational force?[17]

All that the reward theory *can* offer is an account of direction of fit in terms of contingency-based learning. Though unfamiliar, this proves to be a surprisingly interesting possible ground of direction of fit upon closer inspection. The relevant feature of desires for direction of fit, according to the reward theory, is that they *drive the mind of the organism into particular configurations*. Desiring that *P* leads to learning signals that lead to changes in perceptual capacities, changes in behavioral and cognitive habits, and probably other forms of long-term change as well. Thus, desiring tends to *regulate* the mind of the organism with the desires. At the same time, while it is true that some desires are regulated by others (if the acquisition and maintenance of new intrinsic desires depends upon the learning signals produced through one's existing desires), this is not a necessary fact about desires. There is no requirement in the nature of desire itself holding that it must be possible to acquire new desires through contingency-based learning. Hence, it is part of the essential nature of desire to regulate the mind, but not part of the essential nature of desire to be subject to regulation. Desires, by their very nature, shape the world around them, but are not essentially shaped by it. Here is a possible ground for the desire-like direction of fit.

In order to sustain the view that the desire-like direction of fit stems from the matter of regulation, two things would be needed. The first would be an argument that all mental states with the desire-like direction of fit are essentially regulators, though not essentially subject to regulation. Trying and intending, like desiring, would have to have the shaping of the world as an essential feature, while being independent in principle of other shaping forces. Having no settled view on the nature of trying or prior intention, I have no quick argument to this effect, but perhaps such an argument could be constructed: the prospects are not entirely bleak.[18]

The second thing that would be needed is a clearer view of what it is for one thing to naturally regulate another. The only literal and familiar form of regulation is the regulation of things by intentional agents: I can regulate the temperature of my oven through the use of the dial, and you can regulate my driving by voting on traffic bylaws, and so on. But it may be that there is a literal but less familiar form of regulation, such that non-intentional systems can themselves literally regulate one another. Certainly in engineering one speaks of regulatory systems: the oven regulates its interior temperature, once I have set the dial, by means of a thermostat. Is this literal, but non-agential, regulation? Perhaps it is.

Non-mental systems can literally destroy one another, create one another, prevent one another from changing, and so on. Why should they not also regulate one another? Do cells not regulate their own sodium levels? Does the Banff National Park ecosystem not regulate the deer population? (Well, perhaps it no longer does, almost all the predators having been killed off early in the twentieth century. But recognizing a failure of regulation amounts to recognizing the possibility of regulation under other conditions.)

Back in the mid-twentieth century there was an enthusiasm for naturalizing the notion of regulation, and for explaining biological function in terms of natural regulation (Braithwaite 1968; Nagel 1961). Now that biological function more commonly receives explanations in historical or functional-role terms (Godfrey-Smith 1993; Millikan 1984; Davies 2001; but see Adams 1979) the enthusiasm for giving a non-intentional account of regulation has waned. Yet perhaps there is room for an account of natural regulation still, even if the account would have nothing to say about biological function.

If, then, there is a non-intentional account of regulation, and if contingency-based learning proves to be a form of regulation on such an account, then there would at least be the beginning of a story as to how desires come to have the desire-like direction of fit. This would be one route from the reward theory of desire to direction of fit. Other routes might also be possible, given particular accounts of the good or the rational, but because I have even less to say about the good and the rational than I do about natural regulation, I will leave off with merely mentioning them as possibilities. Showing that the reward theory of desire attributes the correct direction of fit to desires remains a challenge, but perhaps not an insurmountable one.

3. A Postponed Controversy: Moral Motivation

A topic that may have been nagging at the reader for some time is the stance of the reward theory on moral motivation. People are sometimes motivated to do what is morally right or good: they help one another, pass just laws, promote fair treatment of the disadvantaged, and so on. If the reward theory of desire is correct, and the supplementary account it supplies of human desires in all their complexities is also correct, then what follows about the nature of moral motivation? Does it allow for moral concern to motivate in the absence of a desire to do what is right? Does it allow for moral knowledge to give rise to desires to do what is right? Does it make moral motivation entirely dependent upon desire?

Until now, I have avoided such questions. In part, I have avoided discussing moral desires because they are controversial, while desires for the victory of a particular sporting team, say, are not controversial in the same way. Obviously, one should avoid building one's theory upon the most contested data as a general rule, and nowhere are the data more hotly contested than in the field of moral psychology. Also, I have avoided questions of moral psychology because, until now, I have not had a proper statement of the reward theory or a proper statement of how it explains the rich, lived experience of human desire. Now that both are in hand, something about moral motivation can be said. I should be clear that what follows is not an *argument* that moral motivation should be understood in a certain way, but rather an explanation of the resources available to the reward theory for explaining moral motivation. If any argument could be made in favor of understanding moral motivation in this way based on the present work, it is that this book as a whole makes the reward theory of desire compelling, and therefore whatever treatment the theory can give of moral motivation must be correct.

The simplest account of moral motivation that I can see in keeping with the reward theory is as follows. Allow that certain actions are moral, others immoral,[19] and that at least some people have perceptual or cognitive capacities allowing them to represent actions as having these properties. In some morality-representing people, these representational capacities are connected to the reward system so as to constitute right action as rewarding. In others, they are connected so as to constitute right action as neither rewarding nor punishing. And in the remainder, they are connected so as to constitute right action as a punishment. These are people who intrinsically desire that people act morally, people who neither intrinsically desire nor are averse to people acting morally, and people who are intrinsically averse to moral action. To keep things simple, consider only the people with intrinsic desires that people act morally. These people go about their business, perceptually and cognitively representing many aspects of the situations in which they find themselves. On a given occasion, these representations may include representations of the situation as offering an opportunity to promote moral action or as threatening to contain or prolong non-moral action. Some of these representations, including (in our morality-desirous individuals) the moral representations, will have impact upon their bearers' reward systems. These various impacts will be in proportion to the strength of the various desires they reflect, and to the estimated likelihood that the situation will make a difference to desire satisfaction or frustration, all else being equal. Taking all of these inputs into account, along with current perceptual and cognitive representation, and current information about motor output, and in part influenced by past learning, the basal ganglia will select from among the possible responses and promote one. If the moral desire is strong and the likely gain or loss to morality felt significant, and the other desires are weak and felt to be less dramatically affected by current action, and if the individual has engaged in some minimum of relevant past behavioral learning, then (all else being equal) the individual will act in the manner he or she takes to be likely to promote morality. Thus, moral motivation might be produced.

A few illustrations may be helpful. Here is Nick, well aware that $1,000 from his savings account could make a clear contribution to a shelter for the homeless, and so make a clear moral contribution. But Nick is equally aware that the money could also be used to further other interests of his, most saliently his enthusiasm for extremely high-fidelity stereo equipment. If he should see the money as equally certain to benefit each desire (he has no doubts that the homeless shelter is run in a financially responsible and efficient manner; he has no doubts that he can select better vacuum tubes to run his amplifier), and if all else is equal, then the reward theory would expect Nick to be moved by the stronger desire.

The same sort of conflict should also arise, according to the reward theory, when the choice is whether or not to perform some clearly immoral action, rather than a morally generous action such as donating money. If Nick is contemplating claiming his holiday expenses as work expenses, and so stealing money from the university employing him, his choice can again be expected to reflect which of his desires is stronger, all else being equal. Or, quite saliently in a case such as this, which *collection* of desires has more strength overall, for Nick's aversion to public condemnation (which would follow any discovery of his misdeed), his various desires the satisfaction of which requires money (which he would not have if he lost his job), and so on are likely to weigh in, along with his desire to act morally, against making a false expense claim. So long as Nick represents these possibilities, the desires to which they are relevant will contribute to producing reward and punishment signals that will have a motivational impact, and it is simply the sum of these impacts that the reward theory expects to carry the day.

In the absence of moral training, or after excellent moral training, things may go differently for Nick. Moral training can in principle take many forms, but the form pertinent to the reward theory is that of habits formed by past reward and punishment signals, and weaker but still habit-like connections of the same sort. If Nick's moral deeds have rarely been rewarded, or often punished, there may be very weak connections in his motor striatum between input from representations of moral situations to output to motor instructions needed to act morally. It may be that it will take a particularly strong signal from his moral desires in order for him to do the right thing on a given occasion, under such circumstances. Perhaps Nick has a modest desire that people do what is right, but his adult life has rarely rewarded moral action. Wanting to do what is right, to some extent, but also having been punished in the past for trying to do what is right, Nick no longer finds it as easy as he once did to do the right thing, and doing the wrong thing comes more readily. Nick might afterward reproach himself for not being moved to do the right thing, and find that his immoral gains are shallow, but this motivational stance will not guarantee right action in the absence of proper learning. If Nick has had a more uplifting moral education, however, things might turn out quite the opposite: he might be inclined to resist temptations to immoral action even more powerfully than would be suggested by the strength of his desires. If Nick has often been rewarded for resisting immoral temptations, and never rewarded (or often punished) for falling to them, then representations of opportunities for immoral action are likely to find no easy route through the motor striatum to action, even when reward signals from Nick's desires are indicating that the situation promises net desire satisfaction if only Nick will do what is wrong. In this situation, though Nick will perhaps feel the strong pull of temptation, he will find himself constitutionally incapable of acting wrongly. Afterward perhaps he will even reproach himself: why did he not accept the sexual advances of his student, why did he not just keep the money he found in the wallet, why did he not just throw the trash out the car window? For moral training can modify behavioral dispositions independently of desire strength, and habit can win a victory for morality even against the wishes of the individual in whom the battle is fought, according to the reward theory.

This picture of moral motivation, though not completely simplistic, is the simplest and most straightforward the reward theory of desire can provide. No doubt many philosophers will rebel at the picture of moral motivation being presented here. Where is the dignity of morality? Where is the force of reason alone? Where is the person who stands apart from her desires and decides whether or not to act upon them?[20] But consider what is biologically possible. We have our perceptual and cognitive representational capacities: somewhere in them is our capacity to represent that things are right or wrong, just or unjust, helpful, harmful, and so on. In order for these representations to have an effect upon what we do, they must act upon some motor pathway or other. What is open to them? Well, they all project directly to the striatum, for a start. But representations that have a powerful effect upon movement just because of their projections to the motor striatum, independent of reward signals, appear most like representations that move us out of habit. If moral representations regularly move us through such a pathway, a pathway that is equivalent to the one that leads me to unthinkingly answer the phone with the word "hello," this will be a comfort to no one. Another route by which moral representations might move us is through their projections to the OFC, and so to the reward system. But this is just the route that would constitute moral desires: the route I have been describing in this section. If this were the main route by which moral considerations moved us, then moral considerations would move us in the same way that considerations of our favorite hockey teams and our favorite sandwiches move us. The strengths of the desires might be different, but the basic mechanism would be identical. The philosopher who seeks a special dignity, force, and independence for moral motivation will not find it here. The final route for moral representations to take to promote action would be through the higher motor control centers, such as the motor PFC or motor AC. Perhaps moral representations can directly promote the formation of motor intentions to act in a way that is appropriate to the moral situation. Certainly it is true that movement possibilities are constantly appearing in the motor centers, forcing the basal ganglia to inhibit them, and so perhaps moral considerations can place morally appropriate movement possibilities directly into the motor centers, and so cause action, independently of desires. Yet if moral representation would not merely promote possible actions, but actually override the inhibitory action of the basal ganglia, this would put moral motivation on a par with Tourettic urges and would make moral action a form of behavioral tic. For the power to move a person directly to action through activation of motor instructions that the basal ganglia cannot readily inhibit is exactly what is characteristic of Tourette syndrome, and not autonomous agency. Perhaps there is some fourth route from representation to action, not yet described by neuroscience but waiting for us to find, distinctive of moral motivation (and so not possessed by other species), and unlike habits, desires, or Tourettic tics in its manner of action. Perhaps. But I do not see any particular reason for optimism on this front. Considering the empirical possibilities, in seems to me that there is no special dignity in the *structure* of moral motivation, only in its content.

6

Clean and Messy Theories

The reward theory of desire is far from the simplest theory of desire one could hope for. It requires the existence of perceptual and cognitive representational capacities, for instance, without explaining in what these capacities might consist. It invokes a form of learning that is so unfamiliar it has no name in everyday language, and is characterized best in purely mathematical terms. It requires one to give complex accounts, sometimes *very* complex accounts, of such apparently simple phenomena as petting the cat because one wants to, eating because one is hungry, or feeling bad because one wanted a particular girl to call last night and she did not. At the same time, the reward theory also has a certain theoretical elegance. Its derivations of the everyday phenomena may be ungainly on this or that occasion, but the theory itself is readily stated. The theory may entail that our desires exist within an incredibly tangled web of causal and representational relationships, but it also entails that desire itself forms a straightforward functional kind, realized in a straightforward physiological system in the brains of animals like us. From the perspective of phenomenology, the theory is a mess, perhaps; from the perspective of science, the theory is clean.

There are those who cannot abide theoretical mess, at least when it comes to the philosophy of mind. If common sense points to one thing and our best science points to something else, the tension is declared intolerable, and the only remedy allowed is the eradication of the offending element of common sense. In the philosophy of mind, this particular form of fastidiousness goes under the heading of *eliminativism*. If common sense declares that pain is a sensation but neuroscience declares it to be the product of two distinct and potentially competing neural systems, then the concept of pain should be eliminated, says Hardcastle (1999). If common sense declares emotions to be a seamless web but neuroscience declares them heterogeneous, then the concept of emotion should be eliminated, says Griffiths (1997). If common sense holds our minds to be filled with discrete, sentence-like beliefs but neuroscience declares that we are really filled with continuous pattern-recognition systems, then the concept of belief should be eliminated, says Churchland (1981). This urge to eliminate that which does not mesh cleanly with the scientific picture of the world is not restricted to the philosophy of mind, of course. When philosophers assert that, given the gappy nature of atoms and molecules, nothing is solid (following Eddington 1928), for example, they appeal to the same urge to tidy up our ontology. But at present, it is perhaps true that the philosophy of mind is the domain in which the most enthusiastic and persuasive eliminativists are working. To the eliminativist, the sharp contrast between the theoretical cleanliness of the reward theory of desire and the messiness of the theory's mesh with phenomenology must naturally excite the urge to tidy things up. Why not declare that the reward theory is a correct theory of something—call it 'reward'—but not a correct theory of desire, because there *is* no correct theory of desire? Why not hold that, rather than explain the nature of desire, the reward theory has in fact made the best imaginable case for *eliminating* the concept of desire? So might say the eliminativist.

At the same time, there are others who cannot see why anyone should prefer a clean theory to a messy one. Such philosophers might have quite a different suggestion to make to the reward theory. Why hold that reward and reward alone is the essential face of desire? Why not hold that reward and motivation, or reward and pleasure, or motivation and pleasure, or—well, why not?—reward and motivation *and* pleasure jointly form the essence of desire? Of course, this will mean that desires will not be natural psychological kinds and that they will not be realized by natural physiological kinds in beings like us. And it will certainly mean that the relationship between the phenomenology of desire and desire itself will be a tangled mess. But who wanted a tidy theory of desire anyway? Some philosophers, most famously Donald Davidson (1980), have gone so far as to hold that one should expect the mind *not* to be realized by theoretically neat physical entities.[1] Far from thinking that the reward theory is too messy, these philosophers are likely to think it is too obsessed with cleanliness, too obsessed with carving off a well-defined theoretical entity when a less well-defined but more suitable entity is in the offing.

In this final chapter, I answer both sorts of objections. The reward theory of desire is neither too messy nor too clean. Like my bedroom when I was a child, it is *just messy enough*. Exactly how messy that is will become apparent as the chapter progresses.

1. Against Fastidiousness

Arguments for the elimination of putative mental states are generally explicit about what is required for elimination. To conclude that there are no desires, they say, one needs both a philosophical claim about what states of affairs must obtain in order for there to be desires, and a (generally empirical) claim to the effect that those states of affairs do not obtain. I will assume that the empirical facts are not in dispute. What is left to dispute is what must be the case for the empirical facts to show that there are, or are not, desires.

What must be the case for there to be desires is also what must be the case for our term 'desire' to refer, as eliminativists generally point out. So it should be enlightening to consider various theories of linguistic reference. Under what conditions does a putative natural kind term refer or not refer, according to philosophical theories of language? Here we get three main types of answers: naïve descriptivist answers, naïve causal answers, and sophisticated intermediates. This is very familiar philosophical ground, so I will traverse it quickly.

According to the naïve descriptive theorist, the term 'desire' has an associated description telling us what a thing must be like in order to be a referent of that term. Anything fitting the description is properly called 'a desire', and anything not fitting the description is not properly called 'a desire'. These descriptions are shared by all competent speakers of the English language, and so are not particularly complex. For 'desire', for instance, the associated description might look something like this: 'a kind of mental thing that inclines people to act; stronger ones provide stronger inclinations to act; sexual desire, hunger, and thirst are paradigm examples'. Of course, this is a gross oversimplification, but it suggests the right sort of complex description everyone has in mind when talking about desires, on the naïve descriptive view.

If the naïve descriptive theorist is right, then all that is required for there to be no desires is that there be no one thing having all the features competent speakers of English associate with the term 'desire'. Since the reward theory does not agree with common sense on absolutely every point, it follows that if the reward theory is the best possible theory of desire, then there is no such thing as desire. The only problem with this argument is that nearly everyone now agrees that the naïve descriptive theorist really is a bit naïve, and his theory of reference is mistaken. The arguments of Kripke (1972) and Putnam (1975) seem to have shown this much, at least. Naïve descriptive theories have trouble with a number of things, such as explaining the possibility of co-reference between speakers (doesn't everyone's personal description differ a little from everyone else's—but then aren't we talking about slightly different things?), especially across theoretical disputes (wouldn't Freudians mean something different by 'desire' from the rest of us—but then, how could we even put our disagreement into words?). If an eliminativist argument depends upon the naïve descriptive theory of term reference, then there seems little reason to worry about it.

On the other hand, according to the naïve causal theorist, descriptions associated with terms are completely irrelevant. All that matters is that for the term 'desire' there was a baptismal event that introduced it into the language. Crudely, someone pointed and said, "Whatever is making Og drink, call that and things of the same kind 'desires'." The thing making Og drink was of a particular natural kind, and it was the causal origin of the naming event, and 'desire' thereby became the name of that kind. Of course, this is a gross oversimplification of the naïve causal theory, but it does get the idea across.

If the naïve causal theorist is right, then it is easy to show that there are desires, and the eliminativist is wrong. For *representation-driven reward-based learning* is, plausibly, a natural functional kind, and so desires turn out to be a natural kind, on the reward theory. They were the things being pointed at when the term 'desire' was coined, and so the term 'desire' refers to them. Whatever crazy ideas we might have got about desire in between coining the term and discovering the underlying natural kind are irrelevant. Thus, the fact that there are various points of disagreement between the reward theory and common sense is no evidence at all that the term 'desire' does not refer. The only problem with this argument is that, like the naïve descriptive theory, the naïve causal theory is terribly implausible—so implausible that the source most often cited (Kripke 1972) actually disavows the theory as a theory, calling it only a "picture." If the naïve causal theory is right, then the term 'mermaid' refers to a real animal (to manatees, these apparently being the most likely origin of mermaid legends), the term 'unicorn' refers (for the same sort of reason), the term 'animal magnetism' refers (it is a name for the causal basis of hypnosis), and so on.[2] Yet it seems obvious that none of these terms refer to any such things. If an anti-eliminativist argument depends upon the naïve baptismal theory of reference, then the eliminativist need not worry about it.[3]

In between naïve causal and descriptive theories are a range of theories more likely to be true. On these theories, desires need not be just as we conceive them in order for the term 'desire' to refer, but they need to be at least a little bit like we conceive them: mere causal connection to something at the other end of a baptismal event is not enough on its own. Exactly where to strike this balance has not been settled, needless to say, but surely some such theory must be right, for its most extreme competitors are clearly mistaken. If any such theory is right, then it will not be trivial to settle whether or not the term 'desire' refers, because the question of whether anything has *enough* of the *right sort* of properties to be a desire will have to be answered, and this is a subtle matter, not quickly judged.

What, then, is there to say to the eliminativist? This is hardly the appropriate forum in which to consider the most general arguments for the elimination of all propositional attitudes, and I have nothing new to add to that debate in any case. But if the question is just whether the concept of desire specifically should be eliminated from philosophical and scientific thinking about the mind, then a more concrete answer can be defended. The best way to answer such a question, it seems to me, is to enumerate again, in summary form, the various things common sense has to say about desire, and what the reward theory has to say about desire, and determine how good or bad the fit is between pre-theoretic expectation and the theory. If the fit looks good, then only a very stringent theory of reference could force us to hold that the term 'desire' nevertheless does not refer, and so force us to eliminate the notion of desire from our philosophy and science. If the fit looks less good, then it would take a very liberal theory of reference to rescue the reference of the term 'desire', and so rescue the reality of desire. But without a final theory of reference, this is where the matter will have to be left. Fair enough: let us get the matter advanced at least that far. Perhaps one or two considerations can be advanced at the end that will tip the scales in favor of the reality of desire.

The simplest way to proceed will be to enumerate the claims the reward theory makes about desire, and then compare them to the corresponding claims made by common sense. Since the most basic fact about the reward theory is that it claims there is a single entity to be theorized, we should begin with the following:

Claim 1 (C1): Intrinsic desires, wants, and wishes form a natural grouping, closely related to one another but distinguished from other pro attitudes such as trying or intending.

C1 introduces a certain systematization into thinking about desire that is not, I think, present in everyday thought. People talk about planning, wanting, and wishing, but they do not generally worry about whether wishing is more like wanting than like planning. Common sense has one grouping, the pro attitudes, and it has many small sub-groupings, desires, plans, wishes, and so on, but it has no intermediate groupings that lump the particular species of the pro attitude kingdom into discrete phyla, classes, and so on. Thus, C1 differs from common sense in this respect. At the same time, everyday thought does not generally object to introducing systematic grouping where once there was chaos. It did not run counter to common sense to distinguish between those natural substances which proved to be elements (e.g., copper, gold, carbon) and those which proved to be compounds (e.g., salt, water, quartz), though common sense had never made the grouping itself. It is part of the job of theories to form coherent groupings of things, and common sense does not object to the project in principle. So I think it safe to say that C1, while not a part of common sense, nonetheless is consistent with it, and so poses no reason to eliminate desire from our ontology. Admittedly, common sense *does* revolt when theory tries to change groupings it endorses (to move whales from the fishes to the mammals, for example, or to force the year 2000 into the same millennium as the year 1999), but this applies only when common sense already had a settled opinion about how a grouping should go, one which theory disputes.

The other basic postulates of the reward theory are as follows:

C2: Intrinsic desires may be distinguished from instrumental ones.
C3: All desires are desires that P ('P' standing for some proposition).

C2 is not particularly controversial. Pre-theoretic considerations are often very sloppy about distinguishing intrinsic from instrumental desires, but the distinction is widely recognized and accepted for all that. No one has difficulty recognizing a distinction between means and ends, and most people will have little trouble naming things they want for their own sake, without need to appeal to some further goal.

More controversial is C3. Common sense recognizes at least desires for objects (for apples, for Helen) and for states of affairs (that I get my way, that π be an irrational number), and is, I think, taken by surprise by the philosophical arguments that all desires are desires that *P* in the end. But common sense is cavalier with the propositional attitudes generally. One plans a party and plans to go out; one believes Fred, believes that the Earth is spherical, and believes in ghosts; and so on. By regimenting the matter, insisting that all desires get propositional contents, the reward theory of desire does a certain amount of violence to common sense, which should not be overlooked. Yet the discrepancy between pre-theory and theory in this case is a standard discrepancy that shows up everywhere in contemporary literature on the mind. This can only count toward eliminativism in the case of desire if it counts toward eliminativism in general, and while that case has been made (Churchland 1981), few have been persuaded.

What about the contents of desires? According to the reward theory,

C4: One can, in principle, intrinsically desire that *P* for any state of affairs *P* one can perceptually or cognitively represent.

Asked to be clear about what they want just for its own sake, I think many people would answer that they would like healthy children, long life, interesting work, good food to eat, happiness, the acclaim of others, world peace—a fairly standard list. Encouraged not to restrict themselves to the grand things they want but to also include the little things, I think most people could also come up with idiosyncratic intrinsic wishes—to write a novel, to perform at Carnegie Hall, to play for a day with the Green Bay Packers. They could also articulate desires regarding mundane concerns—to have a husband that remembers one's birthday, to have leisure time. In all of this, pre-theoretic considerations harmonize perfectly with the reward theory.

Divergence between the reward theory and everyday thought comes when we turn to desires regarding sensuous states. Though in chapter 3 I did my best to argue that it is not theoretically unreasonable to assert that we have intrinsic desires regarding what odors we smell, what sights we see, and so on, it nonetheless runs against common sense to make this a general principle. Common sense would more typically hold that one has preferences for various sensuous states simply because one desires pleasure and is averse to displeasure, and because some of these states cause pleasure while others cause displeasure. The reward theory allows desires for pleasure, but cannot make them fundamental. This is an important point. Indeed, for my own part, I take this to be the source of the greatest tension between the reward theory and common sense. But does it suffice to show that desires do not really exist, if the reward theory is right? I think not. For all that the reward theory does, in the end, is take a number of philosophically ignored pro attitudes, such as tastes and likings, and force them into the realm of desire. If desires really include one's tastes as discrete sensuous desires, this will be a surprise to common sense, but it will be a surprise akin to forcing common sense to admit whales into the collection of known mammals. Common sense rebelled, but the category of mammal was hardly threatened as a result.

One other potential conflict between the reward theory and common sense over C4 lies in the fact that the reward theory permits desires to have any content at all, at least in principle. But one might hold, in the spirit of Anscombe (1963/2000, 70–72) that in order to desire something there must be a desirability characterization one could give of the desired thing. Anscombe seems skeptical that one can desire a saucer of mud, say, or a twig of mountain ash, unless one is ready to say that one desires it "because it would be pleasant," "because it befits a person like me to possess such a thing," "for my health," or something of the sort. For however odd such insistences would be (and however mad they would make one seem), they would at least make intelligible why one would want such a thing as a saucer of mud. I am not sure that common sense requires so much, however. It seems to me that "because he is crazy" is a good enough explanation of why a person would want a saucer of mud or a twig of mountain ash for its own sake, so far as common sense is concerned—which is to say that common sense does not recognize a conceptual impossibility in people having very unusual desire contents, just a psychological implausibility. And since the reward theory is a theory of all possible desires, however psychologically implausible, there is no tension between it and common sense over the matter.

C1–C4 cover the most basic features of the reward theory. What remain to be considered are the details, beginning with the three faces of desire and finishing with the claims the reward theory makes about the way desires are enacted in the minds of beings like us. I will start with reward.

> **C5:** A thing is a reward or punishment only if it is wanted or unwanted (a thing to which one is averse), respectively, by the recipient.
>
> **C6:** To be a desire is to be a representational capacity contributing to a reward or punishment signal.
>
> **C7:** To be a desire is to be a representational capacity contributing to a certainly mathematically describable form of learning.
>
> **C8:** Desires are realized in human beings and other animals like us by the biological reward system, centered around the dopamine-releasing neurons of the SNpc and VTA.
>
> **C9:** Desiring that *P* is what makes it possible for people to learn certain sorts of habits and to have certain sorts of modifications to their sensory capacities, and probably what makes it possible for them to undergo other, less well studied long-term psychological changes.

C5–C9 cover the most important claims about the relation of desire to reward made by the reward theory. Their main feature is that, with the exception of C5, they are highly novel claims, completely foreign to the expectations of common sense. C5 is rather more conservative. Its claim is, I held in chapter 2, a platitude of common sense. But the remaining four claims all invite a question. Does the fact that a theory makes utterly unexpected claims about desire give us any reason to think that the theory is really showing that there is no such thing as desire? There seems little reason to say so. It will be the nature of any theory to give new insight into the thing about which it theorizes. Without new insight, what is the good of a new theory? Without the hope of radical new findings, what is the purpose of investigating a phenomenon? Light was found to have an incredible speed, and yet we did not conclude there was no such thing as light. The mechanism of heredity proved to be a molecule with just four repeating units, and yet we did not eliminate genes from our ontology. All the same, it is clear that *some* surprising discoveries force or threaten elimination. The discovery that there is more genetic variability within racial groups than between them threatens to eliminate the notion of race.[4] The discovery that the same laws of physics apply above and below the orbit of the moon eliminated the superlunary realm from physics. The discovery that birds are more closely related to some reptiles than some reptiles are related to each other argues for the elimination of the term "reptile" from biology. And so on.

A principle would be helpful here. In discussions of elimination, one thing that strikes me as important is whether surprising theoretical discoveries surprise us because they force us to give up cherished beliefs, or whether they only surprise us because we had never contemplated the possibility of the discovery. Only insights that *take away* from what we once thought we knew threaten to eliminate an item from our ontology. People had no settled convictions about light's speed, and there were no presuppositions about the mechanism of heredity. In these cases, elimination was not even considered. On the other hand, we thought we knew that there were large biological differences between people of European ancestry and people of African ancestry, but these large biological differences have not materialized. We thought that a different sort of physics from that applying to the terrestrial realm was needed to explain why the bodies of the heavens move steadily in their courses, but this proved false. We thought that birds formed one clear natural grouping, reptiles another, but this, too, has been questioned. Hence elimination, or its threat. This is not to say that *every* insight that takes away from what we once thought we knew threatens to eliminate the topic of research. The discovery that the atom could be split violated expectations, as did the discovery that mass can be transformed directly into energy. But these discoveries did not seriously threaten to eliminate atoms, mass, or energy from our ontology. Even so, it seems to me that *only* discoveries that take away can threaten elimination. It was not learning that my father brought Christmas gifts to my house that threatened to undermine the reality of Santa Claus, but learning that he brought them only to me, and in a car, and via the door. Had he also delivered to other children, in a sleigh, via the chimney, I would have simply concluded I had acquired a new fact about Santa Claus, namely, that he was my father.[5]

If the only novel theoretical claims that threaten elimination are those forcing us to reject our prior convictions, then C7–C9, for all their novelty, are no threat to the reality of desire. For it is clear enough that common sense has no opinion about the biological realization of desire, or mathematical reward theories, and it has never had any more settled view on habit learning than that rewards can be relevant, as chapter 2 described. On these topics, the reward theory of desire only adds new insights: it takes nothing away. The same, I think, can be said for C6, which offers a statement of the reward theory itself. For common sense by and large operates without philosophical theories of the natures of things, and as a philosophical theory of desire, C6 is concerned only with its nature. Common sense has its means of identifying desires: by the feelings they cause, by watching what others do more than listening to what they say, and so on. But these means of identifying desires are not held up as a theory of the nature of desire by common sense. The *theory* of desire is a topic common sense has been happy to leave to philosophy.

The next face of desire is pleasure, and here there is only one important claim made by the reward theory:

C10: Pleasure and displeasure are representations of net positive and negative (respectively) change (relative to expectations) in desire satisfaction.

C10 is like C6–C9 in that it is a theoretical addition to existing beliefs about desire that undermines no pre-theoretic belief. It is not part of common sense that pleasure and displeasure represent nothing: the question of their representational content simply does not arise in everyday thought. And in fact, the claims common sense makes about the relation between pleasure and desire were the best support chapter 3 could offer for its view of pleasure. According to common sense, really wanting something to be the case makes one vulnerable to sadness if it proves not to be, but also opens one to happiness if things work out as one desires. Also according to everyday thought, one way to learn what you intrinsically desire is to find out what makes you happy. And it is widely held that there is something wrong with a person who feels pleased when confronted with the fact that all he holds dear is falling to ruin or a person who feels morose though, aside from feeling morose, she has everything in her life that she might want. These claims were used as philosophical support for the claim that pleasure represents desire satisfaction back in chapter 3, and so can hardly be inconsistent with the reward theory's view of pleasure.

This brings us to the third face of desire, motivation. According the reward theory, the following are all certainly true or likely true:

C11: People are typically moved to action, or inhibited from acting, because there is something they want to achieve (avoid), and they see a way of achieving (avoiding) it.
C12: Desires can cause one to form prior intentions, and cause one to try.
C13: Desires are not the only causes of goal-directed movement, but of all the pro attitudes, they are the most fundamental causes.
C14: A human being with no desires is incapable of normal goal-directed movement.
C15: Moral thinking has no special power to move us except insofar as we have desires regarding morality.

C11 is a very straightforward claim, so far as everyday thought is concerned, and it is a comfort to common sense to see the reward theory affirm it after some of the more surprising claims the theory made about reward and pleasure.

C12 is a little more complex. It does not merely say that people form prior intentions because they want something, which *would* be uncontroversial, but says that desires *cause* the formation of prior intentions and episodes of trying. When it comes to the causation of mental events, common sense has very mixed feelings. It is easy to attribute a mind full of causes and effects to *you*, but less easy to attribute such a mind to myself. After all, I just have to watch the way you rise to taunts about your English accent (gained during your year in Sheffield, after a youth in Tennessee) in order to think that your impulse to answer the taunts is caused in a most mechanical fashion. But when I think about the way *I* cannot resist defending Canada when its name comes up in casual conversation, well, that seems a much less mechanical matter. Certainly, I try to defend Canada's medical system because I want to have people think well of my country, but to say that my desire *causes* me to try this retort or that is, for most people, to go too far. By adopting a causal view of the role of desires, the reward theory violates the common sense view that our minds operate in a manner distinct from that of the rest of the universe. Yet this discrepancy between the reward theory and common sense can hardly justify even the beginnings of eliminativism unless every naturalistic theory of mind courts eliminativism just in virtue of its naturalism. This has certainly not been the judgment of philosophers of mind, even those most enthusiastic about eliminativism.

People are likely to differ over the hostility to common sense displayed by C13–15. To some it will seem only common sense that desires are the key to motivation. Certainly, one may sometimes act without desiring to act, but normally one acts because one wants to, and normally what one wants to do will trump any competing source of motivation. Likewise, normally if there is nothing at all one wants to do, not even a little, one will just do nothing (though this is not a normal psychological state to be in). Even in the case of moral considerations, to some it seems plain that a person who does not want to do what is right will certainly not do what is right unless forced to by a vigilant legal system. But standing in opposition to the people of common sense who say these things will be other people of common sense saying just the opposite. Some will say that normally one does not worry about one's wants: one does one's duty, meets one's needs, fulfills a role, and so on. Doing what one wants is a luxury, rarely enjoyed. Such people will say that life would carry on quite smoothly if one no longer wanted anything, for then there would be nothing holding one back from doing what one *has* to do. As for moral considerations, such people are likely to insist that they never act morally because they want to: they act morally because they must. In moral philosophy, needless to say, these are matters of some import. But the simple fact of systematic disagreement within common sense shows that there is no ground for elimination here, whichever view is correct. Elimination makes sense only when it turns out that desires lack most of the properties almost everyone was sure they had. When it turns out that desires lack only qualities many disputed their having in the first place, no eliminativist conclusion follows.

Having surveyed the three faces of desire and their treatment under the reward theory, we have covered the main theses the reward theory holds, supports without entailing, or needs to be true. Another pair of claims with a certain amount of controversy to them should be added to the collection.

C16: There are no fleeting desires.
C17: Desires cause happenings in consciousness, but are not themselves elements of consciousness.

In spite of appearances, however, C16 proves to be a fairly harmless claim. For all that C16 holds is that there are no fleeting *intrinsic* desires. Fleeting instrumental desires abound, according to the reward theory, and C16 appears controversial only because common sense has never been very careful to distinguish intrinsic from instrumental desires in casual conversation. Much more serious is C17. For I think that most people have the idea that desires can lie dormant in our minds, but on occasion rise into consciousness and thereby command our attention. Thirst and hunger, wanting one's daughter to be healthy on the occasion of one's terrifying visit to the pediatric oncologist: these seem desires that can fill up large portions of our conscious experience. Yet according to the reward theory, it is not the desires themselves that are found in consciousness, but only their effects. The desires lurk permanently outside of consciousness, having a causal influence upon us but making themselves known only indirectly. I think that, as with some of the other claims made by the reward theory, this is a genuine cost of the reward theory, so far as common sense is concerned. Yet it is something of a comfort to the reward theory to know that many philosophers have been happy to distinguish the realm of consciousness from the realm of the propositional attitudes without worrying that eliminativism must follow.[6]

On reflection, then, the reward theory agrees with common sense at many points, supplements it at many points without disagreeing, and takes issue with it at a few important points. Is this a good reason to conclude that the reward theory has really eliminated the notion of desire, rather than given a theory of it? I suspect not. In the place of a precise theory of reference which would prove that the term 'desire' still refers even if the reward theory is true, consider a few pointed examples from the history of science. Take gravity. Phenomenologically, gravity is a straightforward matter. Things tend to fall downward on the Earth, massive bodies tend to come together in space, and so on. Theoretically, it seemed reasonable to treat gravity as a force, like magnetism. When Einstein introduced the radical idea that gravity would be better treated as the curvature of space itself, this did not result in the elimination of gravity from physics. No one should conclude that, if this is the best theory one can give of gravity, then there just is no such thing: all there is is curved space instead. No one should conclude that the phenomenology was so misleading that the concept of gravity had to be thrown out. Gravity has simply been given a new theoretical treatment. Consider also the history of theories of light. The theoretical claims now made about light (wave/particle duality, speed measured the same by observers in any frame of reference, waves without a vibrating medium) are such that they routinely astound the people of common sense who learn about them, and yet no one should doubt that light is real.[7] Such examples appear to set a high standard for the eliminativist: in order to reasonably say that there is no such thing as desire, the best theory of desire must be more outrageous, more controversial, more defiant of common sense than existing theories of gravity or light, or other comparable phenomena. It seems to me, reviewing the points of agreement and disagreement between the reward theory and common sense, that the reward theory passes this particular test.

2. Against Slovenliness

The reward theory raises eliminativist worries precisely because it elects to focus on the least familiar face of desire and to push desire's more familiar faces to the periphery. It does this in part because of arguments against the standard theory of desire and the hedonic theory, but it also does this in part because of an enthusiasm for a clean, simple theory. If motivation is not the nature of desire on its own, and neither is pleasure, then reward on its own must be its nature. It will naturally occur to some philosophers to suggest a little less theoretical cleanliness and a little more theoretical inclusiveness. Why not hold that to desire is to have a reward system *and* motivation (or pleasure, or all three), and that to have anything less is to have only part of what is involved in desiring?

There seem to me very good reasons for not building a multi-faced theory of desire. A theory of desire should not require a motivational face because desire in the absence of motivational capacities is a physical possibility. A theory of desire should not require a hedonic face because desires, like all robust entities, can exist without being represented. And in general, it is better to build less into a theory of desire, so that the theory can explain more phenomena. At least, these are the rough outlines of the rejoinders I will make. As we shall see, the details are rather complex.

Begin with what I take to be the easiest claim: no theory of desire should require an organism to have motivational capacities, tendencies, dispositions or the like in order to have desires. As we saw in chapter 4, it is possible for people to be deprived of the power of movement through damage to movement-production systems in the brain. People with severe Parkinsonian symptoms and people suffering from akinetic mutism are both people who lack the power to move, who appear to have no motivational capacities, tendencies or dispositions of any sort. Yet it is not particularly plausible to see such people as lacking in desires. Would one treat such a person as having no interests that could be served by being cured? If I genuinely have no desire to get better, and my illness is no burden to society, a doctor will not be justified in interfering with my body without my consent in order to cure me, or in expending resources on me that could be spent on someone else who wanted to be cured. Yet people suffering strokes who are thereby rendered akinetic and mute seem to be reasonably treated without consent (even when there is no one else, such as a relative, who can give consent), and such people are not shoved to the end of the line on the grounds of their indifference. We act as though such people want to be cured, but cannot express themselves. Similarly, people suffering from severe Parkinson disease can find the symptoms quite intolerable (Langston and Palfreman 1995).[8] Upon having their symptoms relieved, they are inclined to thank their doctors because, they will say, they very much wanted to be cured while immobile. People generally take such statements about what people wanted during immobility to be true.[9] In these cases, common sense appears to rule that motivational dispositions are not essential to desire.

It might be objected that people with akinetic mutism and profound Parkinson disease really *do* have motivational dispositions: they only need corrections to their biological machinery in order to execute these dispositions. But in the cases of severe Parkinsonism and akinetic mutism, this seems implausible. These people do not have intact motivational systems whose operations are being impeded by external factors. Rather, their motivational systems are themselves damaged. With time and natural healing (akinetic mutism—if the sufferer is lucky) or drugs, grafts, or surgery (severe Parkinson disease) the damage can be overcome, but without them, no psychologically directed motion will take place. To say that these people have dispositions to move when presented with an opportunity to achieve a goal is like saying that a car with ruptured pistons has a disposition to start when the key is turned in the ignition, or saying that a cored apple has a disposition to bring forth an apple tree when planted. By the same sort of reasoning, everyone has motivational dispositions to say "shit" in public, jerk, twitch, bark, and so on, only we lack the Tourettic wiring needed to execute these dispositions. But people do not have such dispositions, cored apples do not tend to bring forth apple trees, ruptured engines do not dispose cars to start, and people suffering from akinetic mutism and profound Parkinson disease do not have motivational tendencies.[10]

It might instead be objected that, contrary to everyday thought, people with akinetic mutism and severe Parkinson disease do not really have desires after all. To desire, one simply must be capable of movement, and our imagining otherwise in particular cases is illusory and misleading. But at this point, what would be the justification for denying the claims of common sense? To reject the claims of common sense, one needs a powerful, well-supported theory to justify the rejection. But at this point, where would one find such a theory? The standard theory itself has been thrown into question by the results of chapters 1–4, and where will support for denying desires to the victims of akinetic mutism and severe Parkinson disease come from, if not from the standard theory?

Now consider the view that pleasure is a necessary feature of desire. In chapter 3, I argued that pleasure and displeasure represent change in desire satisfaction. If that argument holds, then the philosopher who would have pleasure an essential part of desire is someone who would make a representation of desire necessary in order for desire to exist at all. This strikes me as confused. The whole idea of a representation, after all, is that it is a representation of something existing distinct from the representation of it. And if desire is distinct from its representation in pleasure, then pleasure and displeasure cannot be necessary for desiring.

But suppose that chapter 3 showed only that pleasure and displeasure represent change in reward, and suppose reward is distinct from desire. The cases in which pleasure and displeasure are shown to be misrepresenting are cases in which they do not misrepresent desire satisfaction so much as reward acquisition, one might say. On this supposition, there would be room to hold that pleasure is necessary to desire after all. Pleasure would still not be a good candidate for the *sole* face of desire. After all, there are still the arguments of chapter 1, and the fact that if pleasure were the sole face of desire, desire would have little bearing upon motivation in normal humans (as shown in chapter 4). But pleasure would then be a candidate for a necessary component of a two-faced theory of desire. Pleasure and reward together would constitute desire, rather than reward alone.

The two-faced reward/pleasure theory of desire raises a worry about mental causation. According to this theory, desires play a central role in motivation. But also according to it, it is the reward face of desire that plays this central role in motivation, while the pleasure face plays a much smaller and very different type of role (again, as shown in chapter 4). One might be tempted, then, to say that on this two-faced theory, it is not in virtue of desiring that one becomes motivated but in virtue of constituting states of affairs as rewards. Desiring per se is epiphenomenal to motivation. And this might seem a very counterintuitive conclusion, counting decisively against the two-faced theory. But I am not certain how troubling this argument should be. The argument appears to endorse the principle that if a thing counts as an X only because it stands in a relation to some other, distinct thing, then one cannot attribute causal efficacy to the first thing under the description 'an X'. This principle is, however, open to debate. It is only in virtue of its relation to a designer or user that a wooden rod topped with metal counts as a hammer, and yet one would normally think that things can be broken in virtue of being hit by a hammer. Does the principle show that hammers as such are not causally efficacious, or do hammers refute the principle? Because this is a deep problem in the theory of causation, I will not press the point, but simply say that there is room for concern here.[11]

More straightforwardly troubling for the two-faced reward/pleasure theory is the fact that, according to it, people who lose the capacity for pleasure or displeasure lose their desires, even if they retain the capacity to be rewarded and motivated. Recall (from chapter 3) that some recipients of psychosurgery and some victims of neural injury, whose capacities for displeasure especially have been severely blunted, appear nonetheless to be left intact as desiring agents. Likewise, creatures of science fiction possessed of a coldly logical temperament, with no place for emotions in their lives, will also prove to lack desires according to the two-faced pleasure/reward theory. These conclusions do not strike me as correct, for they seem to reject common sense. As before, it would be open to the philosopher favoring a required hedonic face for desire to say that appearances and intuitions are simply misleading, and that common sense is just wrong about such people having desires. Yet also as before, it would seem that justifying the rejection of common sense requires a powerful theory. With the hedonic theory of desire suffering setbacks at every turn, there seems little hope of finding a powerful overarching theory that would require pleasure to be a part of any theory of desire.[12]

Notice that the intuitive arguments against requiring motivational or hedonic faces to appear in an adequate theory of desire do not apply to the reward face of desire. If one looks at human beings suffering injuries to their reward systems, one sees nothing counterintuitive in attributing modified, diminished, or destroyed desires to such individuals. On the contrary, such attributions are often natural. Damage to the orbitofrontal cortex, for instance, can radically modify what counts as a reward for a person, and is also held to produce radical changes in the desires of people suffering such injuries. As Damasio (1994) recounts, after railway worker Phineas Gage received a massive injury to his OFC and related regions of the brain, friends and relatives found that he had so much abandoned his higher concerns in favor of his base, animal desires that "Gage was no longer Gage" (1994, 8). As for complete but selective destruction of the entire reward system in human beings, the occurrence of such an injury is fortunately rare, and I am aware of no actual cases: it is the sort of injury that never occurs as a result of stroke, bullet wound, or the like. Yet we can imagine what such a person would be like: incapable of movement, like the sufferer from severe Parkinson disease, but also incapable of normal feelings of pleasure or displeasure,[13] incapable of complexly organized mental activities, incapable of all forms of learning other than acquiring declarative knowledge. Such a person would, if we could read his mind, manifest a profound indifference to the world. He might still perceive and think, and with appropriate stimulation could be caused to feel pleasure or displeasure, or to move about, but he would spontaneously manifest nothing suggestive of desire.

The argument so far has been concerned to show that no single face of desire other than reward can be a compulsory face of desire. If the argument has been successful, then the reward-and-motivation, reward-and-pleasure, motivation-and-pleasure, and reward-and-pleasure-and-motivation theories of desire have all been shown inferior to the simple, straightforward reward theory. But one more theory of desire remains to be considered. Call it 'the mix-and-match theory of desire'. The mix-and-match theory accepts that neither motivation nor pleasure can be a compulsory face of desire, but it does not concede that reward alone is the essence of desire. Instead, it concludes that no individual face of desire is compulsory. To desire is to present any two of its three faces. This grants that neither motivation nor pleasure is compulsory, while retaining the idea that the reward theory is an excessively barren theory of desire on its own. Let us take the idea seriously for a moment and see where it leads. According to the mix-and-match theory of desire, desires are ontologically messy. This is clearly far from what one hopes for as a theorist. And yet there is also something appealing to the mix-and-match theory. It is the theory one reaches if one says something along the lines of "a desire is any mental state having most of the features human beings associate with the term 'desire'." So long as one finds that the three faces of desire make up the core features human beings associate with the term 'desire', one will reach something rather similar to the mix-and-match theory. One could, in principle, reach something even messier: a theory on which to desire is to have any twelve from a list of seventeen features, or any eighty-three from a list of one hundred and seven. In comparison, the mix-and-match theory appears quite conservative. It does not treat desires as made up piecemeal of many distinct features, but as made up of three main faces, and thus imposes a certain amount of theoretical order. At the same time, it imposes very little order. Perhaps this should make the mix-and-match theory of desire the just-messy-enough theory, rather than the reward theory.

What distinguishes the mix-and-match theory from each of its main competitors—the standard theory, the hedonic theory, and the reward theory—is that it refuses to do what they do, and treat desire as a natural psychological kind. Rather, it treats desire as any psychological construct or collection of constructs that underlies a certain swirl of characteristic effects. Because it refuses the basic standpoint taken for granted by its rivals, the mix-and-match theory is fundamentally different in spirit from them.

I say that the main theories of desire all treat desire as a natural psychological kind, but this may be confusing. After all, functional-role versions of the motivational theory say that to be a desire that P is to be anything at all which tends to make one bring it about that P. Hedonic theories of desire are similarly general. In what sense do these theories treat desire as a natural kind? They do not treat desire as a natural physiological or biological kind, certainly. But they treat desire as a natural *psychological* kind nonetheless. For all three recognize that there are a host of psychological phenomena associated with desire, and all three seek to explain these phenomena by first postulating a discrete psychological entity and then conjecturing about the relations between this entity and the various phenomena. And, as psychological phenomena, motivation and pleasure are reasonably discrete entities.

The mix-and-match theory is unlike its natural-kind rivals in that it does not seek to create a separation between the desire itself and the things the desire explains. The result is that the mix-and-match theory can explain none of the phenomena of desire in terms of desire, for desires are simply *constituted* by the phenomena, on the mix-and-match theory. On the other hand, because desires are constituted by the phenomena, the mix-and-match theory need never worry that there will be a case in which there are phenomena strongly suggestive of desire without desire itself being present.

But which approach should prevail? Clearly, there are some things for which only natural kind treatments are appropriate, if they are possible at all. Water is the most famous example in the philosophical literature.[14] Early chemistry determined that water is (an aggregation of liquid phase) H_2O. If somewhere there is a compound that, to all appearances, is just like water but that is not H_2O, then it is not water, for it is not H_2O. But there are also things that it would be misguided to treat as natural kinds. The category of disgusting things, for instance, is constituted by its superficial feature—the fact that they create feelings of disgust—rather than by some underlying nature of disgusting things in virtue of which disgusting things normally cause disgust. If I find earwigs disgusting, it makes no sense for me to imagine that scientists might come up with evidence that earwigs are not *really* disgusting to me. So the question is whether being a desire is more like being water or more like being disgusting: apt for treatment as a natural kind or not.

A good argument can be made that any theory of desire should postulate an entity that explains at least a large number of the features of desire. The fact that earwigs are disgusting does not explain the fact that I feel my skin crawl when I look at them: that is what constitutes their disgustingness for me (in part), and so cannot be explained by it. But many of the everyday facts surrounding desire are surely to be explained by the fact of desiring. People normally assume that there are things, desires, the having of which robustly explains a myriad of associated phenomena: actions, feelings of joy and resentment, urges, the acquisition of new desires, and so on. Common sense can perhaps accept that a few of these apparently robust explanations are really tautologous, but it is asking a lot of common sense to accept that they are all like that, that desiring does not explain the lived experience of desire because that is all desiring *is*. We do not expect the fact that earwigs are disgusting to do much explanatory work—and generally, when people try to get it to do such work, other people are quick to point out that it cannot. (You are not revolted by earwigs *because* they are disgusting; they are disgusting (to you) because they revolt you.) On the other hand, we expect much more out of the fact that Paul desires to be an ice-hockey goalie, or the fact that Samir desires to excel at chess.

The tension between natural kind theories of desire and the mix-and-match theory of desire is thus fuelled by a difficult decision: whether to prefer intuitive fitting of cases to explanatory power, or to prefer explanatory power to intuitive fitting of cases. In the sciences, one generally prefers the theory with more explanatory power. This, in the end, is the best reason to prefer a theory that puts a single face at the core of desire over the mix-and-match theory.

The same reason provides a final argument for the reward theory of desire. Because the reward theory of desire places the essence of desire in a phenomenon, reward, which most people link only trivially to a desire (nothing really counts as a reward unless it is wanted), the reward theory allows desires to be independent of the most salient features of desire—motivation, pleasure, felt urges—and so deeply explanatory of them. Both the standard theory and the hedonic theory have a measure of this virtue, but both also give up a measure of it by identifying desire with some of its most familiar phenomena. They render trivial certain explanations that one might have thought were deeper.

Everyday experience suggests that we contain certain mental states, desires, which explain why we act as we do and feel as we do. By maintaining a separation between desires themselves and these consequences of desiring, the reward theory treats experience as maximally correct. The price is that we must be ready to learn things about desire we did not expect to be true. The payoff is explanatory power.

3. Conclusion

In developing the reward theory of desire, I self-consciously followed what I take to be a method just as scientific as it is philosophical. This was something I mentioned at the outset, and something that has just been particularly salient in my arguments in this chapter. By way of conclusion, I would like to say just a few more words about what I take myself to have done.

Three Faces concerns itself equally with the common sense lore of desire, the scientific findings circling around desire, and the existing philosophical literature on desire. As a result, it might equally have been written by a scientist concerned to get her philosophical foundations right as by a philosopher concerned to get his empirical findings right. Of course, there are some obvious marks that make the present work a piece of philosophy, and not a piece of science. The presuppositions and jargon of the work are transparently those of philosophy, and in general the objections to which I have devoted space have been the objections philosophers are most likely to think of, not those scientists are most likely to have raised. Yet these are relatively cosmetic features. At its core, *Three Faces* is simply a book that asks about the nature of desire, and turns to any source of evidence, commonplace or esoteric, contingent or necessary, which might help in answering the question. This is not a methodology proprietary to science, or to philosophy. It is a methodology proprietary to all rational inquiry about the natural world.

Philosophy that draws upon science in this way is not the only sort of philosophy that can be conceived, and it is not the only sort widely practiced. But when it comes to thinking about the mind, it is the only sort of philosophy that I think can be justified. Time and again, empirical findings have shattered philosophical presuppositions about the mind. The absence of a single locus where "it all comes together" in consciousness (Dennett 1991), the separation of pain into two distinct phenomenological components (Dennett 1978; Hardcastle 1999), the irrelevance of conscious experience to certain forms of action-guidance (Weiskrantz 1986): these and many other findings about the mind have had and will continue to have reverberations in the philosophical world. A theory of the mind that ignores these findings is a theory that ignores evidence, and what good is such a theory?

At the same time, it is even rarer for the sciences of the mind to ally themselves with philosophy. Philosophy is generally considered a member of the cognitive sciences (Gardner 1987) and is often given something between lip service and equal treatment, depending upon the cognitive science textbook or research in question.[15] Yet, with a few recent exceptions, philosophers have rarely been used as resources by scientists. This has been a pity. For there are a number of scientists working on the mind whose findings address long-standing questions in philosophy, and who have ambitiously attempted to address these questions in book-length projects, and whose work might have benefited from more philosophy (e.g., Damasio 1994; LeDoux 1996). By neglecting philosophy to the extent they do, scientists neglect a pool of sophisticated evidence about what follows from certain fundamental assumptions, evidence about the apparent necessities in a field, and evidence about how confusingly related facts can best be fitted together. This philosophical evidence sometimes bears upon and illuminates their work, and once again one can ask: why theorize in ignorance of all the relevant evidence?

Research on desire, in particular, has suffered from the incompleteness of the knowledge applied. On the side of philosophy, there has been a dearth of work linking desire to empirical findings. With a few shining exceptions (e.g., Morillo 1990), philosophers have been content to think about and argue about desire using the same data that have concerned the profession since Plato. People desire food and water, they do not always do what they claim they want to do, they may or may not all want to do what is right, and so on. These facts have allowed philosophers many insights into the nature of desire: they have allowed a treatment of desire as a propositional attitude, they have allowed clear distinctions to be made between intrinsic and instrumental desires, between desires as such and pro attitudes in general, and all the rest. But because of their incompleteness, they have not been sufficient to allow philosophers to reach consensus about the nature of desire, or agreement on many of the important questions linking desire to moral psychology. Theorizing in the absence of all the facts is inevitable, but theorizing in willing ignorance of all the facts has been the norm. Yet the same is true in the science of desire. On the scientific side, there has been such a poor understanding of desire in general that it is rare to even see the term 'desire' used in scientific writing. Yet everyone in the scientific community accepts that there is no point to investigating neural systems at random: one investigates those underlying important parts of the human and non-human psyche, or those connected to disease, and so on. The problem has been that acceptance of this principle has been blended with such basic confusion over the human and non-human psyche that it is almost impossibly controversial to interpret scientific findings in terms of desire. In the scientific community, there is not even clear consensus on treating desire contents as propositional, for instance: no wonder that interpreting the workings of the orbitofrontal cortex in terms of desire has been so rare.

In *Three Faces* I have attempted to rectify both sorts of failings. I have drawn from philosophy the conceptual clarity scientific writing lacks, and from empirical science the experimental and clinical findings that philosophy has ignored. By putting together all the evidence available and all the theoretical resources available, I have built a theory of desire that is neither particularly scientific nor particularly philosophical. But the theory at least has a chance at being particularly *right*. And what else does one want from a theory?

Appendix

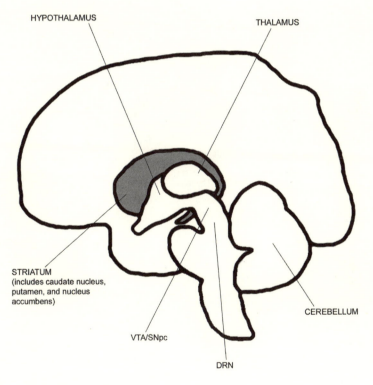

Figure 1 Interior view of the brain.

182 Appendix

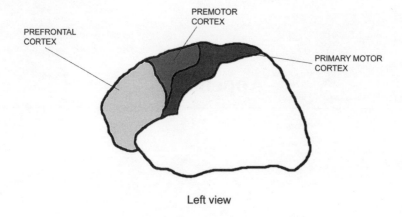

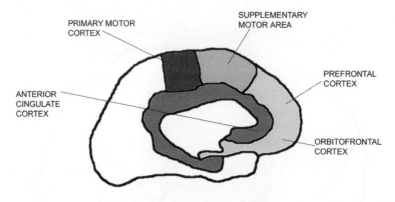

Figure 2   Exterior view of the brain.

Notes

Preliminaries

1. Throughout this work, I use the term 'philosophers of mind' to designate a rather specific group: those philosophers largely preoccupied with intentionality and consciousness, and more allied to cognitive science or the philosophy of language than to such disciplines as moral psychology or metaethics. (Philosophers of psychology are meant to be included insofar as they share similar preoccupations and alliances.) Obviously, this is a rather loose grouping of the 'family resemblance' sort, but it does mark a relevant distinction. My apologies to those action theorists or moral psychologists who think of themselves as philosophers of mind but who fall outside this grouping.

2. Stalnaker (1984) provides an admirably lucid version of the standard account of desiring. From the side of the ethicists, Smith (1987, 1994) provides a very similar account.

3. See, e.g., Cummins (1989, 1996), Dretske (1988, 1995), Fodor (1987, 1990, 1998), Millikan (1984, 1993), and Papineau (1987).

4. Davidson (1980, 1984).

5. See, e.g., Brandom (1994), Sellars (1963).

6. There is also some work that falls on the border between moral psychology or action theory and philosophy of mind deserving special mention. In particular, I have in mind J. C. B. Gosling's (1969) *Pleasure and Desire*, G. F. Schueler's (1995) *Desire*, and many of the essays in Joel Marks's (1986) *The Ways of Desire*.

7. An instructive example is found in the (1999) anthology *Desire*, which collects seven short essays on desire by well-known Canadian writers. Though the contributors were guided in their writing by fairly neutral questions from the anthologist—"When do you trust your desire? When do you censor it? When is it a source of power, and when a source of distress?" (Crozier 1999, 16)—most of the essays only treat the topic of sexual desire.

8. Any intentional item with a world-to-mind direction of fit, to use the terminology of Elizabeth Anscombe (1963/2000) and John Searle (1983).

9. A familiar complication when thinking about intrinsically and instrumentally desired ends is that many ends are desired both instrumentally and intrinsically: my father's welfare is something I desire for itself, but it is also a means to other things I desire for their own sake, such as my peace of mind. This does nothing to diminish a desire's status as intrinsic. It is only those ends that are desired *solely* as means to yet further ends that are desired instrumentally. I will have a little to say about instrumental desires over the course of this work, especially in chapter 5, but in general the focus will be upon intrinsic desires.

10. It should also be noted that the existence of these findings sometimes poses a substantial moral problem. The moral justification of research performed upon non-human animals is uncertain, at least in the case of some of the research I cite in this book. (In fact, in the course of preparing this book, I read a great deal of research that seemed to me to have inflicted substantial suffering without returning any substantial knowledge at all.) And if the research was conducted immorally, can it more moral to use it? I have sometimes assumed that the answer to this question is "yes," but I do not think there are easy answers here.

11. Paul Griffiths's (1997) *What Emotions Really Are* is a particularly good model.

12. A research program including, among many others, P. S. Churchland (1986), P. M. Churchland (1989, 1995), Cummins (1995), Dennett (1978, 1987, 1991), Dretske (1981, 1988, 1995), Elster (1999), Fodor (1975, 1987, 1990, 1998), Griffiths (1997), Hacking (1995), Hardcastle (1999), Haugeland (1985), Millikan (1984, 1993, 2000), Papineau (1987), Prinz (2002), Russell (1921), and Searle (1992).

1. The Standard Theory and Its Rivals

1. For another version of the standard view, see Armstrong (1980).

2. A quick note on jargon: for a state of affairs to obtain is just for it to be actual. So for the state of affairs *the cat is on the mat* to obtain is for the cat to actually be on the mat.

3. See, e.g., Elster and Roemer (1993), *Interpersonal Comparisons of Well-Being*.

4. The standard theory also allows pleasure to cause desires, but only instrumental desires, not intrinsic ones. I might get pleasure from eating fine chocolate, and so desire to eat more, but this will be an instrumental desire, aimed ultimately at getting more pleasure, according to the standard theory.

5. See, e.g., Korsgaard (1996), McDowell (1998), Scanlon (1998), Smith (1994).

6. See, e.g., Schueler (1994), Vadas (1984).

7. See, e.g., Strawson (1994). Searle (1992) holds a weaker version of this view.

8. ST3 is modeled after Papineau's first pass at a theory of desire. Millikan's first pass at such a theory is somewhat more complex.

9. This is a very crude version of the sophisticated story Millikan tells about 'adapted functions' (Millikan 1984, ch. 2).

10. For a sampling of the debate, see Devries (1996), Millikan (1996), Neander (1996), Papineau (1996), Schroeder (2001a), and Seager (1997).

11. Strawson (1994, ch. 9) considers possible objections and responses in much greater detail.

12. Frankfurt (1971).

13. Audi (1973), P. M. Churchland (1970), Davis (1984).

14. Green (1992, 82), Searle (1983, 32).

15. But see Ridge (1998) for a recent argument for the reducibility of intentions to other attitudes.

16. This is evidenced in both philosophical analyses of habit (Brett 1981; Duggan 1980) and in the straightforward fact that habits cannot be satisfied, fulfilled, or executed. Of course, habitual *actions* can be executed, but this would seem to be because habits make one try to bring it about that *P*, not because one has a habit that *P*.

17. Here I draw on Stampe (1986). Stampe's example is that of a tennis player who has the thought that he is going to double-fault.

18. For a sampling of representationalist theories, see Block (1986), Cummins (1988,

1996), Dretske (1988, 1995), Field (1978), Fodor (1975, 1990, 1998), Harman (1973), Millikan (1984), and Papineau (1987).

19. That is, there are structures that working neuroscientists identify as sensory and motor representations, and there seems at this point every reason to agree with them—they meet, at least to a first approximation, most theorists' views of what it is to be a mental representation.

20. With the exception of very primitive ends. There are regions in the brain that can motivate stimulated subjects to eat or drink, for instance.

21. The precise nature of pleasure gets a full treatment in chapter 3. For ease of exposition, this section presupposes a simple if controversial view of pleasure as a basic type of feeling.

22. Hobbes, Hume, and Kant apparently had similar thoughts, though interpretation of these thinkers is difficult. On Hobbes, see Gauthier (1969, 6); on Hume, see Smith (1994, 104–5); on Kant, see Wood (1999, 50).

23. Some philosophers, such as Michael Stocker (1979) and Michael Smith (1994, 120–21), are ready to hold that desires really are diminished in depression, out of allegiance to the motivational theory of desire. In the case of instrumental desires, I would not doubt them. But in the case of intrinsic desires, the position seems strained. Does the depressed man really care less about the well-being of his wife or his children, or does he just have much greater difficulty in focusing upon them and acting in their interests while he is depressed? Depression certainly saps energy and motivation, but does this really amount to draining away all wishes for the well-being of loved ones? The everyday understanding of depression suggests not. Once again, we can always override everyday thinking about desire in order to preserve a tidy and powerful theory, but this is always a cost we should prefer to avoid, if possible.

24. More on direction of fit in chapter 5.

25. In this respect, philosophical theorizing is like scientific theorizing. See Kuhn (1962, ch. 8).

26. Dennett (1978, ch. 5) has been one of the few philosophers to champion the eventual return of thinking about reward and punishment.

2. Reward and Punishment

1. The term 'behaviorist' no longer has the narrow use Skinner (1938) might have preferred. These days, scientists call themselves behaviorists for various reasons. See section 2 for a clarification of terminology.

2. I.e., contrary to the child's best judgment of what he should do, and contrary to his immediately prior practical decision making.

3. For an insightful survey of how behaviorism has been seen by psychologists, see Berlyne (1975).

4. Still other subjects sometimes heard "huh-uh," and the experiment also had other subtle features. For clarity of exposition, I am skipping over a number of details here.

5. Morillo (1990) calls this the "reward event."

6. Much of this work is reviewed in Stellar and Stellar (1985).

7. They have discovered sites in the brain that animals will work to activate via electrical stimulation or drugs, but these are not novel rewards so much as novel ways of simulating aspects of natural reward.

8. There is room to debate the ontology of reward and of the objects of representation (events? states of affairs?), but the topic is not relevant to my argument here.

9. Kandel, Schwartz, and Jessell. Their graduate-level neuroscience text is a standard in the English-speaking world, and I will refer to it frequently when describing well-known facts about the brain. Hence the convenience of the abbreviation.

10. At least, the hypothalamus engages in some activity that neuroscientists typically call 'representing', and that counts as tokening a representation or intentional icon according to some well-known theories of intentionality (Cummins 1989, 1996; Dretske 1995; Fodor 1990; Millikan 1984; Sterelny 1990). There seems no reason to treat the hypothalamus as deploying everyday concepts, however.

11. According to Haber and Fudge (1997), the dopamine-releasing neurons of the VTA are functionally continuous with the dorsal tier of neurons in the substantia nigra, pars compacta. This is a detail I will gloss over. The distinction between VTA neurons and SNpc neurons lies largely in their targets: VTA neurons innervate almost the entire cortex, while SNpc neurons are especially targeted at the striatum, about which more will be said in chapter 4.

12. It is interesting to note that one exception appears to be the cerebellum: dopamine-releasing neurons are not thought to reach into the cerebellum (KSJ 2000, ch. 45). But other than the very large cerebellum, most sub-cortical regions of the brain receive some quantity of dopamine from the VTA. It is also worth noting that the cerebellum engages in its own, very special, form of learning (KSJ 2000, ch. 42), and so it is perhaps not surprising that it does not receive reward-based learning signals.

13. Romo and Schultz (1990), Schultz and Romo (1990), Ljungberg et al. (1992), Schultz et al. (1993), Waelti, Dickinson, and Schultz (2001). Reviewed in Schultz (2000).

14. More cautiously, mild punishment has no effect upon VTA/SNpc activity. Strong stimulation, including strong punishing stimulation, appears to activate the VTA/SNpc along with other, related structures. How this ties in to the role of the VTA/SNpc in reward is not yet understood.

15. It is especially important to note that VTA/SNpc stimulation had no effect on auditory cortex when it *preceded* the tone, or independent of tone. According to existing models of reward-based learning, the structures that should be affected by a reward signal are those involved in bringing about, predicting, and detecting that event: structures active before the reward itself, and so active before the reward signal is received.

16. And in fact, though Bao and colleagues do not explain why they studied the rat auditory cortex, my speculation would be that it was simply a matter of convenience. It is easier (and probably morally preferable) to work on rats than on primates; it is relatively easy to map the primary auditory cortex and detect changes in it; single-frequency tones are not likely to already be linked to reward or punishment centers, the way touches to the body might be; work in Michael Merzenich's lab has generally centered around mapping changes in primary and secondary sensory cortex since the early 1980s; etc.

17. Knutson et al. (2001), Pagnoni et al. (2002), Berns et al. (2001), Schultz et al. (1995).

18. There are other functions of OFC, and this function is restricted to a proper part of OFC, but I will ignore these complications here.

19. But see Eblen and Graybiel (1995) for a study finding no connection between OFC and the nucleus accumbens.

20. But see Wilkinson and Jacobs (1988).

21. Those containing serotonin 2 or 1c receptors.

22. In fact, Deakin (1983) appears to hold that if fluoxetine (Prozac) and other SSRIs (recently discovered at that time) have their clinical benefits through promoting the presence of increased serotonin in the brain, then serotonin cannot carry a punishment signal. He has since revised this view, however.

23. For instance, it might be the case that SSRIs acclimate users to higher serotonin levels, and, after acclimation, punishment signals have less impact than before. It might be objected that drugs such as MDMA (ecstasy) have immediate effects upon both pleasure and serotonin levels, but it has been shown recently that MDMA's effects upon hedonic tone is mediated by its impact upon dopamine systems, while its effects on serotonin release influence only the mild sensory-distortion qualities of MDMA (Liechti and Vollenweider 2000; Liechti et al. 2000).

24. There are variations on this theme, but they can run into problems. Thorndike (1911, ch. 5) holds "Any act which in a given situation produces satisfaction becomes associated with that situation so that when the situation recurs the act is more likely than before to recur." But this introduces the notion of satisfaction, of which a scrupulous behaviorist must be suspicious.

25. See, e.g., Morillo (1990, 181).

26. The psychologically relevant use of the words 'reward' and 'punishment' is, if anything, more basic than use that merely expresses the intentions of the person giving the reward or the social conventions surrounding the punishment. If a parent, intending to punish a child, sends the child to her room, and that is what the child secretly desires, then some would be inclined to say that the parent has not punished the child at all.

27. This follows from such diverse views of the mind as those found in Armstrong (1980), Brandom (1994), Chalmers (1996), Cummins (1989, 1995), Davidson (1980), Dennett (1987, 1991), Dretske (1988, 1995), Fodor (1990), Harman (1973), Haugeland (1985), Lycan (1988), Millikan (1984), Papineau (1987), Peacocke (1992), Putnam (1960), and numerous others.

28. These features being functional organization, or implicit acceptance of norms for utterances, or interpretability as rational agents, or biological function, or information-carrying, or inferential dispositions, or perhaps something else, depending on which particular theory of mind is correct.

29. And perhaps nucleus accumbens, or other brain structures required for the VTA/SNpc to produce its output.

30. See also White and Milner (1992) for an impressively clear view of the nature of reward.

31. This would only cover reward, of course. To include punishment as well, one would need to talk about X causing either of two characteristic forms of what is called 'contingency based learning'.

32. We may assume that receiving recognition from the police was not itself a reward for this particular woman, to make the example stronger.

33. Or state of affairs, depending on the correct ontology of rewards.

34. This is, apparently, the case with manatees (Gerstein et al. 1999).

35. This sort of story will reappear in chapter 3, when the discussion turns to desiring pleasure.

3. Pleasure and Displeasure

1. Also known as positive and negative hedonic tone, positive and negative affect, positive and negative emotional valence, and more. Scientists, especially, have felt compelled to add new jargon to refer to pleasure and displeasure, but I think the simplest terms are equally clear and unequivocal, and will generally prefer them. One exception: for lexical variety, I will sometimes refer to pleasure and displeasure together as 'hedonic tone'.

2. Though I am acquainted with a few individuals in whom they are much more common.

3. Every biologically intact person, at least.

4. A related phenomenon (pointed out to me by William Lycan) is the use of a coin toss to determine what one wants. One narrows the options to two, assigns each to one face of the coin, and tosses the coin. If one is pleased with the way the toss has come up, one can conclude that that is what one most wanted to do all along. If one is displeased (and perhaps wishes to make some excuse to "try again") then one has good reason to believe one prefers the other option. Again, pleasure and displeasure provide evidence for what we want.

5. There may be unconscious pain and other unconscious forms of pleasure and displeasure, but these are not generally recognized as unambiguously painful, pleasant, or unpleasant by common sense.

6. The brain region under discussion here is quite a small one, at most a few square centimeters on the inner surface of each cerebral hemisphere.

7. There is also a limited amount of philosophical agreement. The only philosopher who, to my knowledge, has investigated the neural realization of displeasure has come to a similar view. See Hardcastle (1999, ch. 5).

8. If one prefers an identity theory of pleasure and displeasure, one can read 'realizer' in the degenerate sense in which everything realizes itself.

9. Further from your eyes, closer to the back of your head, in Brodmann's area 24'.

10. In Brodmann's area 25.

11. Although there are deep waters here regarding knowledge of other minds and the like, I propose to skirt them and deal simply with the scientific approach to finding biological bases for mental events.

12. Looking for a last link in a neural chain is also rendered difficult by the fact that a great many neural regions are reciprocally connected and mutually influential. Strict chains are a rarity, though functional approximations to them are somewhat more common.

13. Berridge (2003a, 2003b) clearly maps out the failings in existing research.

14. But see Dennett (1978, ch. 11) and Hardcastle (1999).

15. Bilateral destruction, to be precise.

16. E.g., Hsieh et al. (1995), Rainville et al. (1997), Coghill et al. (1999), Casey (1999).

17. Functional magnetic resonance imaging: a technology for forming images of regions of the brain that are being used at the time.

18. Positron emission tomography: a technology with the same function as fMRI, though a different method of operation.

19. See, e.g., Weiskrantz (1986) on cortical blindness.

20. The ventral pallidum projects to the mediodorsal nucleus of the thalamus (Berridge 2003a), which, in turn, projects to the PGAC (Neafsey et al. 1993).

21. E.g., Kenny (1963).

22. Damasio's view of the emotions in general is one he takes to be derived from the work of William James (1890), and indeed the parallels are obvious.

23. Chapter 4 will also have a good deal to say about the extent to which the link between pleasure and motivation has been overestimated.

24. Discussed by Block (1995b), Carruthers (2000), Dretske (1995), Lycan (1987), McDowell (1994), Peacocke (1983), and Tye (1995), among others.

25. But it must also be said that common sense hints there might also be something more: if pleasure can really be illusory, then it must have content after all.

26. There are some, such as Dretske (1995), Lycan (1987), and Tye (1995), who will hold that a representational account of pleasure will entail everything important about the functional role of pleasure and everything about the qualitative character of pleasure. Though I find this view appealing, I am not committed to it here.

27. It may be the case that Plato holds a similar view in the *Philebus* 33e ff, and that contemporary emotion theorist Nico Frijda also supports a related view in his "Emotions and Hedonic Experience" (1999). It is also interesting to compare this view to that found in Millgram (1997), in which Millgram holds that pleasure is a "rock bottom judgment of desirability" (115).

28. Note that calling such pleasures 'unreal' is not to pass any non-epistemic judgment upon them. I profit from and enjoy the illusions created by filmmakers on a regular basis. Whether the illusions produced by euphorigenic drugs are good or bad is quite independent of their status as illusions.

29. Several other conclusions might also be reasonable, of course, depending upon the individual.

30. It may interest the reader to compare the idea that there are two fundamentally different routes to the felt pleasure caused by desires to Davis's (1986) thesis that there are two different types of desires, one more linked to the appetites, the other more linked to higher cognitive processes.

31. Thanks to an anonymous referee of Schroeder (2001b) for this point.

32. This is the primary role given to desires by Dretske (1988).

33. Thanks to an anonymous referee of Schroeder (2001b) for this point.

34. Thanks to Andrew Melnyk for raising this point.

35. But see Akins (1996) for an account of this sense that makes it more problematic than one might have thought.

4. The Production and Prevention of Movement

1. Suitably qualified, this is the position of Davidson (1980), for example.

2. Hornsby (1980).

3. E.g., Dretske (1988), Searle (1983).

4. Compare, e.g., Mele (1990) and Kenny (1963).

5. See Arpaly (2003) for a discussion of the proposed links between autonomy and action.

6. As with almost every other structure in the brain, there are really two motor cortices, one in each hemisphere. But I will follow scientific convention in suppressing the cumbersome plural unless there is special reason not to.

7. Interestingly, the motor cortex, SMA, and motor AC are all known to be activated by imagined movement and anticipated movement, in ways not unlike their activation by actual movement (see, e.g., Georgopoulos et al. 1993). Exactly how the brain distinguishes imaginary or foreseen attempted movement from real attempted movement is not well understood, but obviously some neural method for distinguishing these exists, since people's limbs do not move in response to imaginary or foreseen attempted movement—at least, not generally, or in just the same way they would were the attempt real. In spite of this complication, neuroscientists nonetheless generally treat the motor cortex, SMA, and motor AC as centers issuing commands to the body for immediate action. Scientific practice in this case is reminiscent of the practice of calling certain representational structures "perceptual representations" in spite of the fact that imaginative activity also triggers their activation (Kosslyn 1994). Perhaps perception and action modules have both "on-line" and "off-line" modes of operation. However exactly it is managed, though, it is generally agreed that the function of motor cortex, SMA, and motor AC is to tell the body what to do.

8. This striking phenomenon has led Francis Crick (1994, 267–68) to suggest, rather precipitously, that the motor AC is the seat of the will. For a dissenting view, see Tibbetts

(2001). Since the nature of the will is a complex topic purely as a matter of philosophical psychology, and since the topic is rendered even more problematic by worries about the freedom of the will, I will skirt this particular debate.

9. For a detailed discussion of the philosophy of prior intention, see Bratman (1987).

10. This suggests that, just as Bratman (1987) argues, intentions cannot be reduced to simple beliefs and desires. For, with declarative memory and behavioral capacities left intact in these experimental monkeys, and with there being no sign of damage to intrinsic and instrumental desires in immediate behavior, there seems little room to say that the damage causes a loss of belief that doing P will lead to Q, or to a loss of a desire to bring about Q, or loss of the capacity to instrumentally desire to do what is necessary for Q. All that appears to be missing in these monkeys is the capacity to hold an enduring pro attitude toward taking the necessary action at the appropriate time in the future. That is, the capacity for future intention appears to be selectively damaged. If separation of function in the brain gives us any information at all about separation of the attitudes, this suggests that intentions really are distinct from beliefs and desires.

11. That is, that part of the striatum concerned with movement—there is another part concerned with the creation of a reward signal.

12. Strictly speaking, only the internal segment of the globus pallidus is a structure with output directed outside of the basal ganglia.

13. Found adjacent to the SNpc, but playing a very different function. Experts will also note that I am skipping over the subthalamic nucleus, though it too plays an important role. Because of the extreme complexity of the basal ganglia, and the irrelevance of most of this complexity to present purposes, I am taking a few liberties in my expository neuroscience.

14. Via the external segment of the globus pallidus and the subthalamic nucleus, in particular.

15. Technically, this influence is indirect, as it is mediated by intervening thalamic nuclei. In practice, however, the control rests very much with the basal ganglia: the thalamic nuclei add little.

16. Though apparently not the primary motor cortex (KSJ 2000, 858–9). Given the fact that the primary motor cortex is largely controlled by the rest of the motor cortex, the SMA, motor AC, and motor PFC, however, failing to control primary motor cortex does not diminish the influence of the basal ganglia upon action.

17. Though see Perry (2001) for a theory of know-how that would dispute this.

18. Just as human infants make characteristic facial responses to pleasant and unpleasant foods, so do many other mammalian species.

19. American Psychiatric Association (1994, 103).

20. Kushner (1999) provides a fascinating account of the history of Tourette syndrome, and forms a good starting point for philosophical investigation.

5. Desire and Aversion

1. Perhaps serotonin, as chapter 2 suggested.

2. See also the discussion of desires and their effects upon consciousness in section 2.

3. With the caveats raised in chapter 2 about the everyday meaning of 'reward' and 'punishment'.

4. To tell the truth, in the college I belong to the more likely dilemma is over how many bottles of beer to drink at *lunch*. But the point is the same, and I will stay with Bratman's more industrious example.

5. It should be said that Bratman has in mind a case involving a genuine change in preferences, while I have left the case described in ways that allow other interpretations. To my mind, a person who experiences genuine changes in preferences in such a short space of time is someone in the extraordinary circumstances of Dr. Jekyll uncontrollably changing into Hyde—at least, if change in preferences entails change in intrinsic desires. I am not sure that there is anything to say about *that* sort of case that has any bearing on the sorts of preference reversals people experience normally.

6. In this context, I mean 'good' and 'evil' in a morally neutral sense: good or evil from one's own standpoint.

7. I expect this more complex scenario is the one Bratman originally intended, for it is the much more philosophically interesting scenario, and it is just as phenomenologically familiar as the simpler scenario.

8. For a survey, see Rolls (2000).

9. Of course, one could object that people do not generally intrinsically desire to acquire money. My own experience of average Canadian and U.S. citizens, however, suggests otherwise. Only a few people have *powerful* intrinsic desires for money, no doubt, but it is not for nothing that love of money is said to be the root of all evil.

10. In the same way, one can decide to have a child for instrumental reasons (to save a relationship, say), but once one has had the child one typically desires its well-being whether this serves one's original goal or not.

11. This is how neuroscientist Jaak Panksepp (1998, 166–67) appears to see things. To a certain extent, this is an empirical bet subject to empirical disconfirmation. If it turns out that there are no stable connections between hypothalamic representations and the reward system, merely the disposition to create such connections when homeostasis fails, then hunger and thirst will turn out to be real fleeting desires after all, and the reward theory will need a more nuanced account of desire stability.

12. Attributing a specific content to such a desire using a natural language is problematic, perhaps, since such attributions make it sound as though a sophisticated concept, blood sugar, is deployed in the hypothalamus, which is probably false. But this is a subtlety that makes no difference to the main thrust of this argument.

13. See, e.g., Smith (1994).

14. This appears close to the view of Anscombe (1963/2000).

15. This is the most natural interpretation of direction of fit if one accepts Millikan (1984) or related teleological theories of desire (Lycan 1988; Papineau 1987; Sterelny 1990), for example.

16. Their distinguished numbers include Chalmers (1996), Dennett (1987), Dretske (1988), Fodor (1990), Haugeland (1985), and Strawson (1994), even if we look only to those philosophers writing books after Searle (1983) had made the concept of direction of fit so salient to philosophers of mind.

17. Equally, the reward theory cannot offer an account of direction of fit in terms of pleasure, though since no one to my knowledge has been tempted to present such an account, this incapacity is of no particular concern.

18. It might also be thought that I need to show that *only* desires are essentially regulatory, since it would be quite mistaken to say that evaluative beliefs, while regulatory, have only the desire-like direction of fit. But I would say instead that if evaluative beliefs are essentially regulatory, then perhaps they have the desire-like direction of fit *in addition to* their belief-like direction of fit. And indeed, the view that there are mental states with both directions of fit is not unknown in the philosophical literature.

19. Or perhaps it would be more precise to say that some states of affairs are better than

others. Though I will write in terms of actions being moral and immoral, this will only be for brevity and convenience, and of course no particular stance on this deep issue is intended.

20. Such questions have a particularly Kantian flavor. For the standard contemporary statement of this view of moral psychology, see Korsgaard (1996).

6. Clean and Messy Theories

1. More carefully, it is Davidson's position that there are no strict laws quantifying over mental events (Davidson 1980, ch. 11), even though token mental events are identical to token physical events and even though there are strict laws quantifying over physical events. This position would appear to entail that there cannot be simple reductions of mental types to physical types, though there may conceivably be room to argue here.

2. It was Avrom Faderman who first made this sort of argument to me, and I borrow his examples here.

3. One could also generate arguments *for* the elimination of mental states based upon naïve causal theories of reference. For instance, one could argue that, because 'emotion' does not have a single natural kind as its causal origin, there is no referent for the term. Such arguments would also be unsound.

4. See, e.g., essays in Boxill (2001).

5. For the purposes of the example, I will ask the reader to imagine that my father was white-bearded and that we lived high in the Canadian arctic. Though not strictly true, the principle of the example is clear enough.

6. The two leading contemporary views of consciousness and the attitudes that do *not* allow for this sort of separation are motivated, not by fear of eliminativism, but by views about the necessity of consciousness to intentionality. See Searle (1992), Strawson (1994). For an argument that, on the contrary, desires could not be literal elements of consciousness, see Hulse, Read, and Schroeder (2004).

7. There are philosophers who are willing to claim that, say, Newton and Einstein did not have two different theories of one and the same thing, but rather that Newton was talking about one thing, Einstein about something quite different, and it was just a confusing fact about them that they both used the word "gravity." My anti-eliminativist argument rests on the assumption that this line of thinking is false. While this assumption is popular at present, it is not universally held.

8. Akinetic mutism is often, apparently, accompanied by felt indifference. This may be a result of the fact that natural causes of akinetic mutism are likely to also affect the PGAC and the attention centers of the anterior cingulate (Vogt et al. 1992). It may also be because akinetic mutism does not result in the painfully rigid poses produced by Parkinsonism. I am not aware of any studies attempting to discover if akinetic mutism is necessarily accompanied by felt indifference.

9. Notice that rejecting such testimony brings one perilously close to the view of Malcolm (1959), according to which dreams are no more than dispositions to produce reports of dreams.

10. See Strawson (1994, ch. 9) for a longer and more nuanced version of related arguments.

11. Dretske (1988) and Kim (1993) hold theories of mental causation on which it seems hammers as such are not causally efficacious, while Davidson (1980) and Millikan (1993, ch. 3) hold otherwise.

12. Strawson (1994) presents an extended defense of the hedonic theory of desire, which I have only begun to answer here in any detail. But the many faults of the hedonic

theory of desire appear to render any refutation of Strawson's particular arguments superfluous. There is one exception: if Strawson is right in thinking that intentionality can only be derived from consciousness, then for all its faults, the hedonic theory of desire may be the best option. But this work is not the place to address the nature of intentionality in general.

13. From many sources. As Berridge and Robinson (1998) emphasize, it is still possible for rats with massive, chemically induced lesions of the reward system to experience pleasure if stimulated appropriately.

14. See, e.g., Putnam (1975).

15. Compare, for example, Weisler et al. (1995) to Jahnke and Nowaczyk (1998).

References

Abrahamson, E., and Moore, R. 2001. "The Posterior Hypothalamic Area: Chemoarchitecture and Afferent Connections." *Brain Research* 889, 1–22.

Adams, F. 1979. "A Goal-State Theory of Function Attributions." *Canadian Journal of Philosophy* 9, 493–518.

Akins, K. 1996. "Of Sensory Systems and the 'Aboutness' of Mental States." *Journal of Philosophy* 93, 337–72.

American Psychiatric Association. 1994. *Diagnostic and Statistical Manual of Mental Disorders.* 4th ed. Washington DC: American Psychiatric Association.

Anscombe, E. 1963/2000. *Intention.* 2nd ed. Cambridge, MA: Harvard University Press.

Armstrong, D. 1980. *The Nature of Mind.* St. Lucia, Queensland: University of Queensland Press.

Arpaly, N. 2003. *Unprincipled Virtue: An Inquiry into Moral Agency.* New York: Oxford University Press.

Audi, R. 1973. "Intending." *Journal of Philosophy* 70, 387–403.

Aydede, M. 2000. "An Analysis of Pleasure Vis-à-vis Pain." *Philosophy and Phenomenological Research* 61, 537–70.

Bao, S., Chan, V., and Merzenich, M. 2001. "Cortical Remodelling Induced by Activity of Ventral Tegmental Dopamine Neurons." *Nature* 412, 79–83.

Bechara, A., Damasio, A., Damasio, H., and Anderson, S. 1994. "Insensitivity to Future Consequences Following Damage to Human Prefrontal Cortex." *Cognition* 50, 7–15.

Berlyne, D. 1975. "Behaviorism? Cognitive Theory? Humanist Psychology? To Hull with Them All!" *Canadian Psychological Review* 16, 69–80.

Berns, G., McClure, S., Pagnoni, G., and Read Montague, P. 2001. "Predictability Modulates Human Brain Response to Reward." *Journal of Neuroscience* 21, 2793–98.

Berridge, K. 2003a. "Pleasures of the Brain." *Brain and Cognition* 52, 106–28.

——— 2003b. "Comparing the Emotional Brain of Humans and Other Animals." In Davidson, R., Goldsmith, H., and Scherer, K. (eds.), *Handbook of Affective Sciences.* New York: Oxford University Press. 25–51.

Berridge, K., and Grill, H. 1983. "Alternating Ingestive and Aversive Consummatory Responses Suggest a Two-Dimensional Analysis of Palatability in Rats." *Behavioral Neuroscience* 97, 563–73.

Berridge, K., and Robinson, T. 1998. "What Is the Role of Dopamine in Reward: Hedonic Impact, Reward Learning, or Incentive Salience?" *Brain Research Reviews* 28, 309–69.

Berridge, K., and Valenstein, E. 1991. "What Psychological Process Mediates Feeding Evoked by Electrical Stimulation of the Lateral Hypothalamus?" *Behavioral Neuroscience* 105, 3–14.

Blackburn, S. 1998. *Ruling Passions: A Theory of Practical Reasoning.* New York: Oxford University Press.

Block, N. 1978. "Troubles with Functionalism." In Savage, W. (ed.), *Minnesota Studies in the Philosophy of Science 9.* Minneapolis: University of Minnesota Press. 261–325.

——— 1986. "Advertisement for a Semantics for Psychology." In French, P., Uehling, T., and Wettstein, H. (eds.), *Midwest Studies in Philosophy 10: Studies in the Philosophy of Mind.* Minneapolis: University of Minnesota Press. 615–78.

——— 1995a. "Mental Paint and Mental Latex." in Villanueva, E. (ed.), *Perception.* Atascadero, CA: Ridgeview. 19–49.

——— 1995b. "On a Confusion about a Function of Consciousness." *Behavioral and Brain Sciences* 18, 227–87.

Boxill, B., (ed.). 2001. *Race and Racism.* New York: Oxford University Press.

Braithwaite, R. 1968. *Scientific Explanation: A Study in the Function of Theory, Probability, and Law in Science.* London: Cambridge University Press.

Brandom, R. 1994. *Making It Explicit: Reasoning, Representing, and Discursive Commitment.* Cambridge, MA: Harvard University Press.

Bratman, M. 1987. *Intention, Plans, and Practical Reason.* Cambridge, MA: Harvard University Press.

——— 1999. *Faces of Intention: Selected Essays on Intention and Agency.* New York: Cambridge University Press.

Breiter, H., Gollub, R., Weisskoff, R., Kennedy, D., Makris, N., Berke, J., Goodman, J., Kantor, H., Gastfriend, D., Riorden, J., Mathew, R., Rosen, B., and Hyman, S. 1997. "Acute Effects of Cocaine on Human Brain Activity and Emotion." *Neuron* 19, 591–611.

Breland, K., and Breland, M. 1961. "The Misbehavior of Organisms." *American Psychologist* 16, 681–84.

Brembs, B., Lorenzetti, F., Reyes, F., Baxter, D., and Vyrne, J. 2002. "Operant Reward Learning in *Aplysia*: Neuronal Correlates and Mechanisms." *Science* 296, 1706–9.

Brett, N. 1981. "Human Habits." *Canadian Journal of Philosophy* 11, 357–76.

Bussey, T., Evritt, B., and Robbins, T. 1997. "Dissociable Effects of Cingulate and Medial Frontal Cortex Lesions on Stimulus-Reward Learning Using a Novel Pavlovian Autoshaping Procedure for the Rat: Implications for the Neurobiology of Emotion." *Behavioral Neuroscience* 111, 908–19.

Casey, K. 1999. "Forebrain Mechanisms of Nociception and Pain: Analysis Through Imaging." *Proceedings of the National Academy of Sciences, U.S.A.* 96, 7668–74.

Carruthers, P. 2000. *Phenomenal Consciousness: A Naturalist Theory.* New York: Cambridge University Press.

Cavada, C., Compañy, T., Tejedor, J., Cruz-Rizzolo, R., and Reinoso-Suárez, F. 2000. "The Anatomical Connections of the Macaque Monkey Orbitofrontal Cortex: A Review." *Cerebral Cortex* 10, 220–42.

Celebrini, S., and Newsome, W. 1995. "Microstimulation in Extrastriate Area MST Influences Performance on a Direction Discrmination Task. *Journal of Neurophysiology* 73, 437–48.

Cervo, L., and Samanin, R. 1995. "5-HT_{1A} Receptor Full and Partial Agonists and 5-HT_{2C} (but not 5-HT_3) Receptor Antagonists Increase Rates of Punished Responding in Rats." *Pharmacology, Biochemistry, and Behavior* 52, 671–76.

Chalmers, D. 1996. *The Conscious Mind: In Search of a Fundamental Theory.* New York: Oxford University Press.
Churchland, P. M. 1970. "The Logical Character of Action-Explanations." *Philosophical Review* 79, 214–36.
——— 1981. "Eliminative Materialism and the Propositional Attitudes." *Journal of Philosophy* 78, 67–90.
——— 1989. *A Neurocomputational Perspective: The Nature of Mind and the Structure of Science.* Cambridge, MA: MIT Press.
——— 1995. *The Engine of Reason, the Seat of the Soul: A Philosophical Journey into the Brain.* Cambridge, MA: MIT Press.
Churchland, P. S. 1986. *Neurophilosophy: Toward a Unified Theory of the Mind/Brain.* Cambridge, MA: MIT Press.
Coffield, J., Bowen, K., and Miletic, V. 1992. "Retrograde Tracing of Projections Between Nucleus Submedius, the Ventrolateral Orbital Cortex, and the Midbrain in the Rat." *Journal of Comparative Neurology* 321, 488–99.
Coghill, R., Sang, C., Maisog, J., and Iadorola, M. 1999. "Pain Intensity Processing Within the Human Brain: A Bilateral, Distributed Mechanism." *Journal of Neurophysiology* 82, 1934–43.
Cohen, A., and Leckman, J. 1992. "Sensory Phenomena Associated with Gilles de la Tourette's Syndrome." *Journal of Clinical Psychiatry* 53, 319–23.
Craig, A., Reiman, E., Evans, A., and Bushnell, M. 1996. "Functional Imaging of an Illusion of Pain." *Nature* 384, 258–60.
Crick, F. 1994. *The Astonishing Hypothesis: The Scientific Search for the Soul.* New York: Simon and Schuster.
Crino, P., Morrison, J., and Hof, P. 1993. "Monoaminergic Innervation of Cingulate Cortex." In Vogt, B., and Gabriel, M. (eds.), *Neurobiology of Cingulate Cortex and Limbic Thalamus: A Comprehensive Handbook.* Boston: Birkhauser.
Crozier, L. (ed.). 1999. *Desire: In Seven Voices.* Vancouver, BC: Douglas and McIntyre.
Cummins, R. 1989. *Meaning and Mental Representation.* Cambridge, MA: MIT Press.
——— 1996. *Representations, Targets, and Attitudes.* Cambridge, MA: MIT Press.
Damasio, A. 1994. *Descartes' Error: Emotion, Reason, and the Human Brain.* New York: Putnam's.
Danto, A. 1963. "What We Can Do." *Journal of Philosophy* 60, 435–45.
——— 1965. "Basic Actions." *American Philosophical Quarterly* 2, 141–48.
Davidson, D. 1980. *Essays on Actions and Events.* New York: Oxford University Press.
——— 1984. *Inquiries into Truth and Interpretation.* New York: Oxford University Press.
Davies, P. 2001. *Norms of Nature: Naturalism and the Nature of Functions.* Cambridge, MA: MIT Press.
Davis, W. 1984. "A Causal Theory of Intending." *American Philosophical Quarterly* 21, 43–54.
——— 1986. "The Two Senses of Desire." In Marks, J. (ed.), *The Ways of Desire: New Essays in Philosophical Psychology on the Concept of Wanting.* Chicago: Precedent. 63–82.
Deakin, J. 1983. "Roles of Serotonergic Systems in Escape, Avoidance, and Other Behaviours." In Cooper, S. (ed.), *Theory in Psychopharmacology, Volume 2.* New York: Academic. 149–93.
——— 1998. "The Role of Serotonin in Depression and Anxiety." *European Psychiatry* 13 (suppl. 2), 57s–63s.
Delgado, P., and Moreno, F. 1999. "Antidepressants and the Brain." *International Clinical Psychopharmacology* 14 (suppl. 1), S9–S16.

Dennett, D. 1978. *Brainstorms: Philosophical Essays on Mind and Psychology.* Cambridge, MA: MIT Press.

——— 1987. *The Intentional Stance.* Cambridge, MA: MIT Press.

——— 1991. *Consciousness Explained.* Boston: Little, Brown.

Derbyshire, S., Vogt, B., and Jones, A. 1998. "Pain and Stroop Interference Tasks Activate Separate Processing Modules in Anterior Cingulate Cortex." *Experimental Brain Research* 118, 52–60.

Devinsky, O., Morrell, M., and Vogt, B. 1995. "Contributions of the Anterior Cingulate Cortex to Behavior." *Brain* 118, 279–306.

Devries, W. 1996. "Experience and the Swamp Creature." *Philosophical Studies* 82, 55–80.

Dretske, F. 1981. *Knowledge and the Flow of Information.* Cambridge, MA: MIT Press.

——— 1986. "Misrepresentation." In Bogdan, R. (ed.), *Belief: Form, Content, and Function.* New York: Oxford University Press. 17–36.

——— 1988. *Explaining Behavior: Reasons in a World of Causes.* Cambridge, MA: MIT Press.

——— 1995. *Naturalizing the Mind.* Cambridge, MA: MIT Press.

Duggan, T. 1980. "Habit." In Van Inwagen, P. (ed.), *Time and Cause: Essays Presented to Richard Taylor.* Boston: Reidel. 203–17.

Durstewitz, D., Kelc, M., and Gunturkun, O. 1999. "A Neurocomputational Theory of the Dopaminergic Modulation of Working Memory Functions." *Journal of Neuroscience* 19, 2807–22.

Eblen, F., and Graybiel, A. 1995. "Highly Restricted Origin of Prefrontal Cortical Inputs to Striosomes in the Macaque Monkey." *Journal of Neuroscience* 15, 5999–6013.

Eddington, A. 1928. *The Nature of the Physical World.* London: Cambridge University Press.

Egelman, D., Person, C., and Read Montague, P. 1999. "A Computational Role for Dopamine Delivery in Human Decision-Making." *Journal of Cognitive Neuroscience* 10, 623–30.

Elster, J. 1999. *Strong Feelings: Emotion, Addiction, and Human Behavior.* Cambridge, MA: MIT Press.

Elster, J., and Roemer, J. (eds.). 1993. *Interpersonal Comparisons of Well-Being.* New York: Cambridge University Press.

Elliott, R., Dolan, R., and Frith, C. 2000. "Dissociable Functions in the Medial and Lateral Orbitofrontal Cortex: Evidence from Human Neuroimaging Studies." *Cerebral Cortex* 10, 308–17.

Engelman, E., Murphey, J., Zhou, F., Aprison, M., and Hingtgen, J. 1995. "Operant Response Suppression Induced with Systemic Administration of 5-Hydroxytryptophan is Centrally Mediated." *Pharmacology, Biochemistry, and Behavior* 52, 525–29.

Evans, G. 1982. *The Varieties of Reference.* Oxford: Oxford University Press.

Field, H. 1978. "Mental Representation." *Erkenntnis* 13, 9–61.

Fischman, M., and Foltin, R. 1992. "Self-administration of Cocaine by Humans: A Laboratory Perspective." In Bock, G., and Whelan, J. (eds.), *Cocaine: Scientific and Social Dimensions (vol. 166).* Chichester, Eng.: Whiley. 165–80.

Fodor, J. 1975. *The Language of Thought.* Cambridge, MA: Harvard University Press.

——— 1987. *Psychosemantics: The Problem of Meaning in the Philosophy of Mind.* Cambridge, MA: MIT Press.

——— 1990. *A Theory of Content, and Other Essays.* Cambridge, MA: MIT Press.

——— 1998. *Concepts: Where Cognitive Science Went Wrong.* New York: Oxford University Press.

Foltz, E., and White, L. 1962. "Pain 'Relief' by Frontal Cingulumotomy." *Journal of Neurosurgery* 19, 89–100.

Frankfurt, H. 1971. "Freedom of the Will and the Concept of a Person." *Journal of Philosophy* 68, 5–20.

Frey, U., Schroeder, H., and Matthies, H. 1990. "Dopaminergic Antagonists Prevent Long-Term Maintenance of Posttetanic LTP in the CA1 Region of Rat Hippocampal Slices." *Brain Research* 522, 69–75.

Fried, I., Katz, A., McCarthy, G., Sass, K., Williamson, P., Spencer, S., and Spencer, D. 1991. "Functional Organization of Human Supplementary Motor Cortex Studied by Electrical Stimulation." *Journal of Neuroscience* 11, 3656–66.

Frijda, N. 1999. "Emotions and Hedonic Experience." In Kahneman, D., Diener, E., and Schwarz, N. (eds.), *Well-Being: The Foundations of Hedonic Psychology*. New York: Russell Sage Foundation.

Frisby, J. 1979. *Seeing: Illusion, Brain, and Mind*. New York: Oxford University Press.

Gamma, A., Buck, A., Berthold, T., Hell, D., and Vollenweider, F. 2000. "3,4-Methylenedioxymethamphetamine (MDMA) Modulates Cortical and Limbic Brain Activity as Measured by [$H_2^{15}O$]-PET in Healthy Humans." *Neuropsychopharmacology* 23, 388–95.

Gardner, H. 1987. *The Mind's New Science: A History of the Cognitive Revolution*. New York: Basic.

Gauthier, D. 1969. *The Logic of Leviathan: The Moral and Political Theory of Thomas Hobbes*. Oxford: Oxford University Press.

Gawin, F. 1991. "Cocaine Addiction: Psychology and Neurophysiology." *Science* 268, 1580–86.

Georgopoulos, A., Taira, M., and Lukashin, A. 1993. "Cognitive Neurophysiology of the Motor Cortex." *Science* 260, 47–52.

Gerstein, E., Gerstein, L., Forsythe, S., and Blue, J. 1999. "The Underwater Audiogram of the West Indian Manatee (Trichechus manatus)." *Journal of the Acoustical Society of America* 105, 3575–83.

Godfrey-Smith, P. 1993. "Functions: Consensus Without Unity." *Pacific Philosophical Quarterly* 74, 196–208.

Goldman-Rakic, P. 1987. "Circuitry of Primate Prefrontal Cortex and Regulation of Behavior by Representational Memory." In Plum, F. (ed.), *Handbook of Physiology, The Nervous System, Higher Functions of the Brain*, sec.1, vol. 5. Bethesda, MD: American Physiological Society. 373–417.

——— 1998. "The Prefrontal Landscape: Implications of Functional Architecture for Understanding Human Mentation and the Central Executive." In Roberts, A., Robbins, T., and Weiskrantz, L. (eds.), *The Prefrontal Cortex: Executive and Cognitive Functions*. New York: Oxford University Press. 87–102.

Gosling, J. 1969. *Pleasure and Desire: The Case for Hedonism Reviewed*. Oxford: Oxford University Press.

Green, O. 1992. *The Emotions: A Philosophical Theory*. Philosophical Studies Series. Boston: Kluwer.

Greenspoon, J. 1955. "The Reinforcing Effect of Two Spoken Sounds on the Frequency of Two Responses." *American Journal of Psychology* 68, 409–16.

Griffiths, P. 1997. *What Emotions Really Are: The Problem of Psychological Categories*. Chicago: University of Chicago Press.

Grill, H., and Berridge, K. 1985. "Taste Reactivity as a Measure of the Neural Control of Palatability." In Sprague, J., and Epstein, A. (eds.), *Progress in Psychobiology and Physiological Psychology: Volume 11*. Orlando, FL: Academic. 1–61.

Groves, P., Garcia-Munoz, M., Linder, J., Manley, M., Martine, M., and Young, S. 1995. "Elements of the Intrinsic Organization and Information Processing in the Neostriatum." In Houk, J., Davis, J., and Beiser, D. (eds.), *Models of Information Processing in the Basal Ganglia*. Cambridge, MA: MIT Press. 51–96.

Haber, S., and Fudge, J. 1997. "The Interface Between Dopamine Neurons and the Amygdala: Implications for Schizophrenia." *Schizophrenia Bulletin* 23, 471–82.

Haber, S., Kunishio, K., Mizobuchi, M., and Lynd-Balta, E. 1995. "The Orbital and Medial Prefrontal Circuit Through the Primate Basal Ganglia." *Journal of Neuroscience* 15, 4851–67.

Hacking, I. 1995. *Rewriting the Soul: Multiple Personality and the Sciences of Memory*. Princeton, NJ: Princeton University Press.

Hardcastle, V. 1999. *The Myth of Pain*. Cambridge, MA: MIT Press.

Harman, G. 1973. *Thought*. Princeton, NJ: Princeton University Press.

Haugeland, J. 1985. *Artificial Intelligence: The Very Idea*. Cambridge, MA: MIT Press.

Heath, R. 1961. "Studies Toward Correlating Behavior with Brain Activity." *Annals of the New York Academy of Sciences* 92, 1106–21.

——— 1963. "Electrical Self-Stimulation of the Brain in Man." *American Journal of Psychiatry* 120, 571–77.

Hefferline, R., Keenan, B., and Harford, R. 1959. "Escape and Avoidance Conditioning in Human Subjects Without Their Observation of the Response." *Science* 130, 1338–39.

Hensman, R., Guimarães, F., Wang, M., and Deakin, J. 1991. "Effects of Ritanserin on Aversive Classical Conditioning in Humans." *Psychopharmacology* 104, 220–24.

Higgins, G., Bradbury, A., Jones, B., and Oakley, N. 1988. "Behavioural and Biochemical Consequences Following Activation of 5HT-sub-1-like and GABA Receptors in the Dorsal Raphe Nucleus of the Rat." *Neuropharmacology* 27, 993–1001.

Homme, L., deBaca, P., Devine, J., Steinhorst, R., and Rickert, E. 1963. "Use of the Premack Principle in Controlling the Behavior of Nursery School Children." *Journal of the Experimental Analysis of Behavior* 6, 544.

Honig, W., Boneau, C., Burstein, K., and Pennypacker, H. 1963. "Positive and Negative Generalization Gradients Obtained after Equivalent Training Conditions." *Journal of Comparative and Physiological Psychology* 56, 111–16.

Hornsby, J. 1980. *Actions*. London: Routledge and Kegan Paul.

Houk, J., Adams, J., and Barto, A. 1995. "A Model of How the Basal Ganglia Generate and Use Neural Signals That Predict Reinforcement." In Houk, J., Davis, J., and Beiser, D. (eds.), *Models of Information Processing in the Basal Ganglia*. Cambridge, MA: MIT Press. 249–70.

Howell, L., Czoty, P., and Byrd, L. 1997. "Pharmacological Interactions Between Serotonin and Dopamine on Behavior in the Squirrel Monkey." *Psychopharmacology* 131, 40–48.

Hsieh, J., Belfrage, M., Stone-Elander, S., Hansson, P., and Ingvar, M. 1995. "Central Representation of Chronic Ongoing Neuropathic Pain Studied by Positron Emission Tomography." *Pain* 63, 225–36.

Hulse, D., Read, C., and Schroeder, T. 2004. "The Impossibility of Unconscious Desire." *American Philosophical Quarterly*, 41, 73–80.

Hutchison, W., Davis, K., Lozano, A., Tasker, R., and Dostrovsky, J. 1999. "Pain-Related Neurons in Human Cingulate Cortex." *Nature Neuroscience* 2, 403–5.

Iadorola, M., Berman, K., Zeffiro, T., Byas-Smith, M., Gracely, R., Max, M., and Bennett, G. 1998. "Neural Activation During Acute Capsaicin-Evoked Pain and Allodynia Assessed with PET." *Brain* 121, 931–47.

Ingvar, M., Ghatan, P., Wisrén-Meurling, A., Risberg, J., Von Heijne, G., Stone-Elander, S., and Ingvar, D. 1998. "Alcohol Activates the Cerebral Reward System in Man." *Journal of Studies on Alcohol* 59, 258–69.

Jahnke, J., and Nowaczyk, R. 1998. *Cognition*. Upper Saddle River, NJ: Prentice-Hall.

James, W. 1890/1952. *The Principles of Psychology*. Toronto: Encyclopedia Britannica.

Jeannerod, M. 1997. *The Cognitive Neuroscience of Action*. Oxford: Blackwell.

Johnsrude, I., Owen, A., Zhao, W., and White, N. 1999. "Conditioned Preference in Humans: A Novel Experimental Approach." *Learning and Motivation* 30, 250–64.

Jordan, S., Kramer, G., Zukas, P., and Petty, F. 1994. "Previous Stress Increases *In Vivo* Biogenic Amine Response to Swim Stress." *Neurochemical Research* 19, 1521–25.

Kandel, E., Schwartz, J., and Jessell, T. 2000. *Principles of Neural Science*. 4th ed. New York: McGraw-Hill.

Kenny, A. 1963/1994. *Action, Emotion, and Will*. Bristol: Thoemmes.

Kim, J. 1993. *Supervenience and Mind: Selected Philosophical Essays*. New York: Cambridge University Press.

——— 1998. *Mind in a Physical World: An Essay on the Mind-Body Problem and Mental Causation*. Cambridge, MA: MIT Press.

Knowlton, B., Mangles, J., and Squire, L. 1996. "A Neostriatal Habit Learning System in Humans." *Science* 273, 1399–402.

Knutson, B., Adams, C., Fong, G., and Hommer, D. 2001. "Anticipation of Increasing Monetary Reward Selectively Recruits Nucleus Accumbens." *Journal of Neuroscience* 21, 1–5.

Korsgaard, C. 1996. *Sources of Normativity*. New York: Cambridge University Press.

Kosslyn, S. 1994. *Image and Brain: The Resolution of the Imagery Debate*. Cambridge, MA: MIT Press.

Kremer, S., Chassagnon, S., Hoffmann, D., Benabid, A., and Kahane, P. 2001. "The Cingulate Hidden Hand." *Journal of Neurology, Neurosurgery, and Psychiatry* 70, 264–65.

Kripke, S. 1972. *Naming and Necessity*. Cambridge, MA: Harvard University Press.

Kuhn, T. 1970. *The Structure of Scientific Revolutions*. 2nd ed. Chicago: University of Chicago Press.

Kushner, H. 1999. *A Cursing Brain: The Histories of Tourette Syndrome*. Cambridge, MA: Harvard University Press.

Laitinen, L. 1979. "Emotional Responses to Subcortical Electrical Stimulation in Psychiatric Patients." *Clinical Neurology and Neurosurgery* 81, 148–57.

Lamb, R., Preston, K., Schindler, C., Meisch, R., Davis, F., Katz, J., Henningfield, J., and Goldberg, S. 1991. "The Reinforcing and Subjective Effects of Morphine in Post-Addicts: A Dose-Response Study." *Journal of Pharmacology and Experimental Therapies* 259, 1165–73.

Lane, R., Fink, G., Chau, P., and Dolan, R. 1997. "Neural Activation During Selective Attention to Subjective Emotional Responses." *NeuroReport* 8, 3969–72.

Langston, J., and Palfreman, J. 1995. *The Case of the Frozen Addicts*. New York: Pantheon.

Lauwereyns, J., Watanabe, K., Coe, B., and Hikosaka, O. 2002. "A Neural Correlate of Response Bias in Monkey Caudate Nucleus." *Nature* 418, 413–17.

Leckman, J., Walker, D., Cohen, D. 1993. "Premonitory Urges in Tourette's Syndrome." *American Journal of Psychiatry* 150, 98–102.

LeDoux, J. 1996. *The Emotional Brain: The Mysterious Underpinnings of Emotional Life*. New York: Touchstone.

——— 2000. "Emotional Circuits in the Brain." *Annual Review of Neuroscience* 23, 155–84.

Levin, B., and Duchowny, M. 1991. "Childhood Obsessive-Compulsive Disorder and Cingulate Epilepsy." *Biological Psychiatry* 30, 1049–55.

Liechti, M., Saur, M., Gamma, A., Hell, D., and Vollenweider, F. 2000. "Psychological and Physiological Effects of MDMA ("Ecstasy") after Pretreatment with the 5-HT$_2$ Antagonist Ketanserin in Healthy Humans." *Neuropsychopharmacology* 23, 396–404.

Liechti, M., and Vollenweider, F. 2000. "Acute Psychological and Physiological Effects of MDMA ("Ecstasy") after Haloperidol Pretreatment in Healthy Humans." *European Neuropsychopharmacology* 10, 289–95.

Liu, Q., Hattar, S., Endo, S., MacPhee, K., Zhang, H., Cleary, L., Byrne, J., and Eskin, A. 1997. "The Developmental Gene (*Tolloid*/BMP-1) Is Regulated in *Aplysia* Neurons by Treatments that Induce Long-Term Sensitization." *Journal of Neuroscience* 17, 755–64.

Ljungberg, T., Apicella, P., and Schultz, W. 1992. "Responses of Monkey Dopamine Neurons During Learning of Behavioral Reactions." *Journal of Neurophysiology* 67, 145–63.

Lycan, W. 1987. *Consciousness*. Cambridge, MA: MIT Press.

——— 1988. *Judgement and Justification*. New York: Cambridge University Press.

Malcolm, N. 1959. *Dreaming*. London: Routledge and Paul.

Marks, J. 1986. *The Ways of Desire: New Essays in Philosophical Psychology on the Concept of Wanting*. Chicago: Precedent.

Marr, D. 1982. *Vision: A Computational Investigation into the Human Representation and Processing of Visual Information*. New York: Freeman.

Mason, G., Cooper, J., and Clarebrough, C. 2001. "Frustrations of Fur-Farmed Mink." *Nature* 410, 35–36.

Mathew, R., Wilson, W., Chiu, N., Turkington, T., Degrado, T., and Coleman, R. 1999. "Regional Cerebral Blood Flow and Depersonalization after Tetrahydrocannabinol Administration." *Acta Psychiatrica Scandinavia* 100, 67–75.

McDowell, J. 1994. *Mind and World*. Cambridge, MA: Harvard University Press.

——— 1998. *Mind, Value, and Reality*. Cambridge, MA: Harvard University Press.

Mele, A. 1990. "He Wants to Try." *Analysis* 50, 251–53.

Melzack, R. 1973. *The Puzzle of Pain*. New York: Basic.

Mertz, H., Morgan, V., Tanner, G., Pickens, D., Price, R., Shyr, Y., and Kessler, R. 2000. "Regional Cerebral Activation in Irritable Bowel Syndrome and Control Subjects with Painful and Nonpainful Rectal Distention." *Gastroenterology* 118, 842–48.

Merzenich, M., and Jenkins, W. 1993. "Reorganization of Cortical Representations of the Hand Following Alterations of Skin Inputs Induced by Nerve Injury, Skin Island Transfers, and Experience." *Journal of Hand Therapy* 6, 89–104.

Meyer, G., McElhaney, M., Martin, W., and McGraw, C. 1973. "Stereotactic Cingulotomy with Results of Acute Stimulation and Serial Psychological Testing." In Laitinen, L., and Kenneth, I. (eds.), *Surgical Approaches in Psychiatry: Proceedings*. Baltimore, MD: University Park Press.

Mill, J. 1861/1957. *Utilitarianism*. Priest, O. (ed.), New York: Macmillan.

Millikan, R. 1984. *Language, Thought, and Other Biological Categories*. Cambridge, MA: MIT Press.

——— 1993. *White Queen Psychology and Other Essays for Alice*. Cambridge, MA: MIT Press.

——— 1996. "On Swampkinds." *Mind and Language* 11, 103–17.

——— 2000. *On Clear and Confused Ideas: An Essay about Substance Concepts*. New York: Cambridge University Press.

Millgram, E. 1997. *Practical Induction*. Cambridge, MA: Harvard University Press.

Mink, J. 1996. "The Basal Ganglia: Focussed Selection and Inhibition of Competing Motor Programs." *Progress in Neurobiology* 50, 381–425.

——— 2001. "Neurobiology of Basal Ganglia Circuits in Tourette Syndrome: Faulty Inhibition of Unwanted Motor Patterns?" In Cohen, D., Goetz, C., and Jankovic, J. (eds.), *Tourette Syndrome*. Philadelphia: Lippincott, Williams, and Wilkins.

Mitoma, H., and Konishi, S. 1999. "Monoaminergic Long-Term Facilitation of GABA-Mediated Inhibitory Transmission at Cerebellar Synapses." *Neuroscience* 88, 871–83.

Morillo, C. 1990. "The Reward Event and Motivation," *Journal of Philosophy* 87, 169–86.

Nagel, E. 1961. *The Structure of Science: Problems in the Logic of Scientific Explanation*. New York: Harcourt, Brace, and World.

Nagel, T. 1974. "What Is It Like to Be a Bat?" *Philosophical Review* 83, 435–50.

Neafsey, E., Terreberry, R., Hurley, K., Ruit, K., and Frysztak, R. 1993. "Anterior Cingulate Cortex in Rodents: Connections, Visceral Control Functions, and Implications for Emotion." In Vogt, B., and Gabriel, M. (eds.), *Neurobiology of Cingulate Cortex and Limbic Thalamus: A Comprehensive Handbook*. Boston, MA: Birkhäuser. 206–22.

Neander, K. 1996. "Swampman Meets Swampcow." *Mind and Language* 11, 118–29.

Nicola, S., Surmeier, D., and Malenka, R. 2000. "Dopaminergic Modulation of Neuronal Excitability in the Striatum and Nucleus Accumbens." *Annual Review of Neuroscience* 23, 185–215.

O'Hearn, E., and Molliver, M. 1984. "Organization of Raphe-Cortical Projections in Rat: A Quantitative Retrograde Study." *Brain Research Bulletin* 13, 709–26.

Otmakhova, N., and Lisman, J. 1996. "D1/D5 Dopamine Receptor Activation Increases the Magnitude of Early Long-Term Potentiation at CA1 Hippocampal Synapses." *Journal of Neuroscience* 16, 7478–86.

Packard, M., and McGaugh, J. 1992. "Double Dissociation of Fornix and Caudate Nucleus Lesions on Acquisition of Two Water Maze Tasks: Further Evidence for Multiple Memory Systems." *Behavioral Neuroscience* 106, 439–46.

Packard, M., and Teather, L. 1997. "Double Dissociation of Hippocampal and Dorsal-Striatal Memory Systems by Posttraining Intracerebral Injections of 2-Amino-5-Phosphonopentanoic Acid." *Behavioral Neuroscience* 111, 543–51.

——— 1999. "Dissociation of Multiple Memory Systems by Posttraining Intracerebral Injections of Glutamate." *Psychobiology* 27, 40–50.

Packard, M., and White, N. 1991. "Dissociation of Hippocampus and Caudate Nucleus Memory Systems by Posttraining Intracerebral Injection of Dopamine Agonists." *Behavioral Neuroscience* 105, 295–306.

Pagnoni, G., Zink, C., Read Montague, P., and Berns, G. 2002. "Activity in Human Ventral Striatum Locked to Errors of Reward Prediction." *Nature Neuroscience* 5, 97–98.

Panksepp, J. 1998. *Affective Neuroscience: The Foundations of Human and Animal Emotions*. New York: Oxford University Press.

Papineau, D. 1987. *Reality and Representation*. New York: Basil Blackwell.

——— 1996. "Doubtful Intuitions." *Mind and Language* 11, 130–32.

Peacocke, C. 1983. *Sense and Content: Experience, Thought, and Their Relations*. New York: Oxford University Press.

——— 1992. *A Study of Concepts*. Cambridge, MA: MIT Press.

Perry, J. 2001. *Knowledge, Possibility, and Consciousness*. Cambridge, MA: MIT Press.

Peterson, B., Skudlarski, P., Anderson, A., Zhang, H., Gatenby, J., Lacadie, C., Leckman,

J., and Gore, J. 1998. "A Functional Magnetic Resonance Imaging Study of Tic Suppression in Tourette Syndrome." *Archives of General Psychiatry* 55, 326–33.

Peyron, C., Petit, J., Rampon, C., Jouvet, M., and Luppi, P. 1998. "Forebrain Afferents to the Rat Dorsal Raphe Nucleus Demonstrated by Retrograde and Anterograde Tracing Methods." *Neuroscience* 82, 443–68.

Ploghaus, A., Tracey, I., Gati, J., Clare, S., Menon, R., Matthews, P., and Rollins, J. 1999. "Dissociating Pain from Its Anticipation in the Human Brain." *Science* 284, 179–81.

Porro, C., Cettolo, V., Francescato, M., and Baraldi, P. 1998. "Temporal and Intensity Coding of Pain in Human Cortex." *Journal of Neurophysiology* 80, 3312–20.

Prinz, J. 2002. *Furnishing the Mind: Concepts and Their Perceptual Basis*. Cambridge, MA: MIT Press.

Putnam, H. 1960. "Minds and Machines." Reprinted in Cummins, R., and Cummins, D. (eds.), 2000. *Minds, Brains, and Computers: The Foundations of Cognitive Science, an Anthology*. Oxford: Blackwell 20–33.

——— 1975. "The Meaning of 'Meaning'." In Gunderson, K. (ed.), *Language, Mind and Knowledge*. Minnesota Studies in the Philosophy of Science 7. Minneapolis: University of Minnesota Press.

Rainville, P., Duncan, G., Price, D., Carrier, B., and Bushnell, C. 1997. "Pain Affect Encoded in Human Anterior Cingulate but Not Somatosensory Cortex." *Science* 277, 968–71.

Rauch, S., Shin, L., Dougherty, D., Alpert, N., Orr, S., Lasko, M., Macklin, M., Fischman, A., and Pitman, R. 1999. "Neural Activation During Sexual and Competitive Arousal in Healthy Men." *Psychiatry Research: Neuroimaging Section* 91, 1–10.

Read Montague, P., Dayan, P., and Sejnowski, T. 1996. "A Framework for Mesencephalic Dopamine Systems Based on Predictive Hebbian Learning." *Journal of Neuroscience* 16, 1936–47.

Ridge, M. 1998. "Humean Intentions." *American Philosophical Quarterly* 35, 157–78.

Rogers, R., Blackshaw, A., Middleton, H., Matthews, K., Hawtin, K., Crowley, C., Hopwood, A., Wallace, C., Deakin, J., Sahakian, B., and Robbins, T. 1999. "Tryptophan Depletion Impairs Stimulus-Reward Learning While Methylphenidate Disrupts Attentional Control in Healthy Young Adults: Implications for the Monoaminergic Basis of Impulsive Behaviour." *Psychopharmacology* 146, 482–91.

Rolls, E. 2000. "Orbitofrontal Cortex and Reward." *Cerebral Cortex* 10, 284–94.

Rolls, E., Critchley, H., Mason, R., and Wakeman, E. 1996. "Orbitofrontal Cortex Neurons: Role in Olfactory and Visual Association Learning." *Journal of Neurophysiology* 75, 1970–81.

Romo, R., and Schultz, W. 1990. "Dopamine Neurons of the Monkey Midbrain: Contingencies of Response to Active Touch During Self-Initiated Arm Movements." *Journal of Neurophysiology* 63, 592–606.

Rueter, L., Fornal, C., and Jacobs, B. 1997. "A Critical Review of 5-HT Brain Microdialysis and Behavior." *Reviews in the Neurosciences* 8, 117–37.

Rueter, L., and Jacobs, B. 1996. "A Microdialysis Examination of Serotonin Release in the Rat Forebrain Induced by Behavioral/Environmental Manipulations." *Brain Research* 739, 57–69.

Russell, B. 1921. *The Analysis of Mind*. London: George Allen and Unwin.

Ryle, G. 1949. *The Concept of Mind*. Chicago: Chicago University Press.

——— 1954. "Pleasure." *Proceedings of the Aristotelian Society*. Supplementary Volume 27. Reprinted in Ryle, G. 1971. *Collected Papers: Volume 2, Collected Essays,*

1929–1968. London: Hutchinson, 325–36.

Sacks, O. 1970. *The Man Who Mistook His Wife for a Hat: And Other Clinical Tales*. New York: HarperCollins.

Scanlon, T. 1998. *What We Owe to Each Other*. Cambridge, MA: Harvard University Press.

Schroeder, T. 2001a. "Monsters among Us." *Canadian Journal of Philosophy*, suppl. vol. 27, 167–84.

——— 2001b. "Pleasure, Displeasure, and Representation." *Canadian Journal of Philosophy* 31, 507–30.

Schueler, G. 1995. *Desire: Its Role in Practical Reason and the Explanation of Action*. Cambridge, MA: MIT Press.

Schultz, W., Apicella, P., and Ljungberg, T. 1993. "Responses of Monkey Dopamine Neurons to Reward and Conditioned Stimuli During Successive Steps of Learning a Delayed Response Task." *Journal of Neuroscience* 13, 900–913.

Schultz, W., Dayan, P., and Read Montague, P. 1997. "Neural Substrate of Prediction and Reward." *Science* 275, 1593–99.

Schultz, W., and Romo, R. 1990. "Dopamine Neurons of the Monkey Midbrain: Contingencies of Response to Stimuli Eliciting Immediate Behavioral Reactions." *Journal of Neurophysiology* 63, 607–24.

Schultz, W., Tremblay, L., and Hollerman, J. 2000. "Reward Processing in Primate Orbitofrontal Cortex and Basal Ganglia." *Cerebral Cortex* 10, 272–83.

Seager, W. 1997. "Critical Notice of Fred Dretske, *Naturalizing the Mind*." *Canadian Journal of Philosophy* 27, 83–109.

Searle, J. 1983. *Intentionality: An Essay in the Philosophy of Mind*. New York: Cambridge University Press.

——— 1992. *The Rediscovery of the Mind*. Cambridge, MA: MIT Press.

——— 2000. *Rationality in Action*. Cambridge, MA: MIT Press.

Seligman, M., and Maier, S. 1967. "Failure to Escape Traumatic Shock." *Journal of Experimental Psychology* 74, 1–9.

Sellars, W. 1963. *Science, Perception, and Reality*. London: Routledge and Kegan Paul.

Shimizu, N., Take, S., Hori, T., and Oomura, Y. 1992. "*In Vivo* Measurement of Hypothalamic Serotonin Release by Intracerebral Microdialysis: Significant Enhancement by Immobilization Stress in Rats." *Brain Research Bulletin* 28, 727–34.

Shin, L., Dougherty, D., Orr, S., Pitman, R., Lasko, M, Macklin, M., Alpert, N., Fischman, A., and Rauch, S. 2000. "Activation of Anterior Paralimbic Structures during Guilt-Related Script-Driven Imagery." *Biological Psychiatry* 48, 43–50.

Shintani, F., Nakaki, T., Kanba, S., Sato, K., Yagi, G., Shiozawa, M., Aiso, S., Cato, R., and Asai, M. 1995. "Involvement of Interleukin-1 in Immobilization Stress-Induced Increase in Plasma Adrenocorticotropic Hormone and in Release of Hypothalamic Monoamines in the Rat." *Journal of Neuroscience* 15, 1961–70.

Skinner, B. 1938. *The Behavior of Organisms: An Experimental Analysis*. New York: Appleton-Century-Crofts.

——— 1948. "Superstition in the Pigeon." *Journal of Experimental Psychology* 38, 168–72.

——— 1971. *Beyond Freedom and Dignity*. New York: Knopf.

Smith, K., Morris, J., Friston, K., Cowen, P., and Dolan, R. 1999. "Brain Mechanisms Associated with Depressive Relapse and Associated Cognitive Impairment Following Acute Tryptophan Depletion." *British Journal of Psychiatry* 174, 525–29.

Smith, M. 1987. "The Humean Theory of Motivation." *Mind* 96, 36–61.

——— 1994. *The Moral Problem*. Cambridge, MA: Blackwell.

Smith, M., and Duffy, M. 1957. "The Consumption of Sucrose and Saccharine by Hungry and Satiated Rats." *Journal of Comparative and Physiological Psychology* 50, 65–69.

Soubrié, P. 1986. "Reconciling the Role of Central Serotonin Neurons in Human and Animal Behavior." *Behavioral and Brain Sciences* 9, 319–64.

Sprengelmeyer, R., Young, A., Schroeder, U., Grossenbacher, P., Federlein, J., Büttner, T., and Przuntek, H. 1999. "Knowing No Fear." *Proceedings of the Royal Society of London B: Biological Sciences* 266, 2451–56.

Stalnaker, R. 1984. *Inquiry*. Cambridge, MA: MIT Press.

Stampe, D. 1986. "Defining Desire." In Marks, J. (ed.), *The Ways of Desire: New Essays in Philosophical Psychology on the Concept of Wanting*. Chicago: Precedent. 149–73.

Stellar, J., and Stellar, E. 1985. *The Neurobiology of Motivation and Reward*. New York: Springer-Verlag.

Sterelny, K. 1990. *The Representational Mind: An Introduction*. Cambridge, MA: Blackwell.

Stocker, M. 1979. "Desiring the Bad: An Essay in Moral Psychology." *Journal of Philosophy* 76, 738–53.

Strawson, G. 1994. *Mental Reality*. Cambridge, MA: MIT Press.

Strawson, P. 1962. "Freedom and Resentment." *Proceedings of the British Academy* 48, 1–25.

Suzuki, T., Miura, M., Nishimura, K., and Aosaki, T. 2001. "Dopamine-Dependent Synaptic Plasticity in the Striatal Cholinergic Interneurons." *Journal of Neuroscience* 21, 6492–501.

Talairach, J., Bancaud, J., Geier, S., Bordas-Ferrer, M., Bonis, A., Szikla, G., and Rusu, M. 1973. "The Cingulate Gyrus and Human Behaviour." *Electroencephalography and Clinical Neurophysiology* 34, 45–52.

Thiebot, M., Hamon, M., and Soubrie, P. 1982. "Attenuation of Induced-Anxiety in Rats by Chlordiazepoxide: Role of Raphe Dorsalis Benzodiazepine Binding Sites and Serotoninergic Neurons." *Neuroscience* 7, 2287–94.

Thorndike, E. 1911. *Animal Intelligence: Experimental Studies*. New York: Macmillan.

Thut, G., Schultz, W., Roelcke, U., Nienhusmeier, M., Missimer, J., Maguire, R., and Leenders, K. 1997. "Activation of the Human Brain by Monetary Reward." *NeuroReport* 8, 1225–28.

Tibbetts, P. 2001. "The Anterior Cingulate Cortex, Akinetic Mutism, and Human Volition." *Brain and Mind* 2, 323–41.

Tye, M. 1995. *Ten Problems of Consciousness*. Cambridge, MA: MIT Press.

Vadas, M. 1984. "Affective and Non-affective Desire." *Philosophy and Phenomenological Research* 45, 273–80.

Vahabzadeh, A., and Fillenz, M. 1994. "Comparison of Stress-Induced Changes in Noradrenergic and Serotonergic Neurons in the Rat Hippocampus Using Microdialysis." *European Journal of Neuroscience* 6, 1205–12.

Vogt, B., Derbyshire, S., and Jones, A. 1996. "Pain Processing in Four Regions of Human Cingulate Cortex Localised with Co-Registered PET and MR Imaging." *European Journal of Neuroscience* 8, 1461–73.

Vogt, B., Finch, D., and Olson, C. 1992. "Functional Heterogeneity in Cingulate Cortex: The Anterior Executive and Posterior Evaluative Regions." *Cerebral Cortex* 2, 435–43.

Volkow, N., Wang, G., Fowler, J., Hitzemann, R., Angrist, B., Gatley, S., Logan, J., Ding, Y., and Pappas, N. 1999. "Association of Methylphenidate-Induced Craving with

Changes in Right Striato-orbitofrontal Metabolism in Cocaine Abusers: Implications in Addiction." *American Journal of Society* 156, 19–26.

Vollenweider, F., Maguire, R., Leenders, K., Mathys, K., and Angst, J. 1996. "Effects of High Amphetamine Dose on Mood and Cerebral Glucose Metabolism in Normal Volunteers Using Positron Emission Tomography (PET)." *Psychiatry Research: Neuroimaging Section* 83, 149–62.

Waelti, P., Dickinson, A., and Schultz, W. 2001. "Dopamine Responses Comply with Basic Assumptions of Formal Learning Theory." *Nature* 412, 43–48.

Watson, J., and Rayner, R. 1920. "Conditioned Emotional Reactions." *Journal of Experimental Psychology* 3, 1–14.

Weiskrantz, L. 1986. *Blindsight: A Case Study and Implications*. New York: Oxford University Press.

Weisler, S., Stillings, N., Chase, C., Feinstein, M., Garfield, J., and Rissland, E. 1995. *Cognitive Science: An Introduction*. 2nd ed. Cambridge, MA: MIT Press.

West, H., Mark, G., and Hoebel, B. 1991. "Effects of Conditioned Taste Aversion on Extracellular Serotonin in the Lateral Hypothalamus and Hippocampus of Freely Moving Rats." *Brain Research* 556, 95–100.

Whalen, P., Bush, G., McNally, R., Wilhelm, S., McInerney, S., Jenike, M., and Rauch, S. 1998. "The Emotional Counting Stroop Paradigm: A Functional Magnetic Resonance Imaging Probe of the Anterior Cingulate Affective Division." *Biological Psychiatry* 44, 1219–28.

White, N. 1996. "Addictive Drugs as Reinforcers: Multiple Partial Actions on Memory Systems." *Addiction* 91, 921–49.

——— 1997. "Mnemonic Functions of the Basal Ganglia." *Current Opinion in Neurobiology* 7, 164–69.

White, N., and Milner, P. 1992. "The Psychobiology of Reinforcers." *Annual Review of Psychology* 43, 443–71.

Wilkinson, L., Humby, T., Killcross, S., Robbins, T., and Everitt, B. 1996. "Dissociations in Hippocampal 5-Hydroxytryptamine Release in the Rat Following Pavlovian Aversive Conditioning to Discrete and Contextual Stimuli." *European Journal of Neuroscience* 8, 1479–87.

Wilkinson, L., and Jacobs, B. 1988. "Lack of Response of Serotonergic Neurons in the Dorsal Raphe Nucleus of Freely Moving Cats to Stressful Stimuli." *Experimental Neurology* 101, 445–57.

Wise, C., Berger, B., and Stein, L. 1973. "Evidence of a-Noradrenergic Reward Receptors and Serotonergic Punishment Receptors in the Rat Brain." *Biological Psychiatry* 6, 3–21.

Wood, A. 1999. *Kant's Ethical Thought*. New York: Cambridge University Press.

Wyvell, C., and Berridge, K. 2000. "Intra-Accumbens Amphetamine Increases the Conditioned Incentive Salience of Sucrose Reward: Enhancement of Reward 'Wanting' Without Enhanced 'Liking' or Response Reinforcement." *The Journal of Neuroscience* 20, 8122–30.

Yoshioka, M., Matsumoto, M., Togashi, H., and Saito, H. 1995. "Effects of Conditioned Fear Stress on 5-HT Release in the Rat Prefrontal Cortex." *Pharmacology, Biochemistry, and Behavior* 51, 515–19.

Zald, D., Lee, J., Fluegel, K., and Pardo, J. 1998. "Aversive Gustatory Stimulation Activates Limbic Circuits in Humans." *Brain* 121, 1143–54.

Zhang, F., and Endo, S. 1997. "Role of Transforming Growth Factor-Beta in Long-Term Synaptic Facilitation in Aplysia." *Science* 275, 1318–21.

Index

Absolute space, 7–8
Action, 107–8
   and belief-desire complexes, 129–30
   and deviant causal chains, 23
Akinetic mutism, 111, 173–4
Akrasia, 41
Alcohol, 79
Allodynia, 80
Amphetamines, 79, 122
Amygdala, 24, 53, 81
Anscombe, G. E. M., 168
Anterior cingulate cortex, 24
   functional heterogeneity of, 77
   motor region of (*see* Motor AC)
   perigenual region of (*see* PGAC)
   stimulation of, 78
Anterograde amnesia, 52, 119
Anxiety, 22, 33, 56, 85, 132
Aplysia, 52, 61
Articulatory loop, 114
Attention, 15, 24, 41, 77, 140
Aversion. *See* Desire
Aydede, M., 78, 83, 86

Basal ganglia
   and motivation, 37, 118, 122, 154, 158, 160
   and reward, 53, 115–16
   and Tourette syndrome, 125
   and urges, 145
Basic action, 110
Behaviorism, 35, 43–4, 57, 147
   and behavioral scientists, 44
Benzodiazepines, 81
Berridge, K., 81–2, 84, 118, 121–2, 127
Brain stimulation, 57–8, 81, 122
Bratman, M., 21, 114 n.10, 139–42

Caloric, 7
Capsaicin, 80
Caudate nucleus, 53
Cerebellum, 56, 119–20
Churchland, P. M., 163, 167
Cingulum, 78
Cingulumotomy, 33–4, 78, 121
Cocaine
   and pleasure, 53, 79–80, 83, 92
   and reward, 60, 117
Conditioning. *See* Reward
Confidence. *See* Pleasure, and expectation; Reward, and expectation
Contingency-based learning theory of desire. *See* Desire, contingency-based learning theory of
Counterfactuals, 17

Damasio, A., 32, 84–6, 93, 111, 117–18, 176, 180
Danto, A., 110
Davidson, D., 4, 110, 163
Deakin, W., 56
Delayed response, 113–14
Deliberation, 145–6
Desire
   acquisition and loss of, 146–50
   asymmetry between it and belief, 133
   and aversion, 25–7, 132
   clean theories of, 162–3
   conflicting, 153
   and consciousness, 14–15, 31, 98, 144–6, 172
   contents of, 12, 99, 133, 166–8
   contingency-based learning theory of, 70, 105–6, 128–30, 131–61
   and direction of fit, 34, 155–7
   epistemology of, 28, 93

Desire (*continued*)
  fleeting, 150–2, 172
  hedonic theory of, 27–35, 69–70, 105, 126–7, 143, 176; advantages over standard theory, 29–30; objections to, 127–9
  innate, 98, 146
  instrumental, 5, 151, 152–5, 166
  intrinsic, 5, 132
  and lack, 137–8
  localization of, 24–5
  messy theories of, 173–9
  mix-and-match theory of, 176–9
  for necessities and impossibilities, 15–20, 29
  in non-human animals, 9
  objectless, 133–4
  for pleasure, 100–1
  and propositions, 11, 166–7
  second-order, 68
  for sensuous states, 97–100, 132
  sexual, 4
  standard theory of, 3, 10–27, 69, 105–6, 123–5, 139, 174; objections to, 15–27, 125–6, 129; teleological version of, 18–19
  strength of, 13, 21, 30–1, 138–44, 159
  and tastes, 98–100
  three faces of, 6, 131
  unconscious, 15
  and urges, 144
  and wants, wishes, 132, 166
Displeasure. *See* Pleasure
Dopamine, 115–19, 121, 132, 148
  and decision making, 54
  focusing effect of, 116–17
  and neural change, 50–2
  and pleasure, 81
  releasing and receptive cells, 50
Dormitive virtue, 59
Dorsal striatum. *See* Striatum
Dretske, F., 4, 129, 134
DRN (dorsal raphe nucleus), 54, 116, 118

Ecstasy. *See* MDMA
Eliminativism, 7–8, 162–73
Elster, J., 92
Emotion, 40, 45, 79, 85, 162
Epilepsy, 111
Ether, 7–8

Euphorigenic drugs, 92. *See also* Amphetamines; Cocaine; Heroin; MDMA; Morphine

Fluoxetine, 56
Freud, S., 8, 164
Frost, R., 10, 25–7, 29–30

Gage, P., 32, 176
Griffiths, P., 162
Goldman-Rakic, P., 24
Globus pallidus, 116

Habit, 115, 128, 143, 145
  dissociated from memory, 51–2, 119
  and moral motivation, 159–60
  as an objection to the standard theory of desire, 22
Hardcastle, V., 76 n.7, 162, 179
Hedonic theory of desire. *See* Desire, hedonic theory of
Heroin, 60–1, 83, 92
Hippocampus, 51–2
Homeostasis, 151–2
Hope, 21
Hunger, 151–2
Hypothalamus
  and desires for food, 151–2
  and motivation, 122
  and pleasure, 78, 96
  and reward, 49, 54, 115

Immobilization, 55
Imperative icon, 136
Inhibition. *See* Motivation
Intensionality, 98–9
Intention, 5, 116, 154, 156
  common sense knowledge of, 112
  neural basis of, 113–15
  and an objection to the standard theory of desire, 20–2
Intentionality, 3
Introspection, 8
Irrational action, 139–43

Know-how, 120

Learned helplessness, 46
Learning, 53. *See also* Neural connection
  functional theory of, 135–6

and memory compared to habit, 51–2
and regulation, 156–7
teleological theory of, 136
unconscious, 41, 54, 63, 115, 118–19
LeDoux, J., 24, 180
Limbic system, 82
Little Albert, 46
Lobotomy, frontal, 33, 78

MDMA (3–4 methylenedioxymethamphetamine), 54
Medial forebrain bundle, 81
Medial raphe nucleus, 56
Mele, A., 21, 154
Melzack, R., 78
Mental causation, 175
Mental representation, 3, 133
  as input to pleasure, 91–3
  localization of, 23–5
  and moral motivation, 158, 160
  and motivational inconstancy, 139–40
  and motor representations, 109
  and pleasure (*see* Pleasure, representational theory of)
  provides desire content, 134
  and reward, 49, 64, 128
  and vision, 88–9
Microdialysis, 55
Midbrain dopamine system. *See* VTA/SNpc
Mill, J. S., 27
Millikan, R., 18–19, 134, 136, 157
Morillo, C., 36, 81, 180
Morphine, 60–1, 81
Motivation, 6, 11, 107–30, 170, 173–4
  and desire, 122–3
  moral, 14, 157–61, 171
  neural basis of, 24, 36 (*see also* Intention, neural basis of; Trying, neural basis of)
  and pleasure, 120, 126–8
  and punishment, 118
  and reward, 115–120, 128–30
Motivational theory of desire. *See* Desire, standard theory of
Motor AC (anterior cingulate)
  and moral motivation, 160
  and motivation, 110–11, 113, 116, 126–8

and pleasure, 77, 79, 121, 126–8
stimulation of, 111
Motor cortex, 37, 110, 116, 120, 128, 154
Multimodal sensory association areas, 24
Multiple realization, 61, 76–7, 135

Natural kind, 5–8, 164, 177–8
Neural connection, 50–1, 118–19, 139, 147–8. *See also* Learning
Nociception, 85
Non-conceptual content, 99
Nucleus accumbens, 53–4, 78, 82, 122

OFC (orbitofrontal cortex)
  damage to, 117–18, 180
  and desire acquisition, 147–8
  and motivation, 115, 121, 160
  and pleasure, 80–1, 99
  and reward, 53–4
Opponent process, 90–1

Packard, M., 51–2, 119
Papineau, D., 18–19
Parabrachial nucleus, 82
Paralysis, 110–11
Parietal cortex, 111–12
Parkinson disease, 54, 118–19, 121, 129, 173–4, 176
Pavlov, I., 44
PFC (prefrontal cortex), 24
  and deliberation, 145
  and motivation, 113–15, 122, 154, 160
  and pleasure, 126
  and reward, 53, 116, 128
PGAC (perigenual anterior cingulate cortex), 37, 83, 91, 105–6
  brain imaging of, 79
  and evidence it does not realize pleasure, 79–80, 82
  and evidence it realizes pleasure, 76–81
  injury to, 78–9
  and motivation, 121–2, 126–7
  and reward, 36
  stimulation of, 78
Pleasure, 6, 13–14, 71–106, 170, 174–6
  behavioral theory of, 83
  body landscape theory of, 84–6
  common sense knowledge of, 71–76
  compared to feelings of warmth and coldness, 72, 103–4

Pleasure (*continued*)
  compared to vision, 88–9
  a continuum of, 72–3, 86–8, 90
  and daydreams, anticipation, 101–2
  and depression, 31–3, 32 n.23, 53–4, 56, 95
  and dopamine, 53–4
  while dreaming, 83
  and expectation, 74–5, 86–8, 93–5, 143
  as a feeling, 71–3, 89
  functional-role theory of, 86–8, 93
  illusory or unreal, 75–6, 91–3, 102, 133
  intellectual and sensuous sources, 73–4, 91, 95–6, 99, 105
  location of, 76, 102–3
  and motivation, 83–4, 120
  neural basis of, 24, 36, 76–83
  and neural injury or surgery, 33–4
  and pain, 72
  qualitative theory of, 86–8, 93
  as representational, 31, 84, 91–3
  representational theory of, 88–105
  and reward, 127
  and serotonin, 56
  and simultaneous displeasure, 72, 86–8, 90–1
  and strength of desire, 143
  trades off against displeasure, 72–3, 86–8, 90–1
  types of, 76, 78, 103–5
  variation in, 74–5
Primary sensory cortex, 24, 51
Primitive action. *See* Basic action
Privileged access, 8
Pro attitude, 4, 21–2, 98, 100, 124–5, 166
Prozac. *See* Fluoxetine
Psychological hedonism, 100, 120
Punishment. *See* Reward

Qualia, 83–4, 86–8
Quinine, 81, 84

Race, 169
Rat facial expressions, 46, 81, 84, 121–2
Reactive attitudes, 42
Reference, theories of, 8, 164–5
Response bias, 117

Reward, 6, 15, 35, 38–70, 168–70, 175–6
  in the absence of pleasure, 60–1
  in action selection, 116–18
  as not the basis of pleasure, 80–1
  behavioral science of, 43–8
  common sense knowledge of, 39–43, 63, 66–9
  and conditioning, classical, 44–5, 56
  and conditioning, emotional, 45
  and conditioning, operant, 44–5, 118–19
  and contingency-based learning, 50, 61–7
  contingency-based learning theory of, 64–5, 70
  conventional, 38, 60
  desire-based theory of, 67–70
  desire for, 68–9
  emotional effects of, 40, 46, 53–4
  and expectation, 50, 53, 115, 128, 140–2
  hedonic theory of, 58–61, 63, 69–70
  and learning, 36, 50
  and motivation, 36–7, 115–120
  motivational effects of, 40–2, 46–7, 51–2, 54–5
  motivational theory of, 57–8, 69
  neural basis of, 36, 48–57
  and pleasure, 37, 92
  positive and negative, 132
  psychological effects of, 42, 47–8, 50–2, 56
  and punishment, 54–7
  and reinforcers, 19, 147
  and trivial explanation, 62–3
  types of, 39, 45–6
Reward theory of desire. *See* Desire, contingency-based learning theory of
Ritanserin, 56
Rolls, E., 54, 99, 147–8, 150
Ryle, G., 83–4, 93

Sacks, O., 32
Schultz, W., 50, 62, 81, 132
Septum, 78, 81
Serotonin, 54–7, 118
Skinner, B. F., 36, 39, 44, 128
SMA (supplementary motor area), 110–11, 113, 120, 128, 154
Smith, M., 10, 34

Spinal cord, 37, 110–11
Stalnaker, R., 10
Stampe, D., 4
Standard theory of desire. *See* Desire, standard theory of
Strawson, G., 4, 20, 27
Stressors, 55
Striatum. *See also* Basal ganglia; Nucleus accumbens
   and moral motivation, 159–60
   and motivation, 51–2, 116, 118–19, 122, 125, 127–9
   and reward, 54
Stuttering, 22, 124
Substantia nigra pars compacta. *See* VTA/SNpc
Substantia nigra pars reticulata, 116
Subthalamic nucleus, 116 n.13

Tastes. *See* Desire, and tastes
THC (tetrahydracannabinol), 79
Tourette syndrome, 124–6, 129, 144–5, 160–1, 174
Trying, 20–2, 116, 154, 156
   common sense knowledge of, 109
   neural basis of, 109–112
Tryptophan, 80
Tye, M., 83–4

Unconscious learning. *See* Learning, unconscious
Urge, 111, 117, 129, 137
   and fleeting desires, 151
   to jump from a balcony, 144–5
   and pleasure, 75
   Tourettic, 124–6

Valence incomparability, 103–4
Ventral pallidum, 78, 82
Vertigo, 144–5
Visceral responses. *See* Pleasure, body landscape theory of
VTA/SNpc (ventral tegmental area and substantia nigra pars compacta). *See also* Dopamine; Learning; Neural connection
   and motivation, 115–16, 118
   and pleasure, 81, 92
   and reward, 36–7, 49–54, 58, 132

Want. *See* Desire
Watson, J., 45
Weather Watchers, 20, 36
White, N., 51–2, 119
Will, 111 n.8
Wish, 19–20. *See also* Desire